GROW TO GREATNESS

GROW TO GREATNESS

*Smart Growth for
Entrepreneurial Businesses*

Edward D. Hess

STANFORD BUSINESS BOOKS
An Imprint of Stanford University Press
Stanford, California

Stanford University Press
Stanford, California

Special discounts for bulk quantities of Stanford Business Books are
available to corporations, professional associations, and other
organizations. For details and discount information, contact the special
sales department of Stanford University Press.
Tel: (650) 736-1782, Fax: (650) 736-1784

Printed in the United States of America on acid-free, archival-quality paper

Library of Congress Cataloging-in-Publication Data

Hess, Edward D., author.
   Grow to greatness : smart growth for entrepreneurial businesses /
Edward D. Hess.
      pages cm
   Includes bibliographical references and index.
   ISBN 978-0-8047-7534-2 (cloth : alk. paper)
      1. Small business—Growth.   2. Small business—Management.
3. Industrial management.   4. Entrepreneurship.   I. Title.
      HD62.7.H483 2012
      658.4′06—dc23

                                                    2011051604

Typeset by Newgen in 10/15 Sabon

This book is dedicated to the memory of Frank Batten, Sr., whose vision, leadership, and generosity founded the Batten Institute at the Darden Graduate School of Business, University of Virginia.

CONTENTS

ACKNOWLEDGMENTS

With each book, I am humbled because this work builds upon my earlier eight books with the unifying focus of illuminating how to build enduring, high-performance organizations. My research has examined public companies, family businesses, start-ups, and now private growth companies. I again thank and acknowledge the continuing contribution of all those acknowledged in previous books--too many to be named here. No one writes a book alone.

This book began with a research question: "What were the major management challenges faced by leaders of high-growth private companies?" Professor Jeanne Liedtka, who at the time of my research was the Executive Director of the Batten Institute, Darden Graduate School of Business, and Professor Sankaran Venkataraman, Research Director of the Batten Institute, supported my curiosity and agreed that the Batten Institute and the Darden Foundation would fund this research.

Fifty-four high-growth private companies located in 23 states generously participated in my study. A special thank you goes to the CEOs who agreed to participate in developing Darden cases with us and sharing their learning experiences.

A special thank you to my Research Assistant, Cassy Eriksson, for her research, critique, good ideas, and perfectionist production of this book.

Once again, she has made my work better and led the production process with exacting high standards and caring professionalism.

Margo Beth Fleming of Stanford University Press has been a good partner in making it possible that others may learn from the entrepreneurs I studied. This is my second book with her and she is a rare professional that can add value and be a joy to work with. Jessica Walsh and Jay Harward did a tremendous job in preparing the book for publishing.

Dean Robert Bruner; Associate Dean of the Faculty Jim Freeland; and Michael Lenox, Executive Director of the Batten Institute of the Darden Graduate School of Business, through their leadership, encouragement, and positivity make the Darden community an energizing, entrepreneurial environment. It is a privilege to be part of that environment.

To the Batten Institute and the Darden Foundation for funding my research and to Elizabeth O'Halloran and Sean Carr of The Darden Graduate School of Business for providing support to make this book possible.

Many of us teach because so many teachers made positive contributions to our life. I have been blessed by many wonderful, generous teachers and mentors who encouraged me along my journey and opened new avenues for me: Tom Aiello, David Bonderman, Professor Lyle Bourne, Professor Kim Cameron, Professor Richard D'Aveni, Professor Charlie Davison, Professor Bill Fulmer, Coach Charlie Grisham, Professor Al Hartgraves, Professor Sidney Jourard, Professor Jeanne Liedtka, Jack McGovern, Judge Harry Michael, Professor Antonin Scalia, and Ira Wender.

My first teachers were my parents, who were both entrepreneurs—although at the time I did not know that. My first paying job, at age six, was distributing flyers for their clothing store in Carrollton, Georgia, for which I was paid 25 cents. My parents worked hard, long hours building a business comprising four clothing stores in rural Georgia. Their hard work enabled me to embark upon my own continuing entrepreneurial journey.

To my wife, Katherine Leigh, thank you again for your continued encouragement and for sharing your expertise by editing this book and giving my ideas life.

I   THE ROADMAP TO
SMART GROWTH

AN INTRODUCTION

Hello, I am Ed Hess. I am a professor of business administration and the Batten Executive-in-Residence at the Darden Graduate School of Business at the University of Virginia. I have spent the last ten years studying how public and private companies successfully grow. Before becoming a professor, I worked with growth companies first as a lawyer and then for over twenty years as a strategy consultant and investment banker. Along the way, I built four small businesses of my own.

THE CONTENT

The content of this book was derived from my business and consulting experience and from research that I conducted called the Darden Private Growth Company Research Project (DPGC) that studied fifty-four high growth private companies looking at the challenges of managing growth. That research became the foundation of a course that I have taught at Darden for years called Managing Small Enterprises. That research also led to the creation of over thirty formal business school case studies about the challenges of growing a private business—all of which were the basis for a business school text/casebook that was published in early 2011 by Stanford University Press entitled *Growing An Entrepreneurial Business: Concepts & Cases.*

In addition, I have written seven other books and have been fortunate to have my work featured in many prominent business publications and media channels. Through these experiences, I encountered more business builders from whom I have learned.

THE AUDIENCE

This book is about growing a small business, not about starting a business. It assumes that you have successfully started a business, have a commercially viable product or service, and have been able to achieve profitability. Now you want to grow your business—to get bigger. This book focuses on the common challenges that a growing business will face and shares the experiences of other successful business builders.

As you grow your business, new challenges will constantly appear. Growth is recurring change. The people, processes, and controls that worked at one level of growth may not work at the next level of growth. In fact, you will learn that the same people, processes, and controls will most likely not be effective as the business grows. In other words, as your business grows, it will continuously face new challenges requiring you to put in place different processes, controls, and people. Growth produces waves of change, and, like waves in the ocean, they naturally keep coming.

I think that you will find the foregoing to be especially true up to the $250M revenue level. Then at some point again—maybe at about $750M in revenue—your business will hit another big inflection point. Many of the issues discussed in this book are being faced now, as I finish this book in 2011, by many of the Executive Education clients whom I teach, whose businesses earn around $5B in revenue.

The lessons, tools, and concepts put forth in this book are applicable at each step of the growth journey. The point is that managing growth is not a one-time event; it is a continuous, ongoing process until you decide that it is time for your business to stop growing.

This book is an attempt to prepare you for the reality of growth so you can better plan for growth, proactively manage the pace of growth, and understand your risks of growth, which must be proactively managed so that growth does not overwhelm your business.

THE LEAD ACTORS AND ACTRESSES

You will meet twelve leaders in this book, all of whom have experienced the challenges and the ups and downs of business growth. Growth requires change. Growth is a bumpy ride. Through their experiences you can learn ways to prepare for and make your growth ride less turbulent.

That is the purpose of this book—to make your growth ride less bumpy and to help you avoid destroying your business in the process.

Yes, growth can destroy your business if not properly managed.

But from the experiences of the twelve leaders featured you can learn how others have successfully managed the turbulence of growth.

LEARNING TOOLS

Real-Life Growth Stories

Each chapter contains at least one story adapted from a Darden Business Publishing case that I wrote. These cases are used in business schools to teach MBA students. From the real-life experiences of these entrepreneurs, you will learn concepts and approaches to successfully manage growth. I suggest you read these stories twice and write down points that you find relevant to your current growth challenges. As you grow, you will face new challenges, so come back to these stories to reread them because new learning points will catch your eye.

These real-life cases are strategically placed primarily at the end of each chapter to maximize your learning. The cases will reinforce points made in the chapter as well as reinforce key points in other chapters. So, I recommend that you read the cases after you have read the chapter.

CEO Quotes

Within many chapters, you will find anonymous quotes from CEOs that participated in my research projects. These quotes represent gems of experience.

Workshops

The book contains six workshops that are designed to give you the opportunity to learn by doing. Three workshops each contain a discussion section outlining possible answers. In the other three workshops, you will apply tools and concepts from the text to your business.

Tools

You will also be given three tools for your use as you grow your business to help you make better decisions about whether to grow, how much to grow, how to grow, and what you need to do to manage growth.

Those tools are a Growth Decision Template, a Growth Risks Audit, and a Growth Planning Template.

Chapter Takeaways

At the end of each chapter, you will find a summary of key learning points that you can refer to easily and quickly as you manage your business. Different learning points will become more relevant at different points in your growth journey, and I recommend you review these Takeaways frequently in a disciplined manner.

THE RESEARCH

This book has been built on my research findings, case studies, and consulting experience. The DPGC involved fifty-four growth companies. The average age of those businesses was 9.6 years, and their average revenue at the time I studied them was $60M. Those companies were based in twenty-three different states. Twenty-one were primarily product companies, and thirty-three were service companies.

Other characteristics of these businesses relate to some basic metrics of their growth. Of the fifty-four companies,

- forty-nine had reached or exceeded $10M in revenue;
- thirty-six had reached or exceeded $20M of revenue;
- twenty-two had reached or exceeded $50M of revenue; and
- twelve had surpassed $100M of revenue.

On average, the approximate amount of time to reach particular revenue levels was

- $1M in revenue in 3 years;

- $5M revenue in 4.8 years;
- $10M revenue in 6 years;
- $20M revenue in 6.7 years; and
- $50M revenue in 8 years.

I also examined characteristics of the entrepreneurs themselves:

- thirty-four CEOs had prior work experience in their business's industry;
- twenty-eight CEOs had no prior start-up experience;
- forty companies were self-funded by the founder, family, and friends;
- thirty-four companies had more than one founder; and
- five companies were started by women.

If the CEOs had prior start-up experience, their companies grew measurably faster than companies with first-time entrepreneurs. If a company had two founders, it reached the $1M, $5M, and $10M levels more quickly than companies with one founder or more than two founders, but it did not achieve higher revenue levels more quickly. There was no real difference in the time taken by product versus service companies to reach the $1M and $5M levels, but product companies reached the $10M, $20M, and $50M revenue levels much faster than service companies.

THE ROADMAP TO SMART GROWTH

This book approaches growth from four perspectives. Growth is viewed in terms of both organizational design and individual behavior and from both strategy and execution perspectives. In addition to looking at growth from different perspectives, this book provides discussions of the key research findings, extensive case studies and practical examples as well as workshop exercises to promote experience in applying the concepts. It is both a "thinking" and a "doing" book.

The book is divided into three parts. Part I includes Chapters 2 and 3, which deal with the issue of whether you should grow your business and arm you with the tools to strategically make that decision. Part II includes Chapters 4 through 6, which deal with the issue of how to grow your

EXHIBIT I.I

Growth is change.
Growth is evolutionary.
Growth requires constant learning.
Growth requires disciplined focus and prioritization.
Growth requires processes and people.
Growth creates business risks.
Growth is constant improvement and scaling.

business. Part III includes Chapters 7 through 10, which focus on the finding that growth requires the right kind of leadership, culture, and processes.

The takeaway lesson from the chapters is that smart growth requires the right leadership, culture, processes, and people. This book gives you tools to start planning and executing growth strategies. Throughout this book, you will see the themes outlined in Exhibit 1.1.

It is important to understand that this book focuses on growing a business after a successful start-up. All businesses go through a lifecycle characterized generally by birth, growth, maturity, and decline. Our focus is growth, not birth, maturity or fighting decline.

PART I: WHETHER TO GROW
Chapter 2, The "Truth" About Growth

This chapter explains what we know about growth from business research so you can think about growth in a realistic way. What does that mean? Well, we know from research that, contrary to popular beliefs:

1. Not all growth is good. Growth can be good or bad. It depends. Growth can stress people, processes, controls, and culture. Growth can create business risks: quality, financial, customer, reputation, and legal. If not properly managed, growth can destroy value and, in some cases, even destroy the business.

2. Bigger is not always better. The bigger a business gets, the more complex it becomes to manage. As it gets bigger, it requires more employees, processes, controls, financial strength, and experienced managers. Becoming bigger exposes your business to bigger and better competition.

3. The business axiom that all business must "grow or die" is not true. Your business does not have to keep growing. However, you do have to continuously improve its customer value proposition and do so better than your competition does. "Improve or die" is true.

Chapter 2 discusses the main themes of this book. They are as follows:

Growth is change. Growth requires the entrepreneur to put in place more processes, procedures, controls, and measurement systems. It also requires that the entrepreneur change what he or she does. Growth increases the likelihood of mistakes because it is dependent on the actions of employees who, being human, will make mistakes. Managing a growing business requires minimizing the number and severity of those mistakes. Some mistakes can create serious business risks.

Growth is evolutionary. Growth requires the evolution of the entrepreneur and the management team and more sophisticated processes and controls. Often, if not always, the business model and customer value proposition evolve, too. Furthermore, this evolution is continuous.

Growth requires continuous learning and constant improvement. The entrepreneur and employees must be constantly open to learning and adapting and improving in an incremental, iterative, and experimental manner. No matter how big you get or want to get, continuous improvement is required.

Growth requires disciplined focus and prioritization. The entrepreneur must strategically focus the business on a compelling differentiating customer value proposition and achieving daily operational excellence and consistency. One CEO described the concept of strategic business focus: "Be 2 inches wide and 2 miles deep."

Growth requires processes. Growth requires implementing processes, which include controls. Processes are like recipes for baking a cake. They are the step-by-step instructions for how to do a task. Processes are necessary to hire employees and train them, to minimize mistakes and institutionalize quality standards, and deliver products and services on time, 99 percent defect free. Controls are necessary to set boundaries on allowable behavior and also alert management to deviations from processes.

Growth creates business risks that must be managed. Growth stresses people, processes, quality controls, and financial controls. Growth can dilute a business's culture and customer value proposition and put the business in a different competitive space. Understanding these risks is critical to managing the pace of growth and preventing growth from overwhelming the business.

The good news is that you can minimize the big risks by planning for growth, pacing growth, and prioritizing what controls and processes you need to put in place prior to taking on much growth. You will use a tool I developed called a Growth Risks Audit to learn how to identify and minimize risks.

You will also learn to use another tool called the Growth Decision Template to think strategically about whether you should grow. The Growth Decision Template will also help you decide what growth methods your business should employ and how fast it should grow. In addition, you will be provided with practical information about how to manage the risks of growth.

Then you will meet Julie Allinson, the founder of Eyebobs Eyewear. Allinson's story is compelling not just because she built a very successful business but also because she did it her way. She was aware that too much growth could overwhelm her business, and she was determined to keep control of her business. It took her six years to reach an income level of $1M, but because she took her time, studied her business, and installed the right processes and controls that were scalable, she was able to at least double her sales every succeeding year for four years.

Chapter 3, Preconditions to Growth

This chapter builds upon Chapter 2 by introducing the concept of preconditions to growth. What must you do before your business is ready to take on more growth? What are your people, process, control, reporting, and daily information needs? What are the costs of growth and how are those costs incurred compared to the timing of more revenue?

All of these questions involve the tension between investing ahead of growth and investing after growth has occurred. Clearly, playing catch-up is more risky but sometimes unavoidable. Playing catch-up could be the result of a failure to predict or plan for growth but instead often reflects the lack of financial resources available to invest ahead of growth.

The questions raised in this chapter will illuminate your growth alternatives. Usually, successful businesses have many growth alternatives. The question is how to decide which alternatives to focus on. Prioritizing the growth alternatives is essential to help keep entrepreneurs aware of the limitations of their business: the time, people, management depth, and money needed to grow. Trying to grow too fast can be disastrous.

Two workshop exercises are included in this chapter. In these workshops, you will begin your analysis by applying the Growth Decision Template and the Growth Risks Audit to a specific business scenario.

Many businesses have a variety of growth opportunities. Sometimes these opportunities just present themselves and sometimes they are actively sought. Strategic focus emerged from my study as a critical component of successfully managing growth and not letting growth overwhelm you or your business. Learning when to say "No!" to growth and learning how to pace growth are key so that growth does not outstrip your capabilities, people, processes, or controls.

In the first workshop, you will meet Susan Feller, a retired teacher and guidance counselor who began a second career when she developed dietary need that was not being met by the market. Without any formal business training, she built a successful gluten-free baking business, 3 Fellers Bakery, through which she creates, manufactures, and sells gluten-free desserts to her retail bakery customers and grocery chains including Whole Foods and Ukrops.

Feller's business growth problem was that she had too many growth opportunities and too little capital, management experience, and time. She had to choose. Her decision was complicated by her love for creating new recipes and baking cakes; she was at the stage in life that she did not have to make more money; and her dream was that someday one or more of her sons would take over the business.

After reading the 3 Fellers Bakery story, you will use the Growth Risks Audit and the Growth Decision Template to decide whether, how, and in what order 3 Fellers should grow. You will also examine, most importantly, 3 Fellers' preconditions to growth.

Then, you will be given an opportunity to do a workshop analysis of your company's preconditions to the next phase of growth.

PART II: HOW TO GROW
Chapter 4, The Four Ps: Planning, Prioritization, Processes, and Pace
Chapter 4 focuses on the recurring findings of my research that managing growth requires planning, prioritization, processes, and pacing the speed of growth.

Planning for growth requires the entrepreneur to think about organizational structure, organizing jobs by function, and creating a layered management structure as well as adding more infrastructure.

Infrastructure includes everything needed to produce and deliver the business's product or service and manage the business. Infrastructure includes space, equipment, technology, supplies, processes, and the means to produce and deliver the goods. Using that definition, infrastructure also includes people.

Planning for infrastructure requires an entrepreneur to think about what activities must be done internally and what could be outsourced. In addition, you will face the question of how much infrastructure to invest in: do you invest and build more capacity than you need now for growth or do you conserve your cash and build just enough infrastructure for current growth needs.

Planning for growth requires an entrepreneur to think about how the business will scale manufacturing or production as well as sales. Planning also becomes a communication tool in that strategic plans can be used to set employee expectations, inspire them, and focus them on critical activities and get people aligned with overall organizational objectives. Lastly, this chapter introduces the concept of "firehouse" time—that is, time to think and plan away from the daily "fires" of every business.

The second topic discussed in this chapter is the challenge of prioritization. Every entrepreneur has limited resources and time. How do you decide where to focus? You will learn from successful business builders about bottlenecks, huddles, and prioritization heuristics.

Growing businesses, by definition, will need more people, processes, and controls. Processes are the checklists, instructions, and ways of doing every aspect of your business. Processes are the means by which you can achieve consistent high performance.

We know that growth can overwhelm a business and, in some cases, destroy the business. Managing the pace of growth using what one CEO calls the "gas pedal" approach is introduced in this chapter, too. One can describe the four Ps as the hardwiring of the business. Driving home all these points is the story of Global Medical Imaging.

Ryan Dienst is the lead actor of the Global Medical Imaging story, and you will learn how he methodically put in place people, processes, and controls to support Global Medical Imaging's growth. After reading this story, you will be introduced to another tool, the Growth Planning Template and have the opportunity to use this template in a workshop to practice planning for growth.

Chapter 5, The Four Ways to Grow Your Business
Chapter 3 focused on some critical questions: Should you grow? Why? How should you grow? What are your risks of growth? What are your risks of not growing? In this chapter, I explore how to grow a business by discussing the four different ways to grow a business: improvements, innovations, scaling, and acquisitions.

Improvements are doing what you do faster, better, and cheaper. They are the fundamental way to stay in business. No matter what you decide about whether to grow or how much to grow, every business must continuously improve to maintain its customers. How much do you have to improve? You must improve enough to stay better than your competition. What must you improve? You must improve what your customers deem to be important and of value to them.

Improvements can also create growth by allowing you to do what you do more efficiently and cheaply. This allows you to sell to more customers. Most value-creating improvements are improvements to business processes—the "how" you do business.

Innovations involve doing something new that your competition is not doing. True innovation—doing something completely novel—is both rare and high risk. It is high risk because customers are often not willing to pay for the new product or service. Innovations can be less risky if entrepreneurs adopt experiential learning and customer co-creation processes that engage customers in the creation to help ensure that the end result is something that customers both need and are willing to buy.

Scaling, the primary way to grow a business, is simply doing more of what you are already doing. Scaling is a replication process. To do it well, you need the right hiring, training, and execution processes along with the right information, measurement, and reward systems overseen by competent managers.

Acquisitions are a more risky way to grow. Acquisitions are buying growth by buying more customers, more products or services to sell, or geographical expansion. Acquisitions are risky because they require due diligence, integration, valuation, and financing expertise.

These concepts will be brought to life through the Sammy Snacks and Enchanting Travels stories. In the Sammy Snacks story, the entrepreneur tried to grow the business through aggressive geographic expansion and lost control of her company. The successor CEO then returned the business to profitability through improvements and then, through iteration, learned how to scale the distribution of its products.

Enchanting Travels is a story of successful scaling that illustrates the necessity and payoff of hard work in creating the processes needed to scale successfully and the difficulties of scaling a personal service business.

Chapter 6, Creating Three Growth Plans

I am a big believer in learning by doing; therefore, in this chapter you will use the concepts of Chapters 2 through 5 to devise growth plans for two companies, C.R. Barger & Sons and Hass Shoes. You will then have a chance to apply what you've learned in Chapters 2 through 5 by creating a growth plan for your business taking into account the four different ways to grow a business.

Barger is a story of a successful business that was in decline. It sells a commodity product. In commodity products, the lowest priced product usually wins. To make money, you must sell a high volume. Barger presents the challenge of how a business escapes the perils of commoditization and reignites growth.

Hass Shoes presents a different challenge. In Hass Shoes, you must examine different avenues to growth of a product business such as selling complementary products or services, expanding geographically, or increasing the number of customers, the amount purchased by each customer, or the number of buying times per customer.

To devise growth strategies for both Barger and Hass Shoes, you will utilize the Growth Decision Template and the Growth Risks Audit discussed in Chapter 2, figure out the preconditions to growth as in Chapter 3, and utilize the four ways to grow to create a portfolio of growth opportunities from Chapter 4. You will also utilize the Growth Planning Template to consider the more granular details of your growth plan.

After you have created your growth plans, Chapter 6 will present some answers for you to consider. Obviously, you will get the most from this chapter by doing your homework before you read the answers.

Lastly, you will do another workshop in which you create your growth plan for the next stage of your business's growth using the concepts learned in Chapters 2 through 6.

PART III: GROWTH REQUIRES THE RIGHT
LEADERSHIP, CULTURE, AND PEOPLE
Chapter 7, Growth Is Much More Than a Strategy
In my research of successful growth companies, I found that alignment into a consistent, linked, internal self-reinforcing system was necessary to produce the enabling environment for consistent, excellent execution of the business model. Aligning a business's strategy, culture, structure, execution process, leadership model, human resource policies, measurement, and rewards on motivating the right behaviors that create long-term value are mission critical. As one can imagine, this is no easy task.

Building such an enabling system takes years of iteration and development. An entrepreneur must start simply with a few critical behaviors and increase breadth and depth as a business grows. Over the last ten years, I have studied over one hundred high-performance companies. One of my favorites is Room & Board, which is based in Minneapolis, Minnesota and led by John Gabbert.

I discovered Gabbert through a *Business Week* article. The article marveled at how Gabbert built Room & Board by refusing to grow as fast as others thought he could and should. Gabbert also refused to use bank debt or private equity or to go public.

Gabbert's story is both inspirational and illuminating. He built an internally consistent system that fostered relationships between the business and all its stakeholders: suppliers, employees, and customers.

You will also meet Steve Ritter, the head of human resources at Leaders Bank, based in Oak Brook, Illinois. Ritter shares with you how Leaders Bank created their unique system that resulted in high employee engagement and high customer satisfaction. Ritter's story demonstrates that human resource investments, both in time and money, pay off.

Chapter 8, The Entrepreneur Must Grow, Too!
Growing a business requires more people, processes, and controls. Growth requires strategic focus and analyzing and managing the risks of growth. A less expected consequence of growth is that it requires the entrepreneur to grow, too. One growth-generated change requires the entrepreneur to learn how to delegate. One CEO told me: "Delegation is not a natural act." As a business grows, an entrepreneur must learn how to manage people. With more growth the entrepreneur must learn how to manage managers.

In addition, growth requires an entrepreneur to learn to live with employee mistakes and to manage constant change, volatility, and the roller coaster ride of growth. At this point, some entrepreneurs decide that they do not want to manage a growth business and bring in outside management. Some entrepreneurs redefine their role to the business, focusing on strategy and culture as the business gets bigger.

Building a growth business is like painting a picture: each entrepreneur will create his or her own work of art. But one constant is that for the business to grow, the entrepreneur must grow. That means change and learning: changing what you do every day and how you do it.

To illustrate these concepts you will read Dave Lindsey's story of how he rebounded from being passed over for a corporate promotion and left the corporate world to build a successful business: Defender Direct. It is the story of iterative learning, installing processes, scaling, adapting to external changes, overcoming a major financial challenge, and then scaling again with different products and a different role for the founder. Lindsey's story is also the story of how he continuously redefined his role in the company and what the business meant to him. After a certain point, making money was not enough for Lindsey.

Chapter 9, *The Silver Bullet: Highly Engaged Employees*

It is the unusual business that can grow without adding more people. Basically, every business is a people business in that they are built on customer relationships and serviced by and through employees and managers. Most successful businesses are dependent on people.

To grow a business, the entrepreneur must figure out how to attract, train, and retain employees who are highly engaged in the excellent daily execution of their jobs. This chapter deals with that awesome challenge. High performance companies generally have highly engaged and happy employees. The research is overwhelming that happy employees create happy customers, which creates financial success.

High employee engagement results from meaning, the right culture, and the right leadership behaviors, policies, measurements, and rewards. This chapter discusses what that means and how to create the right culture and internal environment in which employees will find meaning and be emotionally engaged in more than making you money. How do you make it more than a job for them?

The glue that binds everything together is culture. When entrepreneurs have their often-frightening personal awakening that the business's success depends on others, they learn that what the employee wants is not that much different from what the entrepreneur wants.

This chapter looks at the power of employee "ownership," promotion-from-within policies, hiring for "cultural fit," creating a family atmosphere, information transparency, emotional rewards, and the leader's behavior. Money is not enough.

This chapter pulls together critical lessons about high performance environments from the Room & Board, Defender Direct, Enchanting

Travels, and Leaders Bank stories and introduces you to Trilogy Health Services, another successful company with a highly engaged workforce.

Chapter 10, Building an Effective Management Team
Chapter 9 focused on creating a highly engaged workforce. As you grow your business you will need managers, and, ultimately, you will need a management team that helps you manage and grow your business. Most of the entrepreneurs in my study had between four and seven direct reports—that is, managers reporting to the CEO who had functional responsibilities such as sales, technology, human resources, operations, legal, finance, and customer service.

Building an effective management team turned out to be much more difficult for most CEOs in my study than they expected. You will learn from their trials and tribulations that the right hiring process is critical. Hiring during the "adolescent" stage of growth is very difficult. Often, big company managers fail to adjust to an entrepreneurial growth company environment. Growth often requires hiring several new managers in a short period of time or working with a mix of in-house veterans and new people, which requires expertly managing the managers to ensure they are getting along and "playing nicely together in the sandbox."

Mike Cote of SecureWorks in Atlanta, Georgia, transformed an underperforming company with great technology into a great company. The SecureWorks story is a good conclusion because, not only does it deal with the specific challenges of building an effective management team, but Cote's story reinforces the key themes of this book.

Let's get to work by focusing on the first important questions: How do you decide whether to grow your business and how much should you grow? Exhibit 1.2 outlines ten of the most common growth challenges.

EXHIBIT 1.2
Top 10 Growth Challenges

1. Determining and maintaining a strategic focus.
2. Learning to delegate, manage, and lead.
3. Installing and upgrading the right processes to ensure quality and financial controls.
4. Managing cash daily.
5. Making hiring a rigorous process.
6. Pacing growth so that it does not overwhelm you and your business.
7. Building a high accountability professional "family" culture.
8. Scaling sales and people.
9. Learning to live with change, mistakes, and the need to constantly prioritize, improve, and upgrade processes and people as you grow.
10. Building a management team that works well together.

PART I   WHETHER TO GROW

2 THE "TRUTH" ABOUT GROWTH

CEO QUOTES[1]

- "You don't want to bring on all the business that you can—growth can easily swallow you."

- "Understand that growth puts you into a different competitive space."

- "It takes one set of skills to manage a company and an entirely different set of skills to grow a company."

- "Businesses don't grow, people do."

- "Business is a whole lot like sailing. You know where you are and where you want to go, and it takes a whole lot of tacking to get there."

- I make a good living building four houses a year; why should I build eight a year?"

WHY EVERYTHING YOU PROBABLY THINK YOU KNOW ABOUT GROWTH IS WRONG!

Certain beliefs about growth dominate business thinking and the business press. Those beliefs are: All growth is good, bigger is always better, and

---

This chapter is adapted from Darden Business Publishing Technical Note UVA-S-0172, 2010, authored by Professor Edward D. Hess, "Why Everything You Know About Growth Is Probably Wrong," with permission of Darden Business Publishing.

businesses either "grow or die." In the case of public companies, there is strong pressure from Wall Street for business growth to be continuous and linear, evidenced by ever-increasing quarterly returns.

These beliefs about growth are widely taught in business schools, consistently written about in books and business magazines and espoused daily by business consultants. Few question their validity.

Unfortunately, those growth beliefs are not always true. There is no scientific research that supports the claims that all growth is good or that businesses either grow or die or that getting bigger is always better. There is virtually no support for those beliefs in the fields of economics, finance, accounting, strategy, organizational behavior, complexity theory, or even biology. At best, those beliefs are half-truths. In reality, the business world is filled with companies that survive by improvements, not by constant growth.

This book is not antigrowth. Rather, it puts forth a realistic view of growth, based on research and business reality. Growth can be good and growth can be bad—it depends. Aggressive, untimely, or poorly managed growth can hurt a business and even destroy value. And, in some cases, too much growth can lead to business failure.

Bigger is not always better because the bigger a business gets, the more bureaucratic it gets and the more complex it becomes to manage. Managing a bigger business may exceed the capabilities of the owners.

Likewise "grow or die" is not a universal truth. In fact, we know that, in some circumstances, too much growth can cause business death. What we do know is that a business must continuously improve its customer value proposition so it can beat the competition.

What is needed is a better understanding of how successful businesses actually grow over time, the challenges growth presents for businesses, and useful tools to manage the risks of growth.

Business Research

What does business research tell us about how businesses actually grow? Its findings are as follows:

1. Few businesses evidence any systematic, predictable patterns of growth over the long run.[2]

2. There is not a strong relationship between growth and profitability.[3]

3. Continuous business growth is the exception, not the rule.[4]

4. At some point, the costs and complexity of being bigger outweigh the benefits.[5]

5. Growth can damage a business. Growth can stress people, processes, controls, culture, and customer value proposition, propelling a business into a different competitive space where it has to compete against bigger and better competition.

6. While not every business is required to grow in size, every business must constantly improve and earn revenue in excess of its costs.[6]

7. Growth is an evolutionary process that does not occur smoothly or continuously but usually in spurts.

8. Good growth companies are characterized by strategic focus, operational excellence, continuous improvement, customer centricity, and high employee engagement.[7]

9. Many good growth companies put in place processes to experiment and test growth ideas without risking lots of money or time. They test, learn, adapt, and improve continuously.

10. Consistent good growth requires the right kinds of leadership, culture, and processes.

Biology Research Findings

It is also instructive to look more broadly to growth research in other fields. Examples from biology and complexity theory show that a single-minded focus on growth as the goal may be counterproductive.

1. Many species stop growing to increase their chances of survival because growth beyond an optimal size can increase the risks of being eaten by predators.[8] This happens in the business world, too.

2. Many organisms have a finite amount of energy to allocate to reproduction, growth, maintenance, and survival.[9] Businesses, too, have limited resources that must be allocated among maintenance, improvement, and growth.

3. In some species, growth requires trade-offs that result in periods of growth and periods of nongrowth. Growth is not continuous.[10] This concept is similar to the "gas pedal" theory of growth that we will discuss in Chapter 4.

4. Complexity theory states that growth is an experimental learning process.[11] Experimental means that you test ideas and see whether they work. In this context, learning means that you will need to adapt and change based on feedback as you try things.

A MORE REALISTIC VIEW OF GROWTH

No longer should growth for growth's sake be every business's goal. Understanding that growth if not properly managed can undermine the fundamental strengths of a business is essential to having a more realistic view of growth. One must respect growth by understanding that growth can be good and growth can be bad. It depends on the timing, the amount, and whether you have the right people, processes, and controls in place to manage the growth.

First, growth is change. There are limits to an individual's and an organization's ability to process change. Growth is complex and challenging because it involves people who we know are not always rational or efficient actors. People make mistakes. People have misunderstandings.

Successful and sustainable growth requires the right kind of leadership, the right environment (culture), and the right processes. Growth needs the right environment inside the company as well as the right external environment, which involves customers, suppliers, and competitors.

Second, growth also requires more processes and controls. The right processes and controls must be put in place and taught to employees. In addition, the right information needs to reach the manager regarding variances from processes and controls so mistakes can be fixed quickly and do not escalate into a larger problem.

Third, in addition to requiring more people, processes, and controls, in many cases growth requires different people, processes, and controls than those that a business has in place.

As a business grows, it will continually need to upgrade its processes and controls. In addition, its people will have to grow and learn to do things differently or be replaced with people with better skills. Too much food or drink can make you sick. Too much growth without appropriate people, processes, and controls can make your business sick.

Fourth, growth is a dynamic, interactive, interdependent process that generally involves false starts, learning as you go, adaptation, and failed initiatives. Growth is messy; growth is change; and growth has spurts, detours, downturns, and spikes. Growth requires constant learning and improvement. Growth requires people, processes, and culture to be aligned to drive desired value-creating behaviors.

Businesses often stumble as they grow, making mistakes in personnel, process, and alignment. If not well-planned and well-managed, growth can stress people, processes, and controls and often outstrip the capabilities of people and companies. In fact, growth creates another category of business risks that must be proactively managed.

Growth Should Not Be Assumed

Growth should not be just assumed as a given or foregone conclusion. Rather, whether to grow a company should be a strategic decision made only after both the risks of growing and not growing have been assessed.

Recently, I was consulting with a company that had generated $20M of revenue in its fifth year of existence with a 50 percent net profit margin. I asked the owners why they wanted to grow. Their responses were classic:

- "You have to grow or you will die."
- "You have to grow to create opportunity for younger people."
- "That is what businesses are supposed to do."
- "We need to grow so we will not get bored."

With each response, I asked, "Why," peeling back the outer layers of their thinking to reach the core. Not surprisingly, it turned out that these very bright, well-educated executives had only a flimsy basis for their answers other than "well, everyone knows that," with one exception. After repeated exploration, they identified a key growth-related goal: to be able to afford admitting new partners without reducing their own compensation.

EXHIBIT 2.1

Growth Decision Template

1. Why should we grow?
2. How should we grow?
3. How much should we grow?
4. How fast should we grow?
5. Do we have the right people, processes, and controls in place to support growth?
6. What are the risks of growth?
7. What are the risks of not growing?
8. Do the benefits of growth outweigh the risks?
9. How do we manage the risks created by our decision?

Questions 2–4 are interrelated. They raise issues about the choice of growth strategies with their differing probabilities of success and risks as well as the speed or pace of growth.

A Growth Decision Template

That discussion is not an aberration, especially for private companies. I have conducted five different research projects involving public companies and high-growth private companies trying to uncover the DNA of consistent real growth that creates long-term value, which I call Smart Growth.

That research led me to generate a list of threshold questions for making growth decisions, which I developed into a tool called the Growth Decision Template (see Exhibit 2.1).

THE RISKS OF GROWTH

Integral to thinking strategically about growth is analyzing your company's risks of growth. How can growth stress your people, processes, and controls to the point that it may create serious problems? Many companies do not take the time to make that risk assessment, nor do they take the time to develop and update processes and controls to prepare the organization and its people for growth.

To better manage the risks of growth, every growth company should create a prioritized list of the preconditions to growth. What has to be put in place so you can grow without creating unintended bad consequences?

To illustrate this point, let's look at two public companies that recently undertook aggressive growth goals, resulting in major problems. First, between 2005 and 2007, Starbucks aggressively opened new store locations and made several operational changes that resulted in dilution of their customer value proposition, poor store performance, and the assumption of significant liabilities.

To stem those losses, former CEO Howard Schultz returned to the CEO post in 2008 and immediately closed over 900 underperforming locations. He also had to make operational changes in an attempt to bring back the "Starbucks Experience."

Likewise, in early 2000, Toyota made a corporate decision to become the largest automobile manufacturer in the world—a shift from their previous sole mission of being the best in quality and reliability. To become the biggest, Toyota had to open new plants outside Japan, hire and train many new employees, find new supplier partners, and make engineering and design changes so they could make more vehicles faster and cheaper. Toyota's aggressive growth led to quality issues, major recalls, regulatory issues, and over 200 lawsuits.

Neither Starbucks nor Toyota's management teams intended to destroy value. No one big mistake can be isolated. Rather, value was destroyed by the cumulative effect of several changes made to facilitate growth.

Apparently, neither Starbucks nor Toyota had sufficient people or processes in place to assess how those incremental changes could individually, or in the aggregate, have a negative impact on their value proposition. As a result, both corporations stumbled badly.

In making changes to business processes or the business model to facilitate growth, it is crucial that someone be accountable for monitoring potential pitfalls of growth that can have a material negative impact on quality, customer experience, financial exposure, brand reputation, and culture.

GROWTH RISKS AUDIT

To avoid or minimize the risks of growth, every company contemplating or engaged in significant growth initiatives should conduct a Growth Risks Audit (see Exhibit 2.2). The audit should be done annually and any time growth is contemplated.

EXHIBIT 2.2
Growth Risks Audit

1. For each growth initiative, evaluate if, how, and to what extent that initiative will put material stress on your

   - culture
   - structure
   - management team
   - employees

   - execution processes
   - quality controls
   - customer value proposition
   - customer experience

   - financial controls
   - financial safety net
   - image and brand reputation

2. What specific behaviors create material business risks for you? Will growth increase the likelihood of those behaviors?
3. Based on your answers to questions 1 and 2, prioritize those risks in order of harm to your business.
4. How do you know if those risks are occurring? What is your early warning system for each material risk? How do you monitor and detect those risk-inducing behaviors? How do you manage against creeping additive risks?
5. Does your measurement and reward system encourage or discourage those risky behaviors?
6. Managing growth takes a far different mentality than managing the risks of growth. How do you put in place processes that allow your managers to do both?
7. What changes to your execution processes, quality control processes, financial and information systems do you need to make to better manage the risks of growth?
8. Do you need to balance your internal communications about growth with communications about the specific growth risks you want to avoid?
9. Do you need to pace growth?
10. Under what conditions will you slow down or pause growth?

(continued)

EXHIBIT 2.2 *(continued)*

11. What is your risk management plan for each key material internal risk?
12. Will growth change whom you compete against?
13. If so, how will your new competitors likely respond?
14. Will that new competition impact your ability to maintain current customers? How? How will you ward off those new competitors? On what basis are you at a disadvantage with respect to the new competition? Do they have the capabilities to offer a better customer value proposition than you offer? Could the new competition put your business more at risk?
15. What changes do you need to make from a strategy, structure, cultural, execution processes, quality control, financial controls, information management, measurements, and rewards perspective to manage these risks of growth? In what priority?
16. Have you created a risk management execution plan with timelines, milestones, and accountability?
17. How do you collectivize growth risk management across your management team?

CREATING A GROWTH RISKS MANAGEMENT PLAN

Growth risk management acknowledges that growth is change that can have unintended bad consequences impacting people, culture, quality, and financial controls. Growth can create business risks that, if not recognized and managed, can destroy value.

We know that growth

- stresses people, processes, and controls;
- can dilute a company's culture and customer value proposition; and
- can create quality and financial challenges.

Therefore, the next step after completing the Growth Risks Audit is to create a plan to manage the risks that were identified. I have found that it takes a different mindset to think about growth risks than to think about growth and that very few managers can switch back and forth quickly from a risk-management mentality to a growth mentality.

Thinking about growth is more positive thinking and thinking about risks is more "what can go wrong" thinking. As a result, it is important to implement processes that give early warnings of growth risks and allocate management time specifically to monitoring growth risks.

RESPECTING GROWTH'S DESTRUCTIVE POWER

All business leaders should understand the complexity, difficulty, and the risks of growth. Growth should be viewed both as an opportunity and as a risk-management challenge.

EYEBOBS EYEWEAR, INC.[12]

Let's read a story about one entrepreneur who understood this from the start. Julie Allinson, Eyebobs' President and CEO, built and grew a successful business, respecting the complexity and riskiness of growth from the start.

Eyebobs Eyewear, Inc., is based in Minneapolis, Minnesota. Its business is the design, manufacture, and selling of optician-grade ready-to-wear reading glasses with an attitude. As the company's tagline proclaims, Eyebobs produces "eyewear for the irreverent and slightly jaded."

The artsy frames in striking colors and innovative shapes with tongue-in-cheek names like Board Stiff, Barely Lucid, and Hostile Makeover, have a cult-like following among people with a playful streak. Eyebobs glasses are sold at optical centers, high-end department stores such as Nordstrom and Neiman Marcus, and upscale clothing boutiques from coast to coast. I discovered Eyebobs from my wife who is a customer of Eyebobs' Internet store.

Eyebobs president and CEO Julie Allinson was a 40-year-old former banker and president of a start-up for children's clothing when she quit her job to launch an eyewear business in 2000. She used her life's savings as seed capital and funded growth entirely out of cash flow. It took her six long years and lots of learning to reach $1 million in sales. But, in 2007, her company of 10 employees quadrupled sales, pulling in $4.5 million in revenues. The business has continued to grow significantly every year since then.

Reflecting on her decision to bootstrap her company and eschew external funding sources, Allinson emphasized the long-term benefits of debt-free growth and the freedom it allowed her:

I didn't borrow money; I didn't take on investors, and that allowed me to make all the decisions on how to allocate that tiny pool of money I had myself. I didn't want anybody beating on my back, "Grow faster, grow faster," if I wasn't comfortable with it. I've had many a sleepless night at Eyebobs, going over my decisions. But they are the decisions that I've made, not somebody else pushing me, wanting a certain return. We are trying to be realistic here, and we say that as we make decisions in the office every day: Do we want to take on more private label? Do we want to take on this customer? Do we want to create another brand that's cheaper? And often, the answer is, No, we don't have to have every single dollar in the marketplace. Just be true to ourselves, deliver a beautiful product that's high-end—to stay in that niche. And that's a discipline all by itself.

The Founder: A Country Girl Goes Corporate

Julie Allinson was born in 1958 and grew up on a small farm in Iowa. "We had no idea how poor we were," Allinson said. Her upbringing provided many lessons, which she later applied to running her own business. "What's driven home in a farm situation is common sense, and common sense really isn't very common," Allinson said. "You learn how to take care of yourself on a day-to-day basis, and you learn how to take care of your little business, because every farmer is an entrepreneur."

As a child of parents who, no matter how hard they worked, lived lives of constant uncertainty, Allinson valued planning and predictability. "I hated that type of existence where you couldn't have control," she said. But, reflecting on the similarities between her and her parents' lives, she admitted that maybe she "ended up just like them." She explained:

I can remember my parents praying for rain and then praying for it to stop. I never wanted to live that way. But being an entrepreneur is very much the same: you pray for the business, and you pray that you can handle the business, that you can deliver a quality product. And a lot of that is out of your hands—by virtue of having employees, manufacturers, etc.—because it's not just you who's involved.

Following her parents' advice, Allinson held various steady jobs during her teens. After graduating from high school, she attended the University of Iowa, where she majored in business.

After graduating in 1980, Allinson moved to Minneapolis, Minnesota, and became an operations manager for the brokerage firm Piper Jaffray & Co., followed by a short stint as a stockbroker. She spent the next 10 years managing loan portfolios for FirstBank. Then she spent five years as president of a private, Minneapolis-based clothing start-up, Mack & Moore, Inc.

A Business of Her Own

Five years into her tenure as president of Mack & Moore, Allinson grew increasingly frustrated with her job. "I had no real ownership of the company," she admitted. She also began to feel the entrepreneurial itch. She had wanted to run her own business but "wanting a business and starting a business are two different things," she said. "You really have to find something you have a passion for in order to quit your job and stick your life savings into it."[13]

Ironically, she found that "something" when she developed presbyopia, the farsightedness that accompanied aging and happened to most people entering their 40s and 50s. Allinson realized she needed a pair of reading glasses, so she went to see her friend Jason, who worked at an optical store. "[He] was happy to sell me hip reading glasses, but at a price that I couldn't afford," Allinson said. "So he showed me alternatives—at Walgreens." But Allinson did not like the cheap off-the-rack drug-store readers. "Isn't there anything in between?" she asked her optician friend. "Not really," he said. "That was my *aha* moment," Allinson remembered.[14]

In 2002, sensing a business opportunity, Allinson quit her job at Mack & Moore and plunged into a life of risk and uncertainty—she was going to start her own company. The first year after leaving Mack & Moore, Allinson lived off her savings.

She was "a student of [her] own business," as she put it, "trying to figure out how to get Eyebobs up and running." She went to China, Italy, and Chicago to talk to plastic manufacturers.

Allinson used her personal savings as seed capital and was determined to fund growth from the company's own cash flow, instead of borrowing large sums. "Because my parents grew up during the Depression," Allinson said, "I pay for everything with cash. I've never had a bank loan for the business."

Another reason behind eschewing debt was a family health scare. Soon after she started Eyebobs, Allinson's husband Paul had a heart attack. During his recovery, the couple talked about ways to minimize factors that increased his risk of heart disease. "We asked, 'Okay, what's creating stress in Paul's life?'" Allinson recalled. "And the answer was, 'Well, my starting a business.' What the hell could be more stressful?" She elaborated:

We talked about the numbers—a business could take a lot of cash if you let it—and how do you keep it from just eating-you-alive kind of thing. And the other thing was owning a house, so we moved into a condo, and we just bootstrapped this thing like crazy, because I couldn't have Paul stress out about the business.

Supply Chain Management

When Allinson set out on her entrepreneurial journey, she wanted to produce optical-grade reading glasses with stylish frames equipped with lenses that were scratch and chip resistant. Because she valued quality, she traveled to China to visit manufacturers in order to see their operations. "I interviewed between 24 to 30 people in one week," Allinson said. She learned the importance of staying well-connected with one's partners and suppliers and checking on them in person:

Getting to know your supply side is crucial. If you're going through a middle-man, you don't know stink. You don't know what the hell's going on at the factory. You don't know who owns it, who's getting priority, and what the product looks like. Going back to my upbringing—don't be afraid to get your hands dirty. Don't just make a phone call, get out there. I was gonna end up wiring my life's savings to an optical manufacturer, and the only way I was comfortable doing this was to go there first to meet them eye to eye.

For Allinson, the sourcing trip to China provided many other insights. "I learned so much during that trip about hinges and materials and where the good stuff was coming from," she said, adding that it soon became apparent that she should go talk to the Italian plastic manufacturers in person. "I wanted a higher-end product, and to this day, Italy is the place where they make the latest and the greatest," she said. As it turned out, her Italian manufacturers also had plants in China, so that's where her Eyebobs frames were made.

Allinson believed that the reason she was able to develop successful partnerships with Italian manufacturers was because she made the effort to visit them early on. She explained, "When you're small and you say, 'I'm going to do 1,000 pieces' or some ridiculous amount like that, something I do in a day now, how do you get the attention of these people? Well, they know you're serious because you were crazy enough to go over there to find out."

As a result of her efforts, Eyebobs reading glasses would be made with the same top-grade Italian plastic and hinges used by the more expensive frame companies. Having optical-quality frames also would allow Allinson's customers to have prescription lenses cut for their Eyebobs frames.

Eyewear for the Discerning

Allinson aimed for a niche in the reading glasses market and she targeted customers who valued style as well as quality. The bulk of her clientele were baby boomers that needed nonprescription reading glasses but also wanted to look good. For them, glasses were a fashion accessory. An extrovert, Allinson favored eyewear that was "nonconforming, a little twisted, that [said] something about the nature of the person wearing it." She liked to say that Eyebobs readers were not for most people and that she and her staff wanted to appeal to discerning people like herself.

Allinson looked for colors and styles that would stand out on a person's face and be memorable. "When working on a design, we think about the personality of the individual who might wear it, and what that person would want to communicate about themselves," she said.[15] Because she often drew inspiration from old Hollywood movies, many Eyebobs glasses had a retro feel, yet looked distinctly modern. She was not afraid to do frames with old-fashioned, round lenses, in purple or neon green. "The wackier I get," she said, "the more people love them."[16] She continued:

That's one of the blessings of not having been in the business previously. "We've always done it this way," wouldn't even occur to me. I don't know how they did it—I don't care. Again, that's the advantage of going to your end users to find out what they want, because if I'd gone to the retailer, I would have had a nickel-and-dime product that was a pile of crap that looked like everything else on the shelf.

The Right Distribution Channels

The most obvious distribution channel Allinson tried first was the eye-wear stores. In 2001, she attended an optical trade show, Vision Expo in New York City, hoping that eyewear retail stores would pick up her reading glasses. "I basically sold nothing," she recalled and lamented that she opened only one new account. "The first two years I really struggled. I kept trying to sell in the optical market because you're thinking where do people go with their eye troubles?" Her reasoning was correct, but she did not realize that optical stores resisted selling nonprescription readers for fear these glasses would detract from their high-margin prescription business. Allinson explained:

It was shocking to me how a lot of [eyewear stores] would keep Eyebobs under the counter because they didn't want people to know they carried a reader line. I'd go to these places knowing they'd bought the product and ask, "Where is it?" And they'd be, like, "Oh, we don't show that to anybody." I sat there for two years scratching my head, going, "What am I doing wrong?" I was just dumb enough to stay at it. The first couple of years in the business world you sweat bullets. You have to believe in your vision for a long time.

Hubert White: Allinson's lucky break.   Allinson's belief in her product kept her going forward. The feedback she was getting from her focus groups and her first customers, as well as from friends and family, confirmed that all of them wanted Eyebobs. "I had to find a different way to get them distributed," she said.

One day, Allinson visited Hubert White, an upscale men's clothing store in downtown Minneapolis, to make a pitch. Brad Sherman, the store's general manager, agreed to display a few pairs of Eyebobs readers for eight weeks, but he was not optimistic. "He said to me very honestly," recalled Allinson, "'Julie, I'll work with you because you're local, but I've done it all. I've done belts, gloves, and scarves. None of this stuff sells.'" Two weeks later, Allinson received a phone call from Sherman. "I'm sold out to the piece," he announced.

Sherman ordered more Eyebobs, and he even helped Allinson design an elegant display case for the store. "I still use it today," Allinson said, adding that "everybody in the market had knocked it off." Over time, Hubert White sold "at least one or two pairs a day every single day of the year" and Eyebobs became one of the store's "most successful items," according to Sherman.[17] "And from there—it just went like wildfire," Allinson said.

Hitting the trade-show circuit.   Sherman told Allinson that she should start attending fashion-industry trade shows to generate new sales leads. At the time, renting a 10×10-foot exhibit booth for each show for roughly $10,000 was an expensive proposition for Allinson. "Well, that scared the bejesus out of me," she said. "You know, money's tight in small companies." So, Allinson decided to dip her toes into the world of trade shows, and in 2002, she signed up for the ENK Men's Show in New York City.[18]

Forming relationships with retailers, however, took time and persistence. At the first ENK Men's Show she attended, everyone who stopped by her booth loved the stylish Eyebobs readers. "I sold to every sales rep in the place," Allinson said. "But a lot of them would buy for themselves and wouldn't buy for their store." The following year, at the same show, "it went gangbusters," Allinson said and explained:

[The sales reps] realized that everything I had told them was true: the product was not disposable—it hung together. They realized I was a woman of my word, it built up that trust, and the orders started coming in. But it's not all a bed of roses. My product was too high-priced for some of the stores that bought it. Others were pushing me to go to an even higher-priced product. But I got that swath in the middle, that 60% to 80% that understood it and wanted it.

After her first ENK success, Allinson attended the men's fashion show in New York City, followed by one in Las Vegas and another Chicago, eventually adding the women's accessory show to her roster. "After Brad Sherman introduced me to men's shows, that's when the sales really started to happen," she said and added:

And that's how the company has grown; and I just keep adding these shows. But it's not, like, "I'm going to do all these shows," throwing stuff at the wall and hoping that it sticks. It was very methodical, very bootstrapped. If the show pays for itself, then I can do the next show.

In 2008, Allinson and 12 of her staff members attended 22 national trade shows; however, Allinson believed that her presence alone was not generating new sales leads. "Most of it comes from word of mouth," she said. "It's because somebody else bought my product, and they're a believer. Three retailers are being dragged by one of their friends who sells it already."

Building the Eyebobs' Team
Like many entrepreneurs who bootstrap their start-ups, in the beginning Allinson did everything herself. "I created the designs, got the inventory stocked, took orders," she said. "I was the only salesperson, packer, shipper, and bookkeeper." An extrovert, Allinson went to lunch with the mailman twice a week, "just to have human interaction," she said.

One day, Allinson realized that her company demanded more than she could handle alone. "That's when you start to get really excited about your business," she said. "That's what you dream of—not being able to do it all yourself." In 2002 she hired her first part-time employee. "The first person you hire is a minimum-wage kind of person, just to pickup the phone," Allinson said. "Really, you take all the phone calls, but they'll get the one line that rolls over."

After her first employee moved out of state, Allinson hired a professional customer service rep/bookkeeper, who was excellent at the job, and who hired two of her relatives as packers and shippers. Unfortunately, the new hire started charging personal items to Allinson's business credit card. "She thought that because she paid the credit card bill, I would not catch on," Allinson said.

But Allinson, who monitored her credit-card statement online every day, caught the embezzler in her tracks. "And so I fired all of them," she said. Losing all employees, including an entire shipping department, during one of the busiest times of the year was tough on the fledgling company. "It was one of my big surges when I was catching on right before Christmas when the retailers count on you," she said.

Getting it right.   In 2004, through personal referrals from friends, Allinson hired a part-time operations manager named Saul and a full-time customer-service rep named Kim, who had 20 years of experience in the optical business. By now, Allinson was self-aware enough to know her own strengths and weaknesses and admitted that while she "was not a great customer-service person," Kim was an excellent one.

Allinson understood the importance of having someone to take care of the nuts and bolts of the business, and she particularly valued Saul, who came to Eyebobs from an upscale department-store chain. "He set a really high bar for us," Allinson said. "He never gets sick of checks and balances—'What do we have in today? How do I get these people organized? How can I get them to be more effective in their jobs?'"

Having two knowledgeable and experienced employees freed Allinson up and allowed her to focus more on growing the business. "I was able to go on the road more to talk to customers," she said, and added that she was "completely blessed with [Saul and Kim] . . . it was beyond my dreams." But the transition from working solo for two years to delegating was not without wrinkles. Allinson explained:

Now I can't even go out to the shipping desk and put together a package I'm so proud of, but I'm so glad they have figured out 10 different ways to automate it and do it better then I did. Frankly, my biggest adjustment was handing over my customers to somebody else. Having them take ownership of my customers and letting them talk to my customers. There's a certain tone that I like to have at Eyebobs—it's well-informed smart ass, somebody who can give them the answer but have fun talking to them and kind of pull their chain. Make it a memorable part of their day.

Building the IT function.   When Allinson started building the IT function of her fledgling company, her husband Paul proved to be an invaluable resource. Although working full time for a major bank, he came to Allinson's office after hours to set up servers and computer networks or create Web interfaces. "He saved us money from day one," Allinson said, adding that "when you have a company that's growing like Eyebobs, the technical piece can make you buckle at the knees. When your system goes down—those charges can be enormous." Describing her husband's contributions to Eyebobs, Allinson emphasized the importance of the "technical piece" he provided:

We have a direct interface from our Web site to our accounting software that eliminates rekeying, which eliminates most errors. That's huge for us. Everything we do, he creates an interface for us. We have direct interface with UPS. We never rekey any of that information, either. That's hours of manpower that we don't have to worry about.

Allinson's husband joined Eyebobs full-time in 2007. In addition to being responsible for the IT function, he oversaw the accounting function of the business. Allinson's only regret about hiring her husband was not having done it sooner. "But he was my bread-and-butter-man," she said. "He was the guy who allowed me to be an entrepreneur."

A Team of Hardworking "Nut Cases"

In 2009, Eyebobs had 12 full-time employees. "The people who work at Eyebobs today are the best thing to happen to this company," Allinson said. "Each one is a hardworking nut case, and I derive so much positive energy from them." Allinson was proud of her diverse group, which included one national-sales manager, responsible for the independent sales reps; two people responsible for bookkeeping, accounting, and data entry; and one person who managed the company's Web site, blog, and all of the social networks.

"Everybody else is the packer, shipper, and phone person," Allinson said, and added that all her packers and shippers also served as customer-service reps. "They are all too smart for packing jobs, and I needed to engage them in other ways. By answering the phone, they know that their mistakes are immediately felt by the customers."

Allinson's Evolving Role—Growing Sales

As her company grew and she expanded her staff, in addition to her focus on design, Allinson's priority became growing sales. "Marketing comes very naturally to me," Allinson said, "but not the sales part; I had to figure out how to do it inexpensively and effectively. So my attention went to how to get that done."

Over the years, Allinson developed a sales strategy to help her grow Eyebobs. As she saw it, one of its main components was a well-stocked inventory, which carried a risk, but which helped her differentiate her business and engender customer loyalty:

Reading glasses are not a seasonal product. You're trying to create an annuity for the retailer and for yourself . . . So the whole sales strategy is trying to keep that inventory full so that people always have something to go back to. You're trying to educate the retailer that once a month or once a week they need to be reordering Eyebobs. If a customer loses a frame, if they like that frame, they can continue to reorder it from you. And that's really not what customers are used to. They are used to calling for a special order and being told, no we don't have it. And I want to say, "Yes, we have it, we'll ship it for you today." Most companies do not carry inventory—we do. I've changed that paradigm, and that's my real risk in my business.

Managing Growth

For many entrepreneurs, the business catchphrase: "grow or die" meant "grow at breakneck speed or die." Allinson did not see it that way. Unmanaged, "growth could easily swallow you up," she cautioned. She knew that unmanaged growth was a sure sign of growing too fast.

Unlike the cocky upstarts who took on debt swiftly to fund expansions only to crash and burn, Allinson grew her company slowly, out of her own cash flow, and was careful not to overstretch her resources. It took her six years to hit the $1 million in revenue mark. "I spent my money sourcing the product and trying to get the very best product," she said, "and I didn't have money to blow on marketing. I had to be happy to grow a little bit at a time, to get the word out."

Once the word got out about her product, Allinson started getting offers from retailers across the country, but she was very selective about her clients. "It's important whom you say no to," she said. "Why would I take on customers who can't pay me? We are very careful about who we extend credit to." She explained how her financial background was a huge asset in dealing with clients and managing risk:

Cash flow is king, no doubt about it. Now, I'm in a situation where I'm always looking at the balance sheet, I'm looking at inventory, looking at where the money is. Because I extend terms to my customers, I don't have factors in the middle of this. I take all the risk of all these small customers I do business with. Because I understand the collections process and cash flow, we've stayed on top of that. You can't let that become the last thing—it has to be the first thing.

Allinson also tried to broaden her customer base to prevent a crisis that inevitably happened when a company's chief customers suddenly pulled orders. She was not afraid to say "no, thank you" to prospective buyers who posed too much risk to her company's financial health. She explained why she turned away a lot of business:

I didn't want them to be 80% of my business. What if they go away? I do have two or three big customers—they all have a big slice, but it's still a small part of my business. I feel I'm a boutique business. Not everybody wants an expensive reader or is comfortable wearing fashion. So, I'm better off selling to boutiques.

Allinson thought that "it's easy to get into business, but it's hard to stay in business." She understood the perils of undisciplined growth and the importance of the continuous monitoring of inventory levels:

You think, oh yeah, I want to sell to everybody, bring on the business. Bullshit. You've got to manage that, pay for that inventory. And you better know who you're going to sell it to, and how long it's going to take you to see it out. I feel I have a significant amount of inventory. When I was running Mack & Moore, one of our investors, who used to be the president of Target, would say over and over again, "Julie, inventory is not like fine wine, it does not get better with age." So even if it's $25,000 worth of inventory that's just sitting there, get rid of it.

Allinson considered 2005 a breakthrough year for the fledgling company because Eyebobs pulled in $840,000 in revenues. "When I hit that number, I can remember I thought we've made it," she said. In 2006, her start-up generated $1 million in revenue, followed by $4.5 million in 2007. In 2008, Allinson expanded her Minneapolis office and pumped money into a new phone system better equipped to handle the increasing number of calls. She said:

Because we're growing by leaps and bounds right now, we are expanding our area. One of the ideas for the new phone system is that when you're on hold, we want people telling their Eyebobs story. Some funny story and we want it to be a customer, preferably an end user, who's talking about how they found Eyebobs.

Beating the Copycats

Growing a company from zero to $4.5 million in sales in seven years, with no outside investors or credit lines would make many entrepreneurs complacent, but Allinson did not dwell on her extraordinary achievement. "I never focus on my success," she said. "I always focus on the things I'm going to fix and do next. You just put something else on your worry plate."

In 2009, her "worry plate" was full of copycats who were knocking off her reading glasses and funky designs, using inferior materials and selling them for less. Imitation may be the sincerest form of flattery but, for an entrepreneur like Allinson, whose success was born of creativity and innovation, it was a big problem.

To beat the competition whose only game was imitation, she was forced to be more innovative and take charge of the market, which was not an easy feat in a time of economic downturn. In lieu of offering a lower-priced product, which was what many in the fashion-accessories business were doing, Allinson decided to "add some other value," and make her product "even more interesting." Instead of the usual protective case for her Eyebobs readers, she created an innovative leather case with room for car keys and credit cards. She explained:

I want to add value to the product rather than increase or decrease the price. My costs have gone up, but I'm not passing that on to the customer. Other reading-glasses companies are knocking us off—that's why I'm changing my cases; I want to do more for my customer for $65. I want to add value so the customer sees us as the leader. Eventually, instead of saying, "Where are my reading glasses?" I want people to say, "Where are my Eyebobs?"

And, when asked about keeping her Eyebobs business ahead of the copycat pack in the future, Allinson said:

I have to stay at the front; I have to be more creative. I really work hard not to look at people who are knocking me off. What am I going to do? Stand there with my head looking over my shoulder? No, I want to look straight ahead, doing all the things that they are not thinking of doing. They are busy trying to be me, but they are not me.

LESSONS FROM EYEBOBS

What can you learn from Allinson's experience? How did she approach growth? To grow Eyebobs, what did she need to do from a people perspective? From a technology perspective? Why did she prefer many smaller customers over a few big customers? How did she design her business to play to her strengths? What was she constantly trying to improve? How did she discover an employee was stealing money?

Interestingly, her sales breakthrough came from a men's clothing retail store not a women's fashion retail store. Note, also, that Allinson's initial choice of a sales channel—opticians—was a failure because they viewed her product as competing with more profitable products they could sell. Allinson had to learn and adapt.

Allinson had a strategic focus on product differentiation by providing styling and quality at a good price point. She outsourced manufacturing after spending plenty of time on the ground in China and Italy getting to know her suppliers—and letting them get to know her enough to take her seriously. She sold wholesale to boutique and high-end retailers and directly to customers via the Internet.

She kept control and oversight over the customers by handling the shipping, billing, and customer service complaints. Because she discovered customer service was not her strength, she hired someone who loved dealing with customers over the phone. As Eyebobs grew, she narrowed her focus to design, sales, and management.

Once Eyebobs got big enough, she acquired sophisticated technology to help manage the business and control product flow from orders to customer service. She kept getting better at the details of the business—the processes—which were the foundation to quadruple sales from 2006 to 2007 and double sales every year thereafter.

In successfully growing Eyebobs, Allinson learned everything from acquisition of materials, design, and marketing. She evolved in how she developed her client base, handled competitors, and put in place more and better processes so she could scale the business.

She also implemented controls that allowed her to catch theft and motivated her to "clean house" in her back office, which created the opportunity to upgrade systems and hire more experienced and professional people.

CHAPTER 2 TAKEAWAYS

1. Respect the power of growth—both its positive aspects and destructive capabilities.

2. Do not assume all growth is good and that you must grow to be successful.

3. Approach growth as a strategic decision and frequently weigh its benefits and risks. Growth may be a great opportunity but with that opportunity comes risks. Be vigilant about growth risks.

4. Understand that business growth usually requires more people, more processes, more controls, and more administration. Growth changes everything including the business culture.

5. Growth is hard. Growth can be good and growth can be bad—it depends.

6. Growth requires the right leadership, culture, and processes.

7. Growth will create new risks that must be managed.

8. As a business continues to grow, the management challenges change. The solutions, processes, and controls required for a business with $1M in revenue need to be substantially retooled for a business reaching $4M of sales, as Julie Allinson learned.

9. Use the Growth Decision Template and the Growth Risks Audit to help you think about growth, to manage your pace of growth, and to manage the risks of growth for your business.

3   PRECONDITIONS TO GROWTH

CEO QUOTES

- "It's easy to get into business but hard to stay in business."
- "Focus on the one thing you can do better than anyone else and then figure out how to make that thing attractive to a big market."
- "When scaling, focus first on those processes that generate cash."
- "Focus—be 2 inches wide and 2 miles deep."
- "5 Ps: Plan, People, Passion, Prioritize, Process."
- "Prioritize—what is critical to making it to the next month, next quarter, next year."
- "Understand that growth puts you in a different competitive space."
- "In a high growth business, it is easy to get spread too thin trying to be too many things to too many people."
- "Diversification kills focus."
- "The more we focused and said no, the more we grew."
- "As you grow, it is going to be very appetizing to take on disparate products and technology that may ultimately start to pull the company apart as they compete for resources."
- "Focus on one thing you can do better than anyone else and then focus on finding a way to make it appealing to a big market."

SUSAN FELLER'S STORY[1]

On a July morning in 2009, Susan Feller sat in the eating area of her retail bakery, 3 Fellers Bakery (3 Fellers), in Goochland, Virginia, with her son Mike, a recent MBA graduate of the Darden School of Business, and marveled about how, in just two and a half years, she had been able to build a successful business by baking and selling gluten-free cakes and desserts.

The gluten-free products that 3 Fellers made were now sold in 26 grocery stores, including 10 Whole Foods stores, on the Internet, and in her retail store exceeding $200,000 in sales. She was running a successful entrepreneurial start-up with commercially viable products and repeat customers.

In 2005, when Feller was a happily retired high-school guidance counselor, homemaker, and mother of three adult sons, she was diagnosed with celiac disease. Celiac disease is a disease of the small intestines that forced Feller to avoid eating or being exposed to a list of foods made with wheat, rye, most oats (unless grown in a gluten-free environment), or barley. But it was really the inclusion of flours, breads, pastries, and desserts on the list that got Feller moving toward starting her own business.

Feller loved to bake and make beautiful cakes for birthdays, weddings, and other special occasions. Now she found to her dismay that most store-bought gluten-free desserts did not even come close to tasting as good as what she baked at home. So, she spent more than a year learning how to make her own gluten-free pastry creations, which she knew tasted as good as anything made by the finest pastry chefs.

Her secret ingredient was her own flour mix, the product of 12 months of trial-and-error experimentation. She tested her desserts first on members of her family and then on members of her gluten-free support group, the West End Gluten Intolerance Group. She discovered everyone loved her desserts, and several support-group members encouraged her to sell them.

With no previous business experience or training, Feller decided to make the leap and started a business in her home in the spring of 2007. She baked in her kitchen until December 2008, when she bought and transformed a 2,400 square-foot house into a commercial bakery and retail store.

By July 2009, the woman who had never even thought about becoming an entrepreneur now managed seven part-time employees. Feller handled new-product development, sales, and accounting. She also oversaw production, managed inventory, and ordered supplies. Her modified kitchen had two traditional stoves, two refrigerators, and four stand-up freezers, along with two professional bakery mixers and several small counter mixers.

Like most entrepreneurs of successful start-up businesses, Feller kept accounting records by hand and paid bills the week she received them even though her grocery clients paid her between 30 days and 45 days after delivery. She self-financed her business; she did not advertise; and she did not buy anything she could not pay for with cash. She had no computerized inventory or accounting system, no employee manuals, and no automated processes. She did have a Web site and many loyal, happy customers.

When Feller started selling her products in the late spring of 2007, she set her prices after researching competitive prices, but she did not know her per-unit costs. She began selling in three Richmond gourmet and natural-food grocery stores and acquired new customers by repeatedly calling on them herself and giving them samples to try. In addition, in June 2007, she launched the Web site from which she sold her products and participated as an exhibitor at the National Gluten Intolerance Conference held in Richmond, Virginia.

In July of 2007, she began discussions with the Whole Foods store in Charlottesville, Virginia. By November, she was selling her gluten-free cookie dough in five Ukrop's grocery stores in the Richmond area. Her persistence with Whole Foods paid off when she was approved as a vendor for the Mid-Atlantic region and began selling in the Charlottesville store in June 2008.

The Whole Foods Mid-Atlantic region comprised 35 stores located from New Jersey to North Carolina. By July 2009, Feller's gluten-free products were in ten of those Whole Foods stores, in Virginia and the District of Columbia, Ellwood Thompson's Natural Market in Richmond, and in 16 other grocery stores, including Ukrop's.

Along with Feller's success starting her small business had come more opportunities than she ever had imagined. As a typical entrepreneur, she struggled with deciding which opportunity to undertake first.

Market Size

Between 5 and 7 percent of the U.S. population suffers from gluten intolerance and struggles with having to eat gluten-free food. The producers of gluten-free baked breads and desserts face the additional challenge of having to produce these products in completely gluten-free environments. Thus, for gluten-free production, only gluten-free machines, equipment, utensils, and bowls can be used to make gluten-free products.

This led to the creation of many small gluten-free bakeries and several midsized gluten-free dessert companies that produced and sold frozen desserts in different areas of the United States. The market for gluten-free desserts became big enough to convince Betty Crocker to introduce gluten-free cake mixes. Even Budweiser's Redbridge gluten-free beer landed in grocery stores in the fall of 2009.

3 Fellers' Products

If refrigerated, fresh 3 Fellers' products last approximately two weeks. By experimenting, Feller created recipes for gluten-free products that could be frozen and when defrosted tasted as good as freshly baked ones, giving her the flexibility of selling both frozen and fresh products.

Frozen gluten-free baked desserts had a shelf life of approximately four months, and 3 Fellers sold frozen chocolate-chip, oatmeal-raisin, and sugar cookie dough and frozen buttermilk slice-and-bake biscuits. Baked cornbread and six-inch chocolate, vanilla, carrot, and coconut cakes were also offered for sale.

All of Feller's grocery customers carried her gluten-free frozen dough, and several of them also carried her fresh-baked cakes, pastries, and individually packaged desserts such as cupcakes, muffins, and pies. She planned to add cinnamon-raisin cake, mini-cupcakes, and baking-biscuit dough.

An additional outlet for 3 Fellers' gluten-free products was her retail store in the bakery where custom orders were filled for a variety of cakes, brownies, scones, tarts, pastries, dessert bars, seven varieties of cupcakes, eight varieties of pies, four types of muffins, wedding cakes, banana bread, cinnamon-raisin buns, cheesecakes, and cakes for birthdays and other special occasions. Standard items such as gluten-free breads and rolls were always available.

Feller's research had shown that some bakeries sold gluten-free products that were not manufactured in a gluten-free environment and therefore risked contamination. All of 3 Fellers' products were produced in the 100 percent gluten-free environment of the 3 Fellers' bakery kitchen in Goochland, Virginia where current space and equipment were operating at 70 percent of capacity, and from which products were delivered to each grocery store in a delivery SUV.

All ingredients in these gluten-free products were natural, and only flavorings, fruits, and chocolate of the highest quality were used. Also, all ingredients were certified by the Gluten Intolerance Group of North America, which had higher standards than the gluten-free standards of the FDA.

Opportunities

Like many successful entrepreneurial start-ups, Susan's success generated growth opportunities without her planning for growth or even thinking about it. However, the number of growth opportunities along with the limitations of time, people, and capital forced her now to prioritize how she would grow and in order to prioritize she needed to confront some difficult decisions.

3 Fellers' products were approved for sale in 35 Whole Foods stores in the Mid-Atlantic Region. So far she was selling to 10 Whole Foods stores located in the cities of Charlottesville, Richmond, Washington, DC and in Northern Virginia; however, there was a demand for 3 Fellers' products from other Whole Foods stores in the District of Columbia and Maryland.

In the beginning, most stores sold only the frozen gluten-free products, but then Whole Foods requested the freshly baked cakes and other desserts to sell in its bakeries. At the rate 3 Fellers' sales was growing, the demand from Whole Foods' could soon exceed its current production capacity.

Feller's research had also shown the lack of competitive gluten-free frozen cookie dough or biscuit products on the market anywhere else in the United States. To expand into the national market, however, 3 Fellers would need to buy the equipment to produce, package, seal, and freeze-dry the dough in volume quantities to sell to such centralized national grocery chains as Kroger, Safeway, and Wal-Mart.

In addition, many local bakeries that did not carry gluten-free products had approached Feller about selling her products in their retail outlets. Although this would require more distribution capacity, it would increase the 3 Fellers' made-to-order business significantly.

Recently, Feller had been approached by two businessmen she knew by reputation. They had experience in the baking business and wanted to include her in building and operating a gluten-free baking plant in New Jersey. It would be a joint venture as the three of them would be partners in the baking business and use her recipes. Her Goochland retail store would be excluded.

Sysco, the largest wholesale food distribution company in the U.S. with nearly 400,000 restaurants and food service operators, approached Feller about distributing her products.

Because of the magnitude of the Sysco offer, Susan had to think about how she viewed her success:

I love baking and decorating cakes. I have found my passion. My bakery brings together the artist in me—I was an art major in college—and it's the guidance counselor in me—I enjoy helping people. You would understand if you could see the look of a 10-year-old boy upon receiving his first decorated birthday cake that he can eat that is gluten free.

Issues

Feller faced some big questions:

- How big a business did she want to build?
- What was her "end game"?
- Did she want to build something for her children to take over?
- Should she focus on meeting the needs of Whole Foods first by expanding into all its Mid-Atlantic stores?
- Should she diversify her customer base?
- Should she try to be a first mover and go national with her cookie and biscuit dough by selling through big national grocery chains?
- How would she finance production expansion?

- Could she manage a bigger business?

- Her love was creating new recipes and producing beautiful great-tasting desserts but would growth take her away from that?

- Should she partner with someone?

- Should she outsource production? If so, how would she protect her trade-secret flour recipe?

- Should she open more retail locations?

- Should she wholesale her products to local bakeries throughout Virginia?

In other words, should she grow her business? If so, what should that growth look like? What are her preconditions to growth? Preconditions to growth are the preparatory steps an entrepreneur needs to accomplish to lessen the risks that growth could result in major quality, financial, or customer service problems. For example, what personnel does she need to hire? What processes or controls does she need to install to be able to grow without creating major quality, customer service, or financial problems?

WORKSHOP #1: IS THIS BUSINESS READY TO GROW?
Using the Growth Decision Template and the Growth Risks Audit as checklists, please do the following:

1. List all of Feller's growth opportunities.

2. Evaluate Feller's current business situation, taking into account her skills and weaknesses and her employees, processes, controls, manufacturing capabilities, distribution capabilities, sales capabilities, customer service, and financial capabilities.

3. Evaluate each growth opportunity and determine what Feller would have to add, change, or install to make each growth opportunity happen.

4. What are Feller's big risks of growth?

5. What do you think Feller should do and why? In answering this question, please create two lists: (a) a prioritized list of how she should grow and (b) a list of her preconditions to growth.

WORKSHOP OBJECTIVES

This workshop has the following objectives:

1. to provide you with an opportunity to use both the Growth Decision Template and Growth Risks Audit to think about and analyze growth opportunities and risks;

2. to give you practice making the tough choices of prioritizing growth opportunities; and

3. to teach you to think about the preconditions to growth: what people, processes, and controls do you need to put in place before you grow your business?

The last question raises the tension of investing ahead of growth versus investing after the growth has hit you. It is partly a financial question (how much can you afford) and partly a tolerance for risk question (are you willing to take on execution risks, knowing that you need better processes, controls, and maybe more people).

So, take a break from the book and go to work coming up with your answers. It should take you at least two hours to think through Feller's issues using the tools. Have fun!

I have included the following two blank pages for your final answers.

WORKSHOP DISCUSSION

First, there is no one right answer to Feller's challenging situation. What follows is how I would approach her challenging opportunities if she asked my advice.

Feller's Current Reality

Before analyzing the pros and cons of each growth opportunity and thinking about Feller's risks of growth, I would start with an assessment of Feller and 3 Fellers. This assessment would include evaluating Fellers' current strengths and weaknesses and her personal and business goals, and then I would try to identify her priorities. Answers to these questions would help answer the following fundamental questions: Should Feller grow her business? Why?

Feller is 3 Fellers' product development person and the only person with the knowledge of how to make her secret flour, the key ingredient in her products. She also is 3 Fellers' only salesperson; she oversees her eight part-time bakers and retail store personnel and is in charge of inventory control, ordering supplies, keeping the accounting records, paying the bills, and overseeing production and distribution. Feller is a one-woman band.

In addition, Feller has not yet taken advantage of technology to manage her company, installed commercial kitchen equipment, or developed a distribution system.

Feller's business lacks an accounting software package, inventory control software, or customer relationship management software. She does not know her per product costs.

Her kitchen does not have commercial freezers, refrigerators, ovens, or space to increase production. She only has one delivery vehicle and must make all the sales calls herself as well as make deliveries to Whole Foods in northern Virginia.

She has little time for calling on current customers, but she still loves to spend part of her limited time designing and baking custom cakes for birthdays, parties, and weddings, her true passion.

She would love for her sons to come into the business someday, but the business is not currently big enough to entice her oldest son, who has business experience and an MBA to come aboard. Her youngest son wants to work in the business upon graduation from college.

She is motivated to help others by producing and selling to more gluten-intolerant people. Although she does not want to manage a large business, she does think that it would be fun to be a big player in gluten-free customer segment. She has limited cash to invest in the business but can live on her school system retirement.

So, I ask, why should Feller grow 3 Fellers beyond its current operations? Why should she spend more time managing and growing the business when she loves to design and bake cakes for celebratory events? 3 Fellers is already a success. Feller does not need more income. So why grow? Before she can evaluate the various business opportunities, Feller needs to answer that question.

Let's assume that she answers that she wants to grow 3 Fellers because she wants to help more gluten-intolerant people enjoy good desserts. Now, let's look at her alternatives.

Feller's Growth Alternatives

1. Continue to improve, grow slowly, and spend one-third to one-half of her time doing what she loves to do—custom celebration baking.

2. Expand into more Whole Foods stores and put more products in each store.

3. Wholesale her products to other Virginia bakeries.

4. Attempt to make and sell her frozen cookie and biscuit doughs to national grocery retailers.

5. See if Sysco would sell and deliver her products to its customers.

6. Enter into the big bakery joint venture in New Jersey.

7. Some combination of the above.

Pros and Cons of Each Alternative

Alternative 1: Improve on the status quo.   Focusing on her strengths and growing slowly limits Feller's risks—whether financial, quality control, or hiring and training—and allows her to do more of what she enjoys. She could pace her growth and expansion to enable her to pay for increased production capacity, equipment, and upgrades as the business could afford them.

Regardless of the alternative that Feller selects, she needs to put in software packages for accounting, inventory control, and customer relationship management, and she probably needs a part-time accountant/administrative person to assist her, with the understanding that Feller would continue to have sole control of the checkbook, cash, and credit cards.

The key risk posed by adopting Alternative 1 is that it limits her ability to pursue one of her stated goal to "help a lot of people."

In addition, Feller has customer concentration risks with Whole Foods and Ukrops as her main customers. Either could change its mind on a day's notice and decide to no longer sell her products. This vulnerability is real because Feller currently has limited time now to maintain close relationships with the key people at Whole Foods and Ukrops that make product decisions.

Other risks posed by Alternative 1 are that another bakery will seize the opportunity to become the dominant national frozen cookie dough maker and other Virginia bakeries will enter the gluten-free product market. Furthermore, unless Feller grows aggressively, 3 Fellers will not get big enough to attract and financially support her sons.

Alternative 2: Expand into more Whole Foods stores. 3 Feller's products are currently approved for sale in twenty-five Whole Foods stores in which Feller does not actively sell. Feller could expand into more Whole Foods outlets and broaden the line of 3 Fellers fresh-baked goods in existing stores. The main advantage here should be faster new customer acquisition or a faster sales cycle because she is approved and has a track record in ten Whole Foods stores. This alternative should be easier growth from a sales generation perspective.

The biggest risk of this strategy is that expanding within the Whole Foods spectrum would require Feller to spend more time on the road, away from her baking production and retail store. As a result, she would need to appoint someone to manage the daily production and the retail store. This alternative is made more complicated because all of her employees are part-time now by their choice. There is no existing employee who could step in.

A second detriment to Alternative 2 is that Feller currently has limited unused production capacity in her current space so there is a limit to how fast she can expand to service more stores. She would have to find employees to work a partial night shift, which, in turn, would mean longer days for Feller, unless she trains managers.

Alternatively, Feller could look at the feasibility and costs of physically expanding her current kitchen and at the costs of acquiring commercial-grade and size freezers, refrigerators, and ovens to increase her baking capacity during the regular daytime shift.

Third, a Whole Foods expansion may exacerbate her cash flow challenges because she would incur additional people, equipment, and supply costs more than 45 days ahead of receiving payment from Whole Foods. How much Whole Foods growth can she afford?

Fourth, she would probably need another delivery van and an additional full-time delivery employee because the new Whole Foods stores would be in Maryland, North Carolina, and farther north.

Fifth, expanding sales to more Whole Foods stores, while being relatively easy sales, would increases her customer concentration risks. With so much of 3 Fellers' business concentrated with Whole Foods, Feller would be very vulnerable to Whole Foods decision about her as a supplier. What would happen if Whole Foods decided to private brand with an entity bigger than 3 Fellers that could produce products for multiple regions of Whole Foods? What would happen to Feller if Whole Foods hired a new person in charge of products for the Mid-Atlantic Region who decides to replace 3 Fellers products with another producer? What would Feller do with her excess capacity and employees then?

Alternative 3: Sell wholesale to other Virginia bakeries. In Alternative 3, Feller would concentrate on building a diversified customer base across the state. She could start first with the Richmond metropolitan area and expand out in concentric circles to northern Virginia, Shenandoah Valley, and the Tidewater area. Building a brand name regionally could protect her against local competition. This alternative would be superior to Alternative 2 in that it provides more control and diversifies her client base.

However, first, the major negative to this slow and small approach is that these potential customers are, individually, smaller buyers than a grocery store such as Whole Foods, so it would take a considerable sales effort to generate enough new customers to have a meaningful revenue impact. In other words, because new customer acquisition activities would not be as efficient, her costs would be higher. This strategy would require her to focus on knowing her per unit costs and having different prices per product, based on volume and delivery location.

Second, to expand regionally, Feller would need more sales, customer service, and delivery help as well as an increase in her production capacity. She would need help with accounting, receiving, and keeping track of each store's purchases and payments.

Third, it is an open question as to whether the individual bakery stores would allow her to brand her products.

Fourth, she would still have a mismatch between cash outlays and cash inflows as with the Whole Foods alternative unless she only sold on a cash on delivery basis to these entrepreneurial customers. Otherwise, she would have not only cash mismatching again but also additional credit risks because all of the new customers would be small businesses.

Alternative 4: National sales of cookie dough.   Alternative 4 would be to focus on growth by selling the frozen cookie dough nationally. The pros of this strategy are that cookie dough can be mass produced, frozen, and shipped to the distribution centers of major grocery retailers. Another pro is that the retail grocery retail market is controlled by a small number of buyers. As a result, there are efficiencies in sales, customer service, and distribution. In addition, the potential exists for big volume so you could grow sales into the millions quickly. Sounds good so far.

There are cons, however. This alternative is a perfect example of the saying, "There is no free lunch." First, to execute this strategy, Feller would have to spend a lot of time trying to convince these retailers that she could be a viable producer. To do that, she would have to figure out how she would manufacture the cookie dough in large quantities and how she would ship it. To manufacture cookie dough in large quantities, she has two choices: build her own "plant," which would require a significant capital investment in real estate (ownership or leasing) and equipment (purchase or leasing). It would also require additional employees, a production manager, a shipping department, and contracting with a major trucking company.

Second, large-volume buyers are very cost conscious. It would be critical for Feller to know, before she enters the sales discussions, her projected per unit costs. She has not previously focused on this issue, but without this information she could end up with large buyers negotiating a purchase price below her costs—not a good result for obvious reasons.

Third, even after figuring out the capital needed and her per unit costs, Feller must be able to convince a major retailer to give her small business a try. Remember how long it took her to get her Whole Foods' approval for several stores. Feller must have a strategy for reaching and persuading the right decision makers at Wal-Mart, Kroger, and other potential major retailers to buy her product.

Fourth, Feller must ask herself two difficult questions about growing the business this way: does she want to spend her time and take on the additional financial risks of becoming a national player with large and powerful customers, and will she need experienced, expensive senior production and sales managers to oversee this part of the business? That is, can she do it herself or does she need to bring in expert help?

Fifth, even investigating outsourcing options and production scaling costs takes time and money. How should she proceed? Should Feller hire a consultant to do this? The tradeoff is that if Feller spends a lot of time on this task she will not be able to keep the same level of effort with her current activities. As a result, she would need to hire people to help with her current activities because she cannot afford for her base business to suffer while she explores growth. Again, this alternative would require cash out before cash in.

Alternative 5: Sysco.   Sysco is a world-class food and food products distribution company. Sysco could solve Feller's needs related to distribution to restaurants, a customer segment that she does not now serve, and possibly to retail bakeries. However, Sysco does not deliver to grocery chains. At this point, the Sysco option is a delivery solution if Feller expands by selling to local Virginia bakeries and restaurants as new customers. It is not an expansion option by itself.

Alternative 6: New Jersey bakery joint venture.   This idea could solve Feller's manufacturing scaling challenge. The cons of joint venturing at this stage are numerous. First, it is very risky going into a business partnership with partners you do not know intimately and have no prior business experience with. Feller would no longer "control" her business destiny even though she would own 100 percent of her retail store.

The financial risks would be much larger than Feller currently has. She would need to spend significant time getting to know her new partners and incur significant legal costs negotiating a joint venture that protects her and 3 Fellers' secret flour recipe.

Simply joint venturing still leaves open the question of how Feller would acquire the new national customers necessary to produce enough demand to keep the manufacturing plant running at a profit. Lastly, is Feller willing to spend time every week in New Jersey working with her new partners?

The additional complexity of getting to know partners, negotiating a deal, and putting in the time and effort to learn to work together could be overwhelming. Why does Feller need these risks? Can she instead outsource production, if needed, to an established large-scale bakery closer to her current operations? Can she meet her production needs in a lower risk manner?

FELLER'S GROWTH DECISION

Scaling

While scaling is addressed in depth in Chapter 5, Feller's business decisions revolve around the question of how she should scale production, sales, and distribution. The answers depend in part on the product. Scaling frozen cookie dough is different than scaling fresh baked cookies, biscuits, and cakes. Both of those product segments are different from scaling custom birthday, wedding, anniversary, and special event desserts.

One critical learning point about growing a business is the necessity of strategic focus. Should Feller focus her growth efforts on one of the three product segments? Another way to look at it is customer segments. Should Feller focus on grocery chains, wholesale bakery and restaurant customers, retail customers via the Internet, or by opening more small retail outlets? The difference in customer segments is one of the risks of customer concentration versus the costs and time to acquire many bakery, restaurant, or retail customers.

Product sales drive how much she would need to scale manufacturing and distribution. Choice of sales growth strategy determines the speed and manner of scaling manufacturing and distribution. Should Feller free up more of her time to sell? Should she hire an experienced food product sales person?

Scaling also involves putting in more processes and controls. Scaling may involve adding more experienced full-time people. Scaling will cost money, and much of that money will have to be paid out before more revenue is produced. Feller needs to determine her potential additional costs and decide what she can afford and over what time period. Growth can be phased or paced to accommodate process improvements and financial affordability.

Complexity of Growth

I hope by now you have a better appreciation for the complexity of growth and the interrelationship among growth, scaling, financial risks, and quality risks. It takes time to assess the options, the potential benefits, and the risks. Successful serial entrepreneurs learn how to grow by taking small steps and testing and trying various growth avenues without talking big financial or quality risks.

The prospects of growth can be intoxicating, addictive, and give you a "big head," resulting in overconfidence, a feeling of superiority, and invincibility. Unless the risks are assessed and planned for, unprepared growth can lead to business and financial demise.

WHAT SHOULD FELLER DO?

Feller should reject the idea of doing the New Jersey bakery plant partnership. It is too risky and is not necessary to achieve her goals. Feller should continue discussions with Sysco to see whether they would deliver her products to bakeries as well as restaurants.

Feller probably does not have the size, brand credibility, or financial ability to contract with the major grocers for national distribution of her cookie dough at this point. This idea is probably premature. As she takes her first growth steps, she should consider exhibiting her products at the one or two key national trade shows that retailers frequent yearly.

Based on her success with Whole Foods, she could possibly sell more easily to boutique grocery retail chains such as Trader Joe's, Wegman's, or Rebecca's Natural Food stores. This exposure would give her customer diversification without potentially overwhelming her with growth.

Feller needs to focus on her preconditions to growth. She needs to install accounting, per unit costs, customer relationship, and inventory control processes and software. She needs a part-time experienced controller. She needs to determine the costs of expanding her current baking space as well as the costs of commercial grade refrigerators, freezers, and ovens.

She needs to talk to Richmond area bakeries to determine demand for her products. She should also talk to high-end Richmond restaurants to determine their interest in her desserts. Finally, she needs to talk to the existing customers to determine whether they will expand into more of her products.

Feller then needs to formulate a plan based on that information. That plan could encompass multiple thrusts: wholesale sales to bakeries and restaurants, expansion of product lines in existing grocery store customers, expansion into more Whole Foods in a paced manner, and acquisition of a new boutique grocery chain customer.

Paced growth to bakeries and to existing customers limits her distribution challenges and focuses her new sales efforts. She can bring on new customers as she expands capacity. Then she can determine, based on learning and results, whether to expand to more Whole Foods or to expand to different boutique grocery chains like Wegmans in Northern Virginia or specialty grocers.

Feller needs to implement processes. This was mentioned previously in her preconditions to growth, but it is so critical that I need to explain further. Like most small businesses, Feller has reached a good revenue level by doing a lot of the work herself and by overseeing everything in the business.

Growth will make it impossible for Feller to do or oversee everything herself, but she also can't move to an entirely hands-off approach. To maintain quality and not lose control of what she has built, Feller needs to implement processes—lots of processes. She needs to prioritize in what order she will put these processes in place. Feller cannot scale successfully unless she puts in processes.

With more information, Feller can decide how much and in what product direction she wants to expand her business.

WORKSHOP #2: YOUR COMPANY'S PRECONDITIONS TO GROWTH

Using the Growth Decision Template and the Growth Risks Audit to think about growth and to help illuminate the risks of growth, make a list of your company's preconditions to growth. This thinking process applies whether your company is young or at the $1M revenue level, the $50M revenue level, or the $250M revenue level. The same tools can help you navigate the issues about growing your business to the next level, no matter where it is now.

So, spend at least eight hours using these tools to think about your growth alternatives, risks, and preconditions. Understand that. as you learn more in latter chapters, we will come back to this workshop.

Do not do this workshop in one eight-hour session. My experience with clients and executive education students is that two hours of thinking like this at a time is usually the most productive. So spend two hours and stop. Let this incubate in your mind a day. Then, come back and spend two hours again. Stop and let it incubate and then come back to it again. But spend eight hours over a week's time.

One key point to remember: as your business grows, it is highly likely that the people, processes, and controls that you used to help you grow to your current level most likely will have to be improved or even changed to take you to the next level. As you grow, your business model and business infrastructure (processes, controls, and people) will probably need to be upgraded.

CHAPTER 3 TAKEAWAYS

1. Growth requires more people, processes, and controls.

2. Thinking about growth strategically requires disciplined, focused thinking time and processes.

3. The Growth Decision Template and Growth Risks Audit are two thinking processes to help you think about the complexity of growth and its risks, preconditions, and costs.

4. Growth requires you to scale manufacturing or production, sales, distribution, customer service, human resources, and accounting functions.

5. Growth costs money that must be paid out *before* more revenue is received. How much growth can you afford?

6. Growth requires you to prioritize how you will grow and the order of process implementation.

7. Growth can come in phases and be paced to better manage risks.

8. Growth requires improvements and scaling.

PART II   HOW TO GROW

4   THE FOUR Ps
Planning, Prioritization, Processes, and Pace

This chapter covers key content on essential elements of how to manage the growth of a business. It should be read more than once because these lessons apply every time you set forth on a new growth course. As you read, make a list of key takeaway lessons that can help you with your business's current growth challenges.

No two businesses grow the same or face identical challenges, but there is much overlap and the importance of planning and preparation for growth cannot be underestimated. Likewise, smart growth requires more processes, and the quantity and quality of the growth will be impacted by the pace or speed of growth.

THE FOUR Ps

In researching successful private companies that survived the challenges of growth, four growth themes came up repeatedly: (1) the power of planning ahead for growth; (2) the introduction of the appropriate processes, at the right times, and in the right order to manage growth; (3) adoption of prioritization heuristics to focus the entrepreneur's time on the most critical areas at that time; and (4) proactive management of the pace of growth.

PLANNING AHEAD OF GROWTH
CEO Quotes on Planning

- "Begin with the end in mind."

- "We set up as if we were a larger company right from the start."

- "Work your business plan until it fits on one page."

- "Plan from the beginning—know what it is you are setting out to do with the end in mind."

Structure

Many of the companies that I studied or worked with did not plan for growth. Growth happened, and the entrepreneurs reacted. The exceptions to this serendipity were those companies led by entrepreneurs who had previous start-up/growth experience. They had learned from that experience—sometimes the hard way—that they needed to plan carefully for growth.

How did these entrepreneurs plan for their business's growth? Basically, they asked themselves several questions about how growth might impact the structure and operations of their businesses. What will the organizational structure look like at $5M or $10M in revenue? Will the organizational structure need to change at $25M in revenue? At $50M in revenue? At $100M in revenue?

At what point in the growth of the company will it need to add more processes, managers, and structure? The answers varied with the business, but most entrepreneurs used the number of employees, rather than revenue, to describe inflection points that triggered change. Common inflection points were 10 employees, 25 employees, 50 employees, and 100 employees.

While no entrepreneur explicitly employed the following way of describing those inflection points, their approaches often reflected the organizational structure utilized by the U.S. Army and U.S. Marine Corps for combat troops. This military rule of thumb translates, generally, to a business needing managers once it has more than nine employees.

Additionally, at around 25-30 employees a business (or military unit) will need a different management structure where the managers need managers and yet another at around 90 to 100 employees where you will have functional area heads managing managers who, in turn, manage other managers or teams of people.

Common business structures operate according to the function or job such as production or manufacturing, sales or distribution, supply chain, packing and delivery, human resources, and accounting and finance. Structures are created when the entrepreneur can no longer do everything or oversee everything.

Another way to think about structure is to make a flow chart showing every step from the acquisition of a customer through the creation of the product or service you are selling, product delivery and service, customer care, billing, collecting, and accounting.

Several entrepreneurs stated that they had to create a completely new management structure every couple of years as their business grew. As a result, one entrepreneur compared the process of building a company to that of building a house. That is, "be sure you go ahead and pre-wire the electrical and stub-in the plumbing for rooms you will need to finish in the future." In other words, plan ahead for your infrastructure, processes, and people needs. Make flexible, adaptable investment decisions, especially on software and phone systems.

Infrastructure

The entrepreneurs I interviewed unanimously reported a constant tension between closely monitoring the business's bottom line in the short run and longer-term investing for the possibility of growth. For example, should one buy the minimum computer systems needed in the short run or should one financially stretch and invest in more infrastructure to accommodate possible future growth? There is no easy answer to this.

Some entrepreneurs, however, concretely planned for such decisions by drawing organizational charts of their business at different sizes. Using different growth projections, they would visualize a range of variables, including their space requirements, number of employees by function, management team structure, information and technology needs, and how they would process every step of the value chain.

They assessed the personnel, skills, and processes that they would need at several growth points and took those projected future needs into account when making current hires, installing technology, implementing processes, or deciding which administrative functions to outsource.

They took each functional area such as accounting, manufacturing, human resources (HR), sales, information technology, and customer service and drilled down, mapping each component of the value chain at different revenue levels, including an organization chart and number of employees doing each job.

This visualization and planning helped the entrepreneurs because they had thought about these aspects before the chaos of unexpected growth hit them. In other words, they were able to react and respond to growth better and were able to proactively manage the pace of growth better.

Outsourcing Support Functions

At different phases in the growth process, most entrepreneurs utilized some form of outsourcing rather than hiring personnel. Almost all, at least early in their business's growth, outsourced payroll processing, HR benefits processing, and some accounting functions. As businesses grew, many then brought more of those functions in-house.

In accounting, most traversed the common path by initially hiring a part-time accountant, then a full-time controller, and ultimately a vice-president of finance or chief financial officer. Likewise, in HR, many started out with an administrative person handling HR matters, moving to a junior HR professional at around 25 employees, and upgrading to a senior HR professional at around 50 employees.

Outsourcing Manufacturing

Many of the product companies outsourced manufacturing, primarily to China. Entrepreneurs with prior industry experience outsourced to known reputable sources. Entrepreneurs without that experience, however, had to spend considerable time on the ground in the foreign country interviewing potential outsourcing partners.

Outsourcing of manufacturing also required entrepreneurs to plan for manufacturing quality controls on site. Doing quality control on receipt of the products in the United States was both inefficient and often caused cash flow problems because manufacturers required payment prior to shipping.

To ensure quality, entrepreneurs either hired on-site quality control representatives, made frequent inspection trips to the factories during their product runs, or both. Even with diligent planning for manufacturing quality, many entrepreneurs recounted horror stories of receiving containers of bad products.

Strategic Plans

Planning for growth meant different things to different entrepreneurs in terms of how far ahead they planned, what was contained in the plan, and how it was utilized within the business. One entrepreneur took planning so seriously that he had a rolling three-year plan focusing on head count, revenue plan, and expense plan. Others created a one-year plan annually that was rigorously followed with respect to what additional business the company would take on.

Another entrepreneur assembled his management team meet at the end of the year to create the next year's annual plan. They iterated the specifics until that growth plan fit on a single piece of paper. They distributed this one-page growth plan to each employee so everyone understood where the business was going and not going in the next year. That entrepreneur understood the dual function of strategic planning: it not only prioritizes what the business should focus on but also clarifies what it should not do.

"Firehouse Time"

Thinking strategically or on a macro level about how to grow a business is different than thinking tactically and reactively to more immediate business needs. Several entrepreneurs emphasized the need to allocate time to get away from the business to think clearly about what the business needed to do in the longer term. While at work, the daily "heat of battle" decision making often interfered with thinking broadly about the business's direction. It was necessary to set aside time to get away from the daily business demands to focus strategically.

One entrepreneur emphasized this need by saying, "Give yourself an afternoon a week to think about five critical things going on in the business and make sure you are focused on big opportunities or problems." One of my colleagues calls this specified time for strategic business thinking "firehouse time." It is hard to think strategically when you are putting out "fires" daily—and, yes, that is the norm as you grow a business because growth generally means more employees and results in more mistakes, misunderstandings, and people issues. Thus, the term "firehouse time" means giving yourself time away from fighting the fires to think about the business. Another entrepreneur called this "working on the business" instead of working in the business.

You have learned that planning is critical to managing growth. To help you become a better planner, utilize the Growth Planning Template, shown in Exhibit 4.1, as a tool to guide you or as template of the things you should think about as you consider whether to grow, how to grow, and how to manage that growth. Understand that this template is a guide; your circumstances may require you to think of things not listed here, so feel free to add to this tool.

EXHIBIT 4.1
Growth Planning Template

1. What will my business look like at $ ____ of revenue?

Functional Area	Number of Employees by Job Description	Number of Managers Needed	Daily Information Needed
Accounting			
Human resources			
Manufacturing/ production			
Supplies/raw materials			
Inventory management			
Sales/marketing			
Quality control			
Delivery/fulfillment			
Customer service			
Information technology			

(continued)

EXHIBIT 4.1 *(continued)*

2. What will be my business's weekly cash obligations?
3. What will be the technology needs by function?
4. What should be outsourced?
5. For each functional area, what process additions or improvements will I need to ensure quality, cash management, costs controls, and on-time delivery?
6. What kind of hiring, onboarding, training, and employee review and feedback processes will I need?
7. What will I need to do to teach and communicate our culture, mission, and values?
8. How much cash will I have to advance ahead of new revenue?
9. At this new revenue level, how much cash will I need on hand monthly to operate?
10. How must I reallocate how I spend my time to manage this growth?
11. What are my business's risks of growing to this level of revenue?
12. What must I do to prepare for growth to this level?
13. What must I monitor closely in order not to outgrow my people, processes, and controls so that I maintain high quality, on-time delivery, happy customers, and manageable cash flow?

PRIORITIZATION IS NECESSARY

CEO Quotes on Prioritization

- "Don't get involved in all the brush fires—focus on the thing with the biggest impact."
- "I focus on big opportunities and big crises."
- "I do not pay you to get everything done everyday. I pay you to get the most important things done."
- "Prioritize what we needed to do that was critical to knowing about cash flow."
- "We are a product company. I focus on quality, innovation, and sales."
- "For me, the most difficult part is figuring out what not to do."
- "If the CEO pays attention to something, he can influence it."

- "First thing is to make payroll. Then I focus on sales. Once we got growth, I did not focus enough on profits."

Bottlenecks

One purpose of my research was to learn how entrepreneurs prioritized their time under high-growth conditions. I was looking for templates and heuristics of what approaches worked best. What I found were common-sense approaches.

Some entrepreneurs prioritized similarly to how the military teaches team leaders and junior officers: assess the situation and go where you can have the most critical impact relative to the mission.

Others focused on identifying and remedying bottlenecks. They created flow charts showing each critical step in the process of generating cash—the lifeblood of a business. They thought of the flow chart as a pipeline or funnel and monitored flows to determine where there were bottlenecks or flow delays. Finally, they focused on the bottlenecks and, not surprisingly, found that the bottlenecks they focused on eased.

Setting Daily Priorities

To be successful, businesses must prioritize their focus. This is critical because any growing business has resource constraints: limited people, time, and capital. So it is critical that the entrepreneur spend his or her time on the most important areas that can drive success.

These priorities, however, may vary with the type of business or the phase of growth. What is important is for each entrepreneur to think concretely about setting priorities and reexamine them frequently.

To set priorities, entrepreneurs must have concrete and useful data about their business, communicate the priorities to their personnel, and implement processes to ensure that these priorities are carried out.

One entrepreneur who I interviewed prioritized his focus simply as customers, quality, and cash flow. He stated that if an issue did not impact directly and materially one of those three areas, it could wait.

Managing by Numbers

How to prioritize effectively depends on having good information about the underlying business. It is important to have reliable current numbers.

For example, if you are making a product, you would want to know daily your backlog, units produced, supplies or raw materials used and in inventory, quality issues, units delivered on time, customer calls about defects, customer calls about late delivery, new sales calls, new sales made, cash in, cash out, employee absences, and other issues.

Another way to think about the numbers you need to manage effectively is to think about what customers want and then what you have to do to meet those wants. All customers want defect-free products or services delivered on time with great, caring service. What do you have to do daily to meet those needs? Draw a flow chart for each step of your production, delivery, and customer service chain and think about what to measure daily that will give you the information that tells you whether you have a problem.

For most entrepreneurs and growing businesses, the key numbers monitored pertain to cash flow. One entrepreneur stated her priorities this way, "You don't eat if you don't sell. You don't sell if you don't have a customer. You don't have a customer if you don't offer a good service."

Another successful serial entrepreneur stated his priorities this way, "Set up three or four priorities that take precedence over everything else: (1) manage cash flow, (2) focus on customers and quality service, (3) accelerate revenue growth, and (4) all the rest—unless something is on fire—can wait." Yet, another entrepreneur stated it this way, "Focus on the areas of the business that are critical to making it to next month, next quarter, and next year."

Business priorities are not static, however, and can change often. What we know is that when the entrepreneur spends time on setting and articulating the business priorities, it has a multiplier effect because it directs the focus of other employees to those priorities. It also engages the work force in thinking about what is important and teaches them to adapt as the priorities change.

Huddles
Once set, it is important to communicate priorities to employees. How did entrepreneurs accomplish this task? Several entrepreneurs held a "start-of-the-day huddle" with all employees to set priorities for the day and an "end-of-the-day huddle" to review the day. Another entrepreneur had a

meeting every morning at 8:30 a.m. with his direct reports, and then the direct reports had meetings with their direct reports. Those meetings cascaded down the line until, by 10:30 a.m., every employee in the company had been in a meeting, talking about that day's priorities.

Not only must priorities be communicated, but also the business culture must be developed to facilitate working toward those priorities. A business culture helps keep employees focused on what is important and can deter aberrant behaviors. Timely and reliable measurement systems illuminate deviances, helping entrepreneurs to know about and focus on key problem areas or mistakes to be corrected. Consistent deviances or mistakes highlight the need for more process.

PROCESSES: THE "HOW" TO GROWTH
CEO Quotes on Processes

- "We always want to put out the fire and leave a fire extinguisher behind."
- "I do not want a single point of failure."
- "I've got a philosophy that that which is not audited will always get worse, never better, and will create surprises."
- "Get process good enough then improve it constantly."
- "I've been in small companies to know that you can't strangle them with too much process."
- "Understand that accounting and HR people by nature are process oriented."

What Are Processes?
As businesses grow, the entrepreneur loses the ability to be hands-on with all aspects of the business. There is simply too much to do. So, the challenge is for the entrepreneur to increase the probability that others will do the tasks as he or she would like them done.

To accomplish this goal, the entrepreneur implements processes. There are two basic types of processes. The first type of process includes directions, recipes, instructions, and standards for how to do specific tasks.

These include rules or controls for mitigating financial and quality risks. Most processes are designed to instruct an employee how to do something or what not to do.

The second type of process has a goal of producing reliable, timely data, or feedback that will reveal variances or mistakes. These data collecting processes are designed to get the key data in the hands of the entrepreneur quickly as the business grows.

Purpose of Processes

Process implementations are intended to produce standardization, consistency, and reliability and reduce variance and risks. Process improvement is an ongoing job for a growing business. As a business grows it will encounter problems that it never faced before, requiring new processes. Failing to anticipate potential problems is particularly risky for small businesses that are usually without the financial cushions to absorb those risks.

Processes are needed to manage growth risks. In every functional area, a growth company will need processes to ensure that the production and delivery of products or services on time, defect free, with caring customer service. A growing business needs processes to ensure that cash flow stays positive, inventory is managed, the right people are hired and trained, and bad hires are terminated quickly.

Two points need to be made here. First, as a company grows, an entrepreneur will face problems that he or she may have never experienced before. One serial entrepreneur told me that he hit that "wall" at $100M of revenue and, comparing his business to an airplane hitting its maximum speed tolerance, said his business "started shaking, tilting, and rolling" and he thought he was going to "lose control and crash." Second, to handle such challenges, as a business grows an entrepreneur must hire skilled people who have managed functional areas of a business through such growth inflection points.

Process Challenges

There were many common challenges faced by entrepreneurs in my study. Because of their lack of experience in certain functional areas, many had no knowledge of either the processes that they needed or how to implement them. Many had difficulty balancing the pace of growth with process implementation—that is, the difficulty doing both at the same time.

Often entrepreneurs, even those who conceded its importance, did not enjoy process implementation. This stage of building the business was not nearly as much fun as selling and finding customers. Too often, entrepreneurs assumed that process implementation was a one-time event rather than an ongoing priority that would evolve through the life of the business. In addition, many underestimated the time and costs to install processes.

Other challenges included purchasing software tools that could not scale; not involving employees in the development of critical processes; delegating too much of the process implementation to new, unproven managers; struggling with the choice of investing ahead of future growth or always playing catch-up; and failing to prioritize what processes to implement first and, as a result, trying to do too much at once.

Successful Process Implementation

One of the more successful entrepreneurs I studied, Dave Lindsey of Defender Direct, relied heavily on Michael Gerber's book *The E-Myth Revisited*,[1] stating: "the entrepreneur's job is to create the process, management's job is to make sure the process is followed, and the technician's job is to use the process."[2]

Several other entrepreneurs stressed that the development and writing of processes should be part of an employee's job; everyone should create a process that someone else could follow when the employee was absent because of illness or vacation. This helped the business achieve the goal of "not having a single point of failure." Embedding the development and improvement of business processes into each employee's job description "collectivizes problems" and empowers line employees to think about how to constantly improve.

Successful entrepreneurs prioritized what they needed to know and what processes were necessary to acquire and maintain happy customers. They trained employees to do multiple jobs, measured and rewarded the right behaviors, posted daily production or customer service data so all employees knew how the business was doing, and created a culture of high performance. A key challenge for an entrepreneur is deciding what processes to put in place first and putting in enough processes to get the job done but not so much that it kills the small firm, entrepreneurial feel.

Many entrepreneurs thought they could easily deal with process implementation by hiring managers from big companies. Too many times, however, they learned that such managers could not adapt to the pace and realities of a fast-growing, entrepreneurial environment. They were simply too corporate and were used to having support, tools, and resources that small companies lack. Several found that managers with both big company experience and small, entrepreneurial, growth company experience were more likely to be successful.

Complexity

By now, I hope you are developing an understanding of the complexity of these issues. There is no one right answer. Entrepreneurs are constantly managing tensions arising from too many potential opportunities, too much to do every day, cash flow needs, people and time constraints, and the daily need to manage quality, brand reputation, and legal and financial risks while pushing people to be better, faster, and more cost efficient.

For most entrepreneurs who I studied, process choice and implementation was a risky, iterative, learn-as-you-go process requiring constant adjustment. By the time a business reaches $5M in revenue, it generally has some financial cushion to absorb process iteration and even process implementation mistakes. Most successful businesses made and survived multiple process and people mistakes. One entrepreneur stated, "If you are growing, you will make mistakes."

Where should you start with putting processes in place? Focus on what behaviors and results are mission-critical or absolutely necessary for your success. That usually means quality, reputation, customers, and cash flow.

PACE: THE GAS PEDAL APPROACH
CEO Quotes on Pace

- "You do not want to bring on all the business that you can because growth can easily swallow you."

- "We did not hire unless we had cash flow in house to pay their salary and benefits for three to four months."

- "Going from \$8M to \$13M in sales in one year, I had to promise everyone that we would stop selling until we caught up."

- "We were growing just to grow instead of being as calculated as we should have been."

- "Management challenge is when to let up on the gas pedal and let people and processes catch up to growth."

Pacing Growth

Almost everyone in business has heard of the axiom "grow or die." But "grow *and* die" is more apt. Mismanaged growth can kill a business. Too much growth too quickly can create serious quality, people, and financial problems for a business.

We know that the pace of growth has to be managed so growth does not outstrip capabilities, processes, and controls. Many entrepreneurs learned this lesson the hard way, having to put the brakes on growth to play process catch-up. Several entrepreneurs in my study learned it through the failure of their first entrepreneurial venture. One entrepreneur called this "letting up on the growth gas pedal so the people and business can catch up with the growth."

Growth creates risks that need to be managed. Pushing people and systems too hard will likely create more problems or mistakes than usual. The recognition of this fact was a key finding in my research. One entrepreneur whose business grew too fast, losing millions of dollars, reported the following lessons:

1. Before you grow, prove your concept—make it scalable.

2. Have the right people and processes in place.

3. Walk before you run.

4. Do not overbuy and overpay for corporate managers.

5. Have clear lines of authority and reporting—not matrix reporting.

6. Telecommuting for senior managers does not work.

Pacing growth sometimes requires entrepreneurs to turn away business to allow time to implement processes and controls. This can be either a "catch-up" need or a planned precondition of taking on more business. Many entrepreneurs had to stop taking on new business until they installed the necessary processes because the risks of destroying their brand and quality reputation were too high without more controls and processes. Sometimes these "catch-up" periods lasted as long as a year.

Although many entrepreneurs yearned for that next big customer or that marketing breakthrough that would bring thousands of new customers, they knew that if that happened there was no way they could properly service those customers. Some were fortunate, taking on the big opportunity and somehow performing well enough to get past the first big order and then upgrade the infrastructure. Others were not so lucky and had to retrench and hunker down to repair the damage.

Do Not Reinvent the Wheel

One thing I have learned from my various research projects is that most businesses face the same challenges, issues, and problems. While it may sound overwhelming to choose, write, and put in place processes while struggling to meet growth goals, remember that many people just like you have done this same thing through trial and error.

Learn from their mistakes. Learn what worked by joining an entrepreneurs' network in your town or city, seeking help from product or service trade organizations, and seeking advice on good websites for entrepreneurs sponsored by organizations dedicated to entrepreneurship. Talk to successful entrepreneurs and ask their advice. Learn from those who have done it.

GLOBAL MEDICAL IMAGING[3]

Let's bring the challenges of managing growth to life with a real story— the story of Ryan Dienst who, along with his brother-in-law Scott Ray, built Global Medical Imaging.

The Charlotte, North Carolina-based Global Medical Imaging, LLC (GMI) sells and services medical ultrasound equipment. Managing partners, Ryan Dienst and Scott Ray, used $25,000 to launch their company in 2002.[4] Profitable from the start, GMI pulled in about $2.4 million in revenue the first year and $4.5 million in 2003.[5] Within six years, GMI had 64 employees and $17.8 million in annual sales.

Founders with Complementary Skills

Scott Ray was born in Boone, North Carolina. As the son of a builder, he grew up "driving nails."[6] While a student at the University of North Carolina (UNC) Chapel Hill, Ray turned building lofts for dorm rooms into a profitable business. After graduating with a Bachelor of Science degree in biomedical engineering, he moved to Charlotte, where he worked selling ultrasound machines for General Electric's medical systems division. In 1995, Ray took a job as general manager for Imaging Associates, a Charlotte vendor of used ultrasound equipment.

During these years, Ray witnessed the consolidation of the ultrasound-manufacturing industry, as large original-equipment manufacturers (OEMs) such as Siemens and Philips bought up the smaller ones. As the OEMs grew larger, however, they became increasingly focused on making a profit and less on performing personalized service. "That's the opportunity that's been created for us," Ray said. "To fill in that vacuum they've created and be more responsive, faster, and more cost competitive. Ultimately, to just provide a higher level of customer support and service that isn't currently part of this industry."[7]

Working with his brother-in-law Dienst, who had an MBA from UNC's Kenan-Flagler Business School, Ray developed a business plan for a company that offered not only the cost-effective solution of selling reconditioned ultrasound equipment but also "maintenance and service contracts, warranties, system upgrades, leasing, and trade-ins."[8]

At the time Ray launched GMI in 2002, Dienst was still a partner at Dienst Custom Homes, but he made the painful decision to leave a successful company that he loved and had helped build. In January 2003, Dienst joined GMI to focus full-time on business management and finance. Ray was the "sales-and-relationship guy," and although he had started GMI, the two men were managing partners and split ownership of the company 50-50.[9]

An Evolving Business Model

At first, the two entrepreneurs sold reconditioned ultrasound machines mostly to doctors in private practice and small clinics, but eventually they entered the hospital market.

As the population aged and doctors needed better diagnostic equipment, demand for ultrasounds machines grew; however, purchasing new units that cost between $20,000 and $120,000 was an expensive proposition. The entrepreneurs decided to offer reconditioned machines as an appealing alternative; these machines looked brand new, performed as well as new ones, and had an initial cost of 20% to 50% less than comparable new units. "We're primarily in the aftermarket, so we're a value-added distributor," Dienst said. "About 60% of our products are reconditioned— we do that in-house—and about 40% are new or demo products that we distribute and service. We do not manufacture."

According to Dienst, GMI's freedom from manufacturing obligations contributed to its success. "It allows us to be responsive to what the market's needs are rather than what we are restricted to sell or stock in inventory," he said, adding that, as a distributor rather than a manufacturer, GMI could "focus on getting our customers the best products for their needs, instead of pushing a product or solution that may not be ideal."[10]

GMI bought used and off-lease equipment as well as overstocks of new ultrasound-diagnostic equipment. The machines were brought to GMI's Charlotte warehouse, where in-house technicians inspected and then reconditioned them, so the repainted and repackaged machines looked brand new when they were delivered to customers.

From day one, the entrepreneurs implemented a number of quality-control processes in GMI's reconditioning facility. "We've had a continual process improvement as we've gone along," Dienst said. "We've always been focused on checklists and how we run the business, so that if you had problems you could look back and say what happened, why that issue occurred, and modify your checklist to catch it the next time."

Growth by Adding Service

GMI's business model kept evolving. Constantly looking for new revenue streams, in 2004, the founders added a service component to their core business in the form of a field-service business unit. GMI's field-service engineers, with an extensive network of third-party technicians, provided warranty and service-contract support for all systems GMI sold.

"Service was an opportunity for us," Dienst said. "Ultrasound equipment breaks. We've got the right technicians, software, and customer service reps to open trouble tickets, manage those calls, get the parts out, and get the customer back up and running." In addition to generating far higher margins than equipment sales, the service contracts helped the company develop long-term relationships with customers.

Growth by Adding More Complementary Services

The company expanded the breadth of its offerings by adding financing solutions with in-house leasing and a trade-up program that guaranteed customers cost-effective upgrades. Consistent with their mission to "lower the cost of high quality healthcare,"[11] in 2008, the founders set out to penetrate a new market segment: training. By teaching hospital technicians how to take care of the imaging and ultrasound machines in-house, GMI helped hospitals save 40% to 60% of their maintenance budget.[12]

Planning and Processes

With Ray driving sales, Dienst focused on building a basic business infrastructure that was scalable and capable of providing ongoing support for the growing company, enabling the entrepreneurs to make more effective decisions. "We had the luxury of being able to build processes as we've gone forward," Dienst said. GMI's ultrasound-service business was an area where investing in the right technology to create infrastructure made a big difference.

Dienst said that he "wrote up a scope of what exactly we needed to run that business." For one major software need, he outsourced writing code to a software company. "Putting that software package in place has had a huge impact on our business," Dienst said. "We've got the right platform now and have the data necessary to make good decisions and run that business. It's doubled our margins, increased our visibility, and cut our time managing service calls by 100%."

Several instances of employee theft early on had forced the entrepreneurs to take a hard look at the way they managed inventory. Dienst thought it was fortunate that "we haven't had anything that was major - any big public issues that compromised our brand." He continued:

It's better to have those problems when you're a $10-million company than as a $20-million company, just due to the size of the problems. And it gets you focused on putting the right processes and procedures in place to eliminate that early on; it forces you to really improve your cycle counts, and your inventory-flow practices.

Investing Ahead of Growth

Dienst acknowledged that as far as technology and putting the right processes in place, GMI had invested ahead of the growth curve. "We've over-invested, meaning we could have made more money getting to where we are if we hadn't spent as much time and energy on making sure we had the processes to do it right," he said.

Reflecting on what he could have done differently; Dienst said that he "could have invested a little more slowly." Nonetheless, Dienst believed that it was money well spent, and that "it will certainly pay off in the long run." He continued:

We've been business builders rather than just trying to make the maximum amount of money in the shortest amount of time. A lot of our competitors have made a lot more money in the last five years than we have. But we have an incredible brand reputation, an incredible platform, and we have the ability to become a $100 million company.

Growing Pains

From the start, GMI experienced stellar growth. As far as financing was concerned, "We have always done it with our own money and with lines of credit. Pure bank debt," Dienst said. While funding growth did not seem to be a problem, the increasing pace of change forced the entrepreneurs to start learning how to let go and lead, rather than supervise and control. They also realized the importance of delegating to the right people.

Rule of Seven

"Businesses grow in sort of a rule of seven," Dienst said. "There's the 1 to 7 employees [stage], the 7 to 49 employees [stage], and then the 50 to 350 level." According to Dienst, because of Ray's talent for driving sales, GMI grew to the stage of seven employees "real quick."

Each stage of business growth had its own unique challenges. At the first stage, communicating with the GMI employees was effortless but as its workforce grew, Dienst understood that the old way of doing things would have to change. He explained:

You're doing stuff, you go to lunch every day, and you're all on the same page, and everything's easy. After you cross over that seven-person line, it starts to get tough again, because you've got too many people doing too many things to know every detail about everything. So you start building an organizational structure, with people having ownership in parts of the organization they're in charge of.

Delegating responsibility presented new challenges. The employees hired at the first stage of the business were not always equipped to grow with it, often lacking the skills to manage others. Dienst said, "You've got an inflection point at that 7- to 10-person range, where you have to start putting people in charge of parts of the business." He continued:

Typically then you get your phase-one management team in place over the 10-to-25-employee range. And then things start to grow again, because you're getting some synergy, you're gaining some leverage; you're back focused on creating revenue rather than putting out fires and managing the process.

Reshuffling the Team

Dienst identified the next inflection point as the 45- to 55-employee range, when the demands of growth outpaced the skills of the phase-one management team. To take the company to the next level, Dienst found it necessary to "reshuffle the deck and bring in new talent."

At this point, the employees who were unable to grow with the company or become top performers—the C players—were moved to lower-level positions, where they could be A players. As Dienst said, "They're

C players as managers, but they're A players if you can get them back to what they were originally hired to do."

When employee headcount at GMI topped 50, the founders were able to afford a "different level of talent," Dienst said, and he revealed that GMI brought in a professional management team that had the capacity to get the company to the level of 300 employees.

Learning from Mistakes

At first, during periods of rapid growth, Dienst and Ray were under pressure to fill open positions quickly. "Rather than critically interviewing and making sure we're hiring the right person, [we] often started recruiting bodies," Dienst said. In his experience, this time constraint, combined with ineffective job-screening methods led to frequent hiring mistakes early on. "It's not having a defined hiring process, not doing enough on the profiling standpoint," he said. "And the hiring process was more of a sales job on candidates about how badly we need them rather than us critically analyzing a candidate's abilities for the role."

In 2004, the start-up had an especially strong year, characterized by explosive growth. But Dienst told a cautionary tale. "You bring in 20 people for really fast growth over six months, and if 10 don't make it and you've got to let them go, that's extremely costly." Dienst said that hiring too fast in 2004 resulted in significant turnover at GMI in late 2005 and early 2006.

Dienst explained:

If you've got the wrong people in the wrong seats, no amount of rules or processes will get the right behavior. The right people in the right seats will overcome any problems; they'll put in any processes you need, they'll fix any issues you have, because they're the right people. Focusing on that early on can save the organization a lot of money and accelerate growth.

Installing Hiring Processes

After a few years spent hastily filling positions, Dienst and Ray became more disciplined about the hiring process. "We became aware of the high cost of turnover and poor hiring and what that does to the organization,"

Dienst said. He dealt with the issue first by attending HR conferences and seminars and reading about the hiring process.

Then he read a book by the industrial psychologist and consultant Bradford Smart that made a big impression.[13] The eponymous hiring method Smart had developed was a rigorous executive-grading process that helped CEOs (including GE's Jack Welch) to recognize superstars or A players, redirect or retrain B players, and weed out the underachievers or C players who failed to prevent or fix problems. According to Smart, a hiring mistake at any level typically costs business owners more than the employee's original salary.

From late 2006 and into 2007, the entrepreneurs implemented significant changes to GMI's hiring and employee-ranking processes. They embraced Smart's rigorous in-depth interviews, meticulous reference checks, and other hiring techniques to identify top players. They also used Smart's following performance-review tools:

We try to be a lot more structured and strategic in our hiring now, with a good hiring process, and multiple people doing interviews. We do a lot of personality profiling. We are very focused on top grading and force ranking our employees as As, Bs, and Cs, giving them quantifiable performance rankings, and trying to make sure we are getting the bottom 10% and 20% out of our organization and refilling those spots. It was a lot of learning, and just getting really focused on maximizing the effectiveness of our hiring, on-boarding, and training practices, and getting the wrong people out.

The changes to the hiring and employee-ranking processes produced immediate results. After the performers at the bottom of the company were let go, GMI was "much better and much more productive," Dienst said. "I think [it's] the biggest reason why we're, again, growing very quickly and very profitably." He continued:

We went through a stage where we brought in a lot of folks, and we got the wrong people in the wrong seats. We took too much time leaving the wrong people in the wrong seats, so when we finally got serious about cleaning them out, everything got better and smoother and faster again. You're better off being a 30-person company than a 40-person company if you get the wrong 10 out of there.

In 2008, 18 of the 64 GMI employees worked as revenue-generating sales reps. The general and administrative staff—HR and accounting—numbered 12 employees. Dienst identified the rest as "the technical people in our organization that manage service issues and recondition the equipment and repair broken parts."

Building a Management Team
That the founders took more time to fill positions at the top was reflected in the results. "We've gone a little slower, a bit more focused in hiring those key people, and we've had more turnover in the middle than at the top," Dienst said.

In 2006, the founders brought in a bank consultant with a "big-business background," Dienst said. After looking for someone who could grow with the company, Dienst explained "we overhired to get the right caliber of person. It's a guy who has exceptional talent, who has the ability to be the general manager of this business with its 100-plus employees."

Accounting/Financial Information Software
From his experience managing a custom-home-building business, Ryan understood the importance of monitoring financial information and managing cash flow. Therefore, from the start he had invested in the technology to develop effective controls and balance at GMI. He explained:

We have always believed very heavily in software, and we've always been on good business packages. We haven't gone the QuickBooks route or anything like that. You need the data, and you need that core software package to be able to get the information you need out of your business to run it. My previous experience growing a business, my MBA, have helped us always be pretty well off there.

Having tight financial controls was important in any start-up, where cash was a scarce resource, but it was especially critical at GMI where, as Dienst pointed out, "I can't tell you what our sales are going to be like next month. We're a month-to-month transactional business, so we're always impacted by good months and bad months and cash flow."

Building the HR Function

In hindsight, Dienst recognized the importance of finding and cultivating talent from day one. "I think that strategic HR early on is pretty critical," he said. He admitted he should have brought in a "very overqualified HR person earlier to make sure we didn't have the cost of hiring mistakes and lack of on-boarding processes and those kinds of things. The cost of those mistakes is so high that you could afford a rock-star HR manager."

The HR manager, who had been with GMI since its launch in 2002, was unable to grow with the company and was let go in 2007. "Those are painful changes, when you have somebody who was with you from the start," Dienst said. The position was filled with an internal candidate, who also served as controller. "We've identified somebody with the skill set who fit that role well. We hired for personality, ability, and the things we thought we needed rather than hiring a traditional HR person," Dienst said.

Evolving Compensation Policies

The two managing partners had always owned 100% of the business. Only one member of GMI's eight-person leadership team had been offered equity, but, in 2008, the founders started looking into creating a stock-option pool for a few long-time employees who had contributed significantly to growing the business. "We need to find ways to retain them above and beyond just compensation," Dienst said.

Senior management's compensation consisted of a base salary, which was set at a market or above-market level, and a bonus tied to performance. To rate his key managers, Dienst used a comprehensive scorecard listing the skills and competencies that were important to the company at each particular stage of growth. "We've had quarterly scorecards, we've had annual scorecards," Dienst said. "Right now, we've got a six-month scorecard, which is about as far as we can accurately forecast and set goals."

GMI's balanced scorecard consisted of a mix of financial and "soft" metrics, such as teamwork that changed as the company grew. Members of the eight-person leadership team had an opportunity to earn a bonus up to 30% of their base salary. Dienst said, "They have a team-based card that's dependent upon the overall performance of the business, so our repair manager is tied to the same metrics as our sales manager." He continued:

Twenty percent of their 30% bonus is based on the overall performance of the organization. So, hopefully, they're breaking down barriers and working together. They have another 10% balanced scorecard that gets to be tactical within their specific area of impact . . . That 10% is in their control so that they feel like they've got complete ownership of that 10% of their scorecard.

The Art of Prioritization

For Dienst, who was in charge of day-to-day operations from day one, time was a scarce resource. Understandably, he tried to focus on areas that had the greatest impact on the fledgling business. "If you have 20 fires burning, it's knowing which ones are going to impact money, profitability, cash flow, and customer satisfaction and running after those things first," he said. Even though Dienst did not have a "great process," he had a lot of task lists and a set of priorities. "It was walking in and saying, 'Come hail or high water, I'm going to get these three things done today and, hopefully, these other 10 as well,'" he said.

Dienst recalled that in the early stages of building a business, when he was busy putting out fires, he also looked for the "right trends, where you can make a decision that allows you to fix something that would have a big enough impact, so it's worth the effort of fixing it once and for all, with a process change, or people, or whatever else."

Working on the Business

Although it would have been easy to get caught up in the minutiae of running a business was easy, Dienst understood the importance of finding the time to step back from the daily grind to look at the big picture. He continued:

You always try to make sure you're balancing, as best as you can, the amount of time you spend working *in* the business versus working *on* the business. You make sure you're getting out of the office, which is the only time to think about working on the business. Because every day you walk through the front door of the office, inevitably, you're going to get pulled into working in the business and not on the business.

As GMI at times grew more than 400%, Dienst, Ray, and the rest of the organization had to constantly reinvent their roles and priorities and readjust their schedules. According to Dienst, "It's been constant improvement, not only on the personal level but on the corporate level and how we restructure roles." He added:

I got to the point that I couldn't manage a $17 million business the same way I managed the $12 million business. Because of the pace at which we grow, about every six months we're almost a new organization. We have to redo our meeting schedules and our meeting rhythms and how we're communicating to make sure we're always addressing where we are as an organization.

In mid-2008, Dienst again revised his meeting schedule to better fit his role. The first two days of the week were devoted to internal meetings with the heads of those business units that added the most to the company's bottom line at a particular phase of growth. "I spend one hour with no phone, no BlackBerry, no computer, with each of the key managers, focusing on that impactful part of the business," Dienst said. He tried to keep his calendar free on Wednesday, Thursday, and Friday, to have time "to be able to do business development, travel, and meet customers, and do projects, and all of the other things I need to move it forward."

From Doing Everything to Delegating

Early in the game, Dienst and Ray were in total control of GMI, taking care of every detail and managing every area personally. Now, Dienst found it difficult to let go and allow others to take ownership of parts of the business he had nurtured from the start. As he recalled, "When I started with Scott, and there were four of us, you did everything. Literally, touched it, did it, wrote it, and fixed it." Dienst acknowledged that his transition from doing to managing had been painful and that learning to delegate "had been very hard."

"I don't think that learning to delegate is a linear process," Dienst said. He added that, at some point, he realized that there were not enough hours in the day and that he had to delegate. He described the process:

You delegate, and you find things fall apart, and you reach out and you gather them up and you pull them back in. And then you get to the point of pain again that you know you have to delegate and you push it back out. And it falls apart in different places, and you pull some of it back in. And you just keep figuring out where and how you go through that process by sort of hitting points of complexity in your personal operation, that you have no choice but to delegate. If you delegate out 10 major parts of your day, and six people grab that and are doing great, and maybe four of the folks aren't the right people, you grab those four things back, but at least you got rid of six.

The Strategic Coach Program
What helped Dienst switch from managing everything to delegating was Strategic Coach, a recognized organizational development program that encouraged successful entrepreneurs to stick to the three or four tasks they performed extremely well and delegate the rest. A crucial component of Strategic Coach was identifying these three or four unique abilities with the help of the Kolbe psychometric-profiling test; once these abilities were identified, entrepreneurs partnered with others with the same abilities.

It took Dienst and Ray two years to identify their skill sets and abilities. As Dienst described it, part of the Strategic Coach program was determining "how to maximize the amount of time you spend on that unique ability, because you're going to amplify your impact on the organization if you do what you do better than anybody else. And everything else that's outside of that unique ability, you've got to get off your plate."

When Dienst and Ray recognized their strengths, it was beneficial to the company. For example, in 2008, after Ray realized that his sales talent did not correlate with being a sales manager, a seasoned national-sales manager, who was a better fit for managing a sales force was brought in. Dienst continued:

Scott's unique ability is giving customers the confidence to make commitments to do business with us. He needs to be out, talking to customers and closing business, and not managing a sales force. That's not his skill set. Now Scott is out, selling more than he ever has, driving revenue and transactions, and having as much fun as he's ever had.

The national-sales manager built an outside-sales model for GMI. "We now have outside reps, and we're growing that pretty aggressively," Dienst said. With a strong executive team in place, the founders felt comfortable focusing on hiring more revenue producers. Dienst explained:

We're trying to go from $17 million to $24 million this year, and then our goal is to get to $100 million in three years. I've spent the last six years focusing on building the backend processes, writing the software, getting everything in place so that we've got a scalable platform and the right technical and service people.

The Evolving Leader

One of the key factors in achieving stellar growth had been the two entrepreneurs' ability to continually evolve and change their management styles to meet the needs of the business at different points on the growth curve. In 2008, Dienst said:

Personal transformation is amazing in the growth of all of these businesses. Today I have to learn to be a true CEO of a 60-person organization. I've had to restructure my meeting schedules, I've had to restructure my management style, I've had to find different ways to impact the organization that are drastically different than two or three years ago.

Dienst's statement that "fast-growing businesses outgrow people quickly," came from his experience and understanding that, just because they had successfully launched a business, entrepreneurs were not immune to becoming irrelevant. Dienst emphasized the importance of constantly having to "read, educate yourself, and reinvent yourself." He explained:

If you can't keep up with the business, you may not get fired, but you're either going to go out of business because you make some critical mistakes, or you're going to stop growing because the business gets to the point where with your current management style, processes, and leadership abilities—it can't get any bigger. After businesses make it for three or four years, they hit a ceiling. And the ceiling is not the ceiling on the business or the ceiling on the opportunity; it's the ceiling on the entrepreneur as the leader of that business.

Dienst, whose career advice was "work hard every day, and have a quest for knowledge, talk with smart people, read books, listen to CDs, and make sure you are learning every day,"[14] set the bar higher for himself in terms of professional growth.

He expected no less from his management team. "If people aren't willing to do the same, if managers that have been with you for two or three years can't keep up, you're going to outgrow them, and they're going to be gone." He continued:

Business is a game like baseball or golf or anything else. I enjoy being a student of the game, and reading, and learning, and going to conferences, whether it's building custom homes or selling or servicing medical equipment. A good entrepreneur can be a good entrepreneur in any industry because if you're a student of the game, the rules and the lessons are very much the same. And that's the fun part about it.

GMI's success proved that, with Dienst running the business as de facto CEO and Ray making the sales, its leaders were "the right people on the bus, in the right seats."[15] Dienst once described his goal as "growing a business to the point it has outgrown me and needs smarter, better leadership to continue to succeed."[16] Considering his passion for learning and continuous improvement, that goal could take longer to achieve.

LESSONS FROM GMI

GMI's story shows the power of prioritization, processes, learning, and understanding that the solution to today's problem may become a problem itself as a business continues to grow. Dienst put in place process checklists. Think about why an airline pilot does a preflight checklist before every flight no matter how many flights he or she has flown. Checklists focus you on what is important.

Dienst also stressed the importance of constantly improving processes—learning as you go from experience and adapting to prevent future defects. Remember, the goal is 99% defect free, on-time delivery with great, caring customer service.

Dienst used software to facilitate his management and to give him data that allowed him to focus on variances and problem areas as well as manage the business so it had the cash flow to pay the bills. Likewise, he used software to manage inventory and employee theft.

Dienst put in place inventory controls after experiencing theft, and he put in place hiring and employee scorecards after experiencing many hiring mistakes and retention issues. He put in place these processes to solve or reduce problems.

Dienst used the "Rule of 7" to manage; that is, he learned than any one person only can effectively manage or oversee seven people. He also talked about what "fires" he focused on each day.

Dienst's story illustrates the key points of this chapter—which is designed to educate you about the overarching issues rather than answer specific questions, which are dependent on your background, the size of your business, the type of business you operate, and your cash resources. You should go back and read Dienst's story frequently because it contains a treasure chest of lessons for every business builder.

Think about growth; focus strategically; put in place critical processes and controls involving quality, costs, cash flow, and customers; prioritize where you spend your time each day; and understand that growing a business is a learning, iterative, constant improvement way of living.

Find successful entrepreneurs to learn from and join an entrepreneur's network so you have people to learn from whom have worked through similar issues.

WORKSHOP # 3: GROWTH PLANNING WORKSHOP

Now is a good time for you to put to use some of the key concepts you have learned in these first four chapters. Using the Growth Risks Audit on pages 28–29 and the Growth Planning Template on pages 74–75, assume that you want to double your revenue over the next two years.

Use the Growth Planning Template to devise a plan to *double* your revenue. What does doubling your revenue require you to do with respect to every aspect of your business?

The purpose of this exercise is to give you practice learning how to analyze, think about, and manage growth.

CHAPTER 4 TAKEAWAYS

1. Successful business builders institutionalize "firehouse time," that is, time that they get away from the daily fighting of fires to think about "working on" the business instead of working in the business. They use

this time to think strategically and tactically about growth, processes, controls, and building their infrastructure.

2. Successful business builders strategically focus the business in an area where it can excel and they focus themselves daily on the areas where they are most needed to have positive impact. Quality, customers, and cash flow dominate.

3. Successful business builders try to plan ahead for growth, visualizing what the business will look like management and people-wise at certain revenue levels. Use the Growth Planning Template to do this.

4. Growth creates challenges related to people, process, and controls. Many successful business builders managed growth's pace by turning down work until they were comfortable that it could be done the right way. Managing the pace of growth was analogized to the "gas pedal" on a car—letting up on the growth pedal until people, processes, and controls caught up.

5. Growth requires processes—checklists and recipes (instructions) for every critical step in the value creation process. Processes are intended to create standardization and consistency, resulting in reliable, high execution. Processes must be constantly improved and employees should be engaged in creating and improving processes. Processes are used to train and teach, lessening the likelihood of a "single point of failure."

6. As a business grows, in many cases it must update and even in some instances create new and better processes to manage its increasing size and complexity. Especially in the area of technology, processes drive productivity, manage costs and inventory control, and give the entrepreneur quality data in a timely manner that illuminates variances and exceptions that need to be fixed.

7. Think of processes as the electrical wiring and plumbing of your business—the infrastructure.

8. "Leave a fire extinguisher" behind. When you fight a business "fire" remember that your job is much more than solving the problem. It is

to leave behind processes to make it unlikely that problem happens again or processes that make it possible for others to fix the problem.

9. Conduct daily "huddles" with managers that cascade to include all employees. Ultimately, as the company grows, your managers are critical for teaching and setting daily priorities and objectives.

10. You will constantly be challenged by the issue of whether to invest ahead of or behind growth and with the tension of the type and extent of process at different inflection points. Remember that customers want 99 percent defect-free service and products delivered on time with great caring service. Also, remember that cash flow is the lifeblood of your business—control it yourself and manage it daily.

THE FOUR WAYS TO
GROW YOUR BUSINESS

WHAT WE KNOW SO FAR

The first four chapters introduced the concepts that:

1. Growth can be good and growth can be bad—it depends.

2. Bigger is not always better because growing bigger increases the complexity of managing the business and may propel your business into a different competitive space with better competitors.

3. Businesses will not die from not growing so long as they continuously improve their customer value proposition better than the competition.

4. Growth should not be assumed but rather should be a strategic decision, taking into account the pros and cons of both growing and not growing.

5. Growth can stress people, processes, and controls. Growth can dilute a company's culture and customer value proposition and can create risks that need to be recognized and managed.

6. Growth requires strategic focus and more processes and controls and, in most cases, needs to be paced so as not to prematurely outstrip the capabilities of the management team and the quality and financial controls in place.

7. Growth necessarily means more people, process, controls, structure, and risks to manage.

In the previous chapters, we focused on building a strong foundation for growth. Preparation is key. Considering whether and when to grow, systematically thinking about how growth will affect the business, analyzing the risks of growth at different inflection points, and developing processes to manage those risks are all critical to successfully growing a business.

THE NEXT QUESTION

Now that your business has shown itself to be successful, survived the start-up phase, and you have decided to grow your business, you are ready to move on to the next question: "How should you grow your business?"

What are the options for growth? In the start-up phase, successful entrepreneurs create a customer value proposition sufficiently attractive to customers to generate enough profit to support both the business's capital needs and the entrepreneur's income needs. In other words, the entrepreneur reaches a revenue level of survival, which varies by type of business. For our purposes, let's assume a revenue level of at least $250,000.

This chapter focuses primarily on how entrepreneurs grow *after* this start-up, commercialization, and stabilization phase. What are the growth options? Please read this chapter carefully because you will use these concepts to create growth plans in Chapter 6.

THE FOUR WAYS TO GROW YOUR BUSINESS

There are only four ways to grow a business:

1. improvements;

2. innovations;

3. scaling; and

4. strategic acquisitions.

Growth can result from these methods individually or through a combination thereof.

Making improvements to a business means doing what you do faster, better, and cheaper. They are the fundamental way to stay in business. No matter what you decide about whether to grow or about how much to grow, every business must continuously improve to maintain its customer base.

Improvements: Better, Faster, and Cheaper

How much must you improve? You must improve enough to stay better than your competition. What must you improve? You must improve what your customers deem to be important and of value to them.

Improvements can also create growth by allowing you to do what you do more efficiently and cheaply. This allows you to sell to more customers. Most value-creating improvements are improvements to business processes—the *how* you do business.

Innovations: Something New

Innovations involve doing something new that your competition is not doing. True innovations—doing something no one has ever done—are both rare and high risk. Trash cans are full of great products that customers were unwilling to pay for. Innovations can be less risky if entrepreneurs adopt experiential learning and customer co-creation processes that get customers engaged in creating what customers need and are willing to buy.

Scaling: Doing More of What Works

Scaling, the primary way to grow a business, means doing more of what you are already doing. Scaling is a replication process. To do it well you need the right hiring, training, and execution processes; the right information, measurement, and reward systems; and competent managers.

Strategic Acquisitions: Buying Growth

Growing through acquisitions involves buying growth by buying more customers, more products or services to sell, or by expanding geographically. Acquisitions are risky because they require due diligence, integration, valuation, and financing expertise. Acquisitions require competencies and experience that most small businesses do not have and should be undertaken with great care and caution.

METHODS OF GROWTH

Growth by Improvements: The DNA of Growth

Continuous improvement is the DNA of growth. Improving your product or service, how you deliver it to your customers, and every customer touch point is necessary to stay in business and to grow your business. Continuous improvements lead to more loyal customers who can be your best advertising.

Think about improvement as becoming better, faster, and cheaper. What in your business can you improve? You can improve your product or service with the following goals in mind:

1. to better meet customer needs;

2. to meet more customer needs;

3. to cut out features your customer does not need; or

4. to deliver what the customer needs faster.

Improvements should not be limited to improving dealings with customers and meeting their needs better and faster. You can improve every internal business process from answering the phone to billing, hiring, training, communicating with and evaluating employees, aligning measurements and rewards, and detecting and correcting variances and mistakes.

Every step, action, and behavior that impacts quality, customer satisfaction, revenue generation, cost efficiencies, and productivity is a candidate for improvement.

Improvements are designed to generate more revenue or lower costs—both of which are good for the bottom line. My research of growth companies showed that a culture of continuous improvement was the DNA of growth.

Growth Through Innovations: Rare

Innovation is the buzzword in the business press as I write this book. Innovation can be terrific. Who doesn't want to deliver a product like the iPhone to the market? But, realistically, very few people or companies are genuinely innovative if the definition of innovation is restricted to creating something new that no one has ever created.

However, innovations need not completely change the marketplace. In fact, definitions of innovation run the gamut from marginal improvements to a disruptive, game-changing product or business model. Most innovations result from combining things that already exist in a novel way or from transferring an idea from one kind of business to another. Most creative innovations are built on the works of others and from iterative improvements.

The risks associated with innovation can be greatly lessened when done jointly with a paying customer. That approach to innovation is called customer co-creation. Especially in the technology area, the value of innovations is measured by having customers ready and willing to pay for them.

I have a small investment in a technology company that claims to have the world's best multi-database search capacity. It is a great technology, but it has yet to make a profit in its ten years of effort. The critical key to innovation is that it must be matched with a customer who wants it and is willing to pay for it. No matter how good your product or service might be in absolute terms, businesses keep score by customer sales. Customer co-creation helps to ensure that there will be a customer ready to pay for the new product or service when it comes to market.

Wal-Mart is a good example of innovation. Wal-Mart is the dominant retailer in the world. I am convinced it can probably sell any product or service other than consulting services. Is Wal-Mart an innovative company? It depends on your definition of innovation. Although Wal-Mart didn't invent anything, what it did was learn and copy from other retailers around the world and combine already-known things into a business model. Wal-Mart is an execution champion and a constant improvement company.

So, if you view innovation outside the realm of major product breakthroughs, then you have a viable option for your business's growth. If you are trying to create something entirely novel, then my advice is to manage your risk by engaging customers in the co-creation of your new product or service.

Growth Through Scaling: The Growth Accelerator
Ever since my first research project on high organic growth public companies, I have explored the concept of how businesses scale. How do they

get big quickly in a cost efficient and profitable way? The requirements of successfully scaling weave together all the themes of this book. Scaling requires planning, processes, and more people. In some cases, business models must evolve to make scaling easier.

By necessity, scaling requires decisions about what an entrepreneurial business should do itself and what it should outsource. Those decisions may impact quality, control of the customer relationship, and capital considerations. Scaling means doing what you are doing now but in much bigger volumes—replicating many times over what has worked in the past. Scaling volume requires scaling production, sales, and distribution without sacrificing quality and financial controls.

Scaling is the key to high growth.

Planning to scale. Entrepreneurs can scale reactively or they can proactively plan for scaling. Interestingly, first-time entrepreneurs in my study generally scaled reactively, iterating as they went along. Those entrepreneurs with prior start-up experience approached scaling more methodically and proactively.

Planning for scaling a business requires many decisions and involves many variables:

1. What needs to be scaled to grow your business fourfold?

2. What aspects of your business model are so critical that you must control them?

3. Is your business model a direct-to-consumer model or an indirect model?

4. How can you use technology to scale quickly and cheaply?

5. How do capital constraints affect your scaling alternatives?

6. If you need capital, what are your alternatives for obtaining capital and what are the pros and cons of each alternative?

7. Are your current processes and people scalable or do you need to upgrade?

8. What parts of your value chain should you scale yourself and what parts should you outsource?

9. What are the advantages and disadvantages of outsourcing from quality control, customer relationship control, and capital investment perspectives?

What do I need to scale? 1) **Manufacturing/production.** Once a decision is made to scale, it is necessary to examine what specific elements of the business have to change to accomplish this goal. A business must be able to accommodate a growing number of customers while producing consistent, high-quality products or services at the same time. How can a business do that?

Let's look first at how production is done. Depending on the business, production is done by people or machines and aided by technology. A business can produce the goods or services in house, or it can outsource the production. Service companies generally utilize people to produce the service. Product companies generally use machines. To scale production, you also need processes that, if followed, will consistently make high-quality products or services. In producing both goods and services, a business generally should be looking for 99 percent on-time, defect-free production.

To scale production in-house requires capital because the business must add some combination of people, machines, and technology before realizing the financial gains from the scale-up. Further, if a business scales by adding people or machines, it will need more space to house production. This, too, generally requires capital, which is usually needed before the added production assets produce revenue.

If a business scales by outsourcing, capital is also needed, albeit usually a smaller amount. If production is outsourced, the manufacturer generally will want to be paid on delivery or, if using a foreign manufacturer, before shipping. Financing production growth complicates the scaling decision for most growing, private companies because financing can be as big a concern for an entrepreneur as maintaining quality.

2) **Sales.** Scaling production is not, by itself, growth. Scaling production generates inventory that must be sold. Selling must be scaled, too. How do you scale sales? Sales can be scaled through people, technology (e.g., the Internet), or outsourcing. The decision of how to scale sales depends on the type of business and, in part, on whether a business is selling to

the ultimate user or to an intermediary who resells to the consumer. Sales can be scaled in several ways, such as building an in-house sales force, outsourcing sales to independent representatives or wholesale distributors, using the Internet or other media, opening more locations, or franchising.

3) **Fulfillment.** Scaling also requires delivering the product or service to your customer whether you sell directly or indirectly. Again, you can scale fulfillment of customers' orders by adding people, machines, and technology or by outsourcing. Most of the product companies that I studied outsourced manufacturing but kept control of fulfillment to ensure the quality and control of the customer relationship.

4) **Business model.** Although scaling production, sales, and fulfillment seems tangible to entrepreneurs, many often forget that the business model must scale as well. Scaling the business model was a challenge for several companies in my research study. Evaluating whether the business model is scalable is critical because it is possible to build a profitable small business that cannot scale—or, at least, not easily. For example, a business may sell high-priced products or services that only a few people can afford.

Scaling may be difficult because the potential market size is small or the customers' purchasing decision times are too long for the business to survive the wait. Sometimes, even with a good product, potential purchasers may have concerns dealing with a small company that may be relatively new in the marketplace if the sales price is high.

To scale, a business often must change its pricing model to appeal to a broader marketplace; particularly when the cost of the product or service price is relatively high and the business's track record is relatively short. Lowering the upfront costs to customers may be essential to gain market share. Five of the private companies that I studied had to change from a high-price purchase model to a lower price rent or subscription model to attract customers.

Others had to modify their sales model from a retail model to a wholesale model because they could not afford to build a sales organization or to expand geographically. Interestingly, only a few of the companies in my study generated meaningful sales via the Internet.

The chicken or the egg?   Some entrepreneurs struggled with whether to scale production ahead of or behind sales. At issue was minimizing the risks associated with scaling. Service companies generally scaled behind sales, booking business opportunities and then expanding the service capabilities by hiring people to meet the demand.

The conundrum was more challenging for product companies who faced the question of whether and how to expend capital in expanding production capabilities. Those product companies that outsourced production minimized their short-term capital needs and could test the viability of their scaling plans by contracting for more production.

Those companies that chose to keep control of production, however, were forced to address the capital costs of adding more production capacity. These companies either built smaller facilities based on the limited capital they had available, even if such facilities were likely to be inadequate if the scaling plans were successful, or they raised equity capital to finance the expansion of production capabilities. Raising equity capital often complicated the scaling efforts, however, by generating a set of issues related to the company's governance, control, and the ultimate exit scenario for the equity partner.

Scaling has its limits. Scaling a business generally involves doing more of what has made the business successful to begin with. It means leveraging existing capabilities to sell more of the business's products or services to more customers in more locations. Scaling, however, has its limits because the market for a particular product or service is not infinite.

"Growth Boosters"

What do private growth companies do when the capacity for scaling a particular product or service is reaching its limits? To continue to grow, a business must explore "growth boosters."

Businesses that reach this stage of growth must ask the following questions:

1. What complementary products or services can I sell to existing customers?

2. Can I add noncomplementary products or services that my customers need, are easy for me to add, and make vendor management easier for my customers?

3. Is there another customer segment that I can sell to that requires part of my existing offering? Can I go up or down market?

4. What can I do to generate more frequent purchases from existing customers? Can I create more reasons to purchase my products or services?

5. Can I add a new distribution channel to reach new customers?

6. Can I increase net margin by focusing on cost efficiencies through technology?

"Growth boosters" are those activities that involve either delivering products or services more profitably, expanding the breadth of products and services sold to existing customers, selling to new customer segments, or making it easier for customers to buy more products or services.

Types of growth boosters. What avenues should an entrepreneur explore in seeking potential growth boosters? Of course, there is no single answer but successful growth boosters include:

1. new products;

2. product upgrades;

3. adding services;

4. operating more efficiently;

5. new channels of distribution;

6. changing the customer experience;

7. pricing innovations;

8. branding innovations;

9. bundling products and services;

10. payment innovations;

11. different guarantees;

12. geographical expansion; and

13. expanding along the value chain to capture a new source of value from other value chain players.

Five of the fifty-four companies in my DPGC research that had reached limits to their initial scaling efforts were at the growth booster stage.

The big customer.   Sometimes, a business catapults to a new level of growth by acquiring a new major customer. Seven of the fifty-four companies in my study got a major boost by landing a significant customer. The acquisition of a big customer, however, cannot be counted on, and, occasionally, even when the opportunity arises, a business opts to scale according to their previous business plan. For example, Eyebobs Eyewear, Inc. turned down a big customer to keep tighter control of its operations and not run the risks of customer concentration. Eyebobs still grew at a compounded growth rate of more than 50 percent for several years.

A big customer creates customer concentration risks. What happens if you scale up production, sales, and customer support for a big customer and then that customer decides to drop you? You may be left with an unsupportable big cost structure and be forced to seek new customers.

Acquisitions: Be Careful

The fourth growth alternative is to buy revenue by making a strategic acquisition. Acquisitions require due diligence, financing, and integration competencies that very few entrepreneurs have. I get many questions from entrepreneurs about buying a weak competitor so they can get access to their competitor's customers. In substance, they are paying for a customer list without customer obligations to purchase from them. That is a bad enough prospect. But, in many acquisitions, the purchaser is also getting additional employees and lease obligations.

Acquisitions are risky, but they do have their place in a growth strategy once a company gets big enough to run the financial risks. There is no magic number as to how big you need to be. In my study, less than 10 percent of the companies had made an acquisition. Done correctly, acquisitions can add a new geographic or a customer segment or a new complementary product or service to your business.

As you can tell, I do not view acquisitions as a viable growth alternative for most entrepreneurs. Until businesses have a proven track record of successful growth via constant improvement and scaling, the financial resources, and personnel with applicable expertise to mitigate the risk, acquisitions are frequently too risky.

THE BOTTOM LINE ON HOW TO GROW

For most businesses, there are two key ways to grow: improvements and scaling. Whether you choose to grow, it is necessary to constantly improve your customer value proposition to continue to beat your competition. Like the story of the two guys walking in the woods who come on a bear, one guy says, "We need to run faster than the bear." The other guy responds, "No, I do not have to run faster than the bear—I just have to run faster than you." That is business competition.

Mission-critical improvements to your business processes—the *how* you do business—are as important as improvements to your product or service.

Scaling is the main engine of growth. Once you exhaust your scaling opportunities with your existing product or service, you must either utilize growth boosters to find other products or services to scale for your existing customers or find more customers by geographical expansion or moving into another customer segment.

The following stories describe two companies, Enchanting Travels and Sammy Snacks, that grew their business by scaling.

ENCHANTING TRAVELS[1]

The Enchanting Travels story involves the careful scaling of a personal service business.

Scaling a Service Business

In the early days when we were trying to build a brand and it was imperative that every single guest who booked a trip with us had a wonderful time, focusing on the operations or the issues that would have a direct impact on guest feedback or the guest experience would be of prime importance to anyone who was involved with the company—an almost fanatical approach toward guest feedback. And one of the big challenges that we faced and we continue to face is continuing to do what we have done during the past five years. Every entrepreneur goes through that very difficult task. I would say that to be able to build people's skills and abilities you have tzo at one point take away the safety net and let them figure it out; if the issue or the problem at hand involves solving the problem yourself as opposed to giving someone an opportunity even if they may fail, you reach a point when that focus becomes investing the time and effort in getting that person able to solve the issue or problem rather than doing it yourself.

I think that mindset is the big difference between a small start up and a larger high-growth company that needs to enable its people to grow and do things that you would have done. I think in the first year if you had asked me what our focus areas were, I would say that I was involved in creating our product, actually "doing" rather than "managing" operations and personally fixing what went wrong. Now, if you ask me what my focus would be, I would say that investing the time to teach someone or enable someone to fix something would be the focus rather than fixing it myself. And I think that is a point to reach when growing a company. Enabling people around you to do what you do and help you grow the company is a big thing, and one of the big changes we have seen in the last couple of years.

—Parikshat Laxminarayan

History

Founded in 2004 by Parikshat Laxminarayan and Alexander Metzler, who met during their MBA education at INSEAD, Enchanting Travels (ET) is an India- and Germany-based travel company. Its discerning clients, mainly from Western countries, are interested in visiting exotic destinations that pose travel difficulties. ET sells guided, customized, high-end tours to locations that Western tourists find challenging.

ET expanded its operations from India to East Africa and South America, growing by 100 percent a year its first three years, and by 30 to 50 percent in 2008–09. By 2009, ET employed close to 100 people on four different continents and had booked more than 4,000 travelers mainly from the United States, Germany, the United Kingdom, and Australia.

ET's business model was based on: (1) thoroughly knowing its customers in order to customize trips that met their expectations; (2) vertically integrating and controlling every aspect of the trips; and (3) seamlessly executing all operations. This business model differentiated ET from most travel companies that typically outsourced all activities involving clients after their arrival at a destination. ET's business model required that its employees be highly engaged with customers and used extensive measurement and information systems to quickly identify problems that could be remedied without delay.

Creating a Different Value Proposition

The birth of the idea for ET was somewhat of an accident and a surprise. At the end of 2003, while a student at INSEAD, Laxminarayan had visited India with several of his classmates. During their travels around South India, one student commented that his impression of India turned out to be quite different from his mental picture of the country. Laxminarayan recalled, "That set me wondering why there was a gap between the perception that outsiders bear and what India can really be if promoted and presented in an excellent manner." He wondered if he was in the presence of a business opportunity.

Back at INSEAD, Laxminarayan and Metzler discussed opening an exclusive travel service as a potential business venture after graduation. Their research about this market was encouraging because the travel industry was fairly traditional. According to Laxminarayan, "If you take out the online space, it is very traditional in the way it works, and there were a lot of unnecessary players in the value chain that weren't adding much value." He continued:

We found out that a foreign tour operator who might be offering India as one of the many destinations often did not have an on-the-ground presence in India. So he would contact a consolidator in Delhi or Mumbai, who would then subcontract to a final service provider in the final destination or in the region that the trip was actually happening. So there were three to four, or maybe even five parties between the traveler and the actual experience, which we thought was completely unnecessary and not an efficient way of doing things.

Laxminarayan and Metzler's business plan was focused on streamlining the value chain so that ET would be the single point of contact for each customer during a trip. The entrepreneurs attracted 16 investors and raised almost half of the initial money for their start-up before their June 2004 graduation. They flew to India in early July and, as Laxminarayan said, "We pretty much hit the ground running and started from there."

Early Challenges

At first, the big challenge for the partners was managing everything themselves. They started ET with a small team: two partners, two spouses, and one employee. The five of them were responsible for sales, marketing, and operations. The initial task of deciding on a location consistent with their model seemed daunting. They spent three months combing the length and breadth of India visiting every hotel they wanted to offer to their clients. They tested everything: drivers, activities, restaurants, and cars, in detail and with a level of quality control that was taxing. They did it because they were not going to work through intermediaries. Laxminarayan explained:

It wasn't as simple as going to Delhi and telling someone I am going to plan trips to Rajasthan so can you help me out. It was actually going to every small village and destination in Rajasthan, staying at and visiting every hotel that we wanted to sell and promote in our itinerary. I think just setting up the entire operation was a huge challenge early on.

Laxminarayan and Metzler decided that the biggest differentiator between a successful travel company and one that fails before it starts or shortly thereafter was in the execution. The five-member team had a tough first six months but managed to overcome the challenges. Laxminarayan said:

All entrepreneurial ventures have risk, otherwise they won't be entrepreneurial ventures, but I think it is not about feeling 100 percent sure about your business plan or that making complete sense. I think it is about having sound business logic, but then much more time should be spent on executing and actually pulling it off. So for me the appetite for risk is far more important than writing a business plan. The ability to pull off a successful operation and execute on a promise is much more challenging and important than having a very picture-perfect setup or picture-perfect brand or things like that.

Stage Two Growth

When ET opened in 2004, the plan was to operate in India. The partners had agreed that, while their customer base would be Germany and North

America, the destination for customers would be India. But, by 2006, ET's success in India encouraged expansion. Laxminarayan continued:

Our India model worked very successfully, and we grew very well in the first two years. We then asked ourselves—what is it that makes us successful in India? Clearly, more than knowledge of India or the background of being Indian and our presence there, it was our concept of being able to master challenging destinations, the ability to tackle unreliability, lack of professionalism, lack of transparency, the ability to manage the entire operation in a challenging destination. And secondly the ability to connect with and basically understand the mind of a customer was our key strength and value proposition and what made us different and successful. And finally, and most important, our ability to provide world-class service from India at an Indian cost base made us very different from other travel companies.

ET also feared losing its customer base unless it offered more places for them to travel. Laxminarayan explained:

Our goal was to develop a customer base that sort of stays with us for 10 years or more and takes an exotic trip every year or two. Now we have had several people who have come back to India with us on repeat trips, but our kind of guests often have a list of six, seven exotic trips they want to take. So having a lifetime customer base locked in was one of the biggest drivers of our destination expansion.

East Africa. Enchanting Africa was started up in 2006 in Nairobi with the goal of selling and operating trips initially to Kenya and Tanzania. This was a joint ownership venture between ET and Florian Keller, a European national and management consultant, who had lived in East Africa and was familiar with business and life in Africa. This partner also had experience working with several large international companies that had expanded to Africa. Having a partner who lived in Africa and was knowledgeable about the country was thought to mitigate some of the risk of testing the waters outside of India.

The complexity of Africa presented a huge challenge for ET. In an area the size of India, there were 10 countries with different laws, regulations, and ways of operating. Although ET maintained that one of the biggest differentiators of its model was its ability to offer world-class quality and service at an Indian cost base, the infrastructure challenges such as no high-speed bandwidth and the lack of an affordable, yet highly skilled and qualified labor pool to draw from, presented significant challenges.

In spite of the challenges, Africa was an attractive travel destination for Americans and Europeans. The ET team was convinced it could make Africa even more attractive to travelers if it could adapt its Indian business model to the African environment. By the end of 2009, Africa was ET's second-biggest destination having expanded to eight countries in East and Southern Africa. "We are fairly pan-African now, and we continue to grow. We have had challenges . . . But we recovered and are on our way to building what I imagine is a second pillar of profitability in Africa," said Laxminarayan.

South America. By 2008, ET had incorporated and founded Enchanting South America, which focused on Argentina and Chile from its head office in Argentina. The main driver behind ET's expansion in South America was twofold. First, it was a destination that fit well with ET's concept and value proposition of providing a hassle-free experience of exceptional quality in a destination that was known to be difficult. Second, its proximity to the United States, its second-biggest customer market, made South America an attractive destination.

During the expansion to South America, the partners had to decide whether to hire and train a local manager and pay compensation or to enter into a joint ownership venture as they had done in Africa. Taking the first route required one of them spend several months in Argentina to get a feel for the market, set up operations, and hire and train local employees. They chose to build the business organically. Although they knew it would take several months to start ET in that region, they also knew that the end result would be a value proposition—the end-to-end control of the luxury travel business in South America that protected their brand. This gave those customers who had traveled with them to India or Africa the chance to explore South America and enjoy the same high-quality experience with the same reliable customized service they had received in other destinations.

The Right People

The organizational structure of ET was linear, uncomplicated, and international in culture, with 90 employees from 14 nationalities working together across five countries. Most of them worked in India out of offices in Bangalore and Delhi, where there were employees from nine nationalities. According to Laxminarayan:

It is a very healthy and open environment because it is international, and it is not a very typically Indian hierarchical business . . . Our entire recruiting model is hiring freshers without any past experience but with a lot of potential, lots of drive, and lots of intelligence that we can mould into careers rather than laterally hiring people with experience . . . Of our 90 or so people, I think only three had any idea of tourism and travel before they joined us. So it was a conscious decision not to hire people from the travel industry.

Laxminarayan admitted that hiring without requiring experience working in the travel industry posed some risk. "Our training on basic travel skills takes more time, so all of this is a challenge, but I think it more than pays off by having someone who doesn't have any preconceived notions and can adapt easily to a different process." ET stuck with this hiring strategy to eliminate people who already had learned operating procedures that were not appropriate for the company.

Another crucial and unique part of ET's HR strategy was to hire foreigners from its customer markets (e.g., Germany, United States, United Kingdom, and other European countries) in India to further bridge the gap between a customer and the travel experience. This focus evolved into a truly multinational and multicultural team in each of ET's offices around the world.

Structure

At the top, Laxminarayan and Metzler managed in tandem as managing directors. Laxminarayan oversaw trip operations on the ground and the sales and marketing and PR for the company's English-speaking markets (United States, United Kingdom, Australia), while Metzler did the same for ET's European customers. Corporate strategy, finance, and new destinations were evenly split between them, with Laxminarayan in charge of South America and Metzler responsible for Africa with their partner in Nairobi and Asia.

In line with its horizontal management structure, at the second layer, seven functional managers with an average age of 32 supervised a team and managed finance and accounts, operations, marketing, customer management, and reservations.

To keep an international work environment, Laxminarayan and Metzler created an open structure that allowed numerous opportunities for employee growth, which was not typical of an Indian work environment. Because of this philosophy, ET had not lost a person to another company in the travel industry.

ET had a healthy and aggressive performance-linked bonus that was one of its big drivers. Because the company believed that incentivized performance was a fragile way to keep employees, it invested a lot of time in training and giving employees a sense of emotional attachment to the company. This enabled ET to retain people at a time when attrition was the biggest business challenge in India. ET's turnover in the first five years was 15 to 20 percent, but that number was reduced to just 5 percent in subsequent years.

The Business Model
One of the aspects of the business model that was clear to Laxminarayan and Metzler right from the beginning was its strong focus on only offering tailor-made travels and to never have catalogues with standardized itineraries. In order to pull this off and to efficiently create highly customized travel experiences for each guest, they implemented a highly flexible and tailor-made IT system to automate an otherwise hugely time-intensive activity of individual itineraries. They recalled an apt Michael Porter quote from business school: "Strategy is about being different and it means deliberately choosing a different set of activities to deliver a unique mix of value."[2]

Processes Became a Competitive Advantage
With this in mind, ET set up processes geared to offer high-quality tailor-made travels and a unique mix of activities to enable the company to clearly differentiate themselves from competitors and leverage competitive

advantages in its market space. As Metzler said, "We feel that large tour operators would find it nearly impossible to copy our business model and processes given that their entire setup is geared and catered for providing standard packages and mass tourism."

The first differentiator in ET's unique business model of vertical integration was that it handled all operations from beginning to end. Then there were the various nationalities and cultures of the people working in its offices in India with some often coming from the same places as the customers. In short, ET was an international organization in India; out of its 60-odd employees, 25 percent were foreigners.

The partners also invested heavily in training their employees about company processes and about India, a complex and diverse country. Getting the right people and building up their destination knowledge through training, test trips, integration with ET operations, and integrating customer-facing employees with operations was another characteristic that set ET apart. Laxminarayan explained:

If you ask our customers why they book with Enchanting Travels, this is what often comes up: "We felt very well taken care of, the quality of interaction was fantastic, the documents we got were fantastic, but most importantly, the person we were speaking to was really able to understand our needs and had a very good competence level on how to bring India alive in an itinerary that was a good fit with our personality and our needs at a very compelling value for money equation."

Quality controls.   One of the most appreciated value propositions that helped guests feel comfortable was ET's guest management strategy of assigning a hands-on contact person to see to all the activities of guests during their stay at a destination. Carefully selected tour guides were independent contractors who went through a quality check and a training process that taught them ET's different concept and way of doing things. Tour guides who had worked with other companies underwent a stringent selection process and ultimately approximately 80 percent of the guides worked solely for ET.

On average, the overall level of education, quality, sophistication, and skills was extremely low in the travel industry worldwide. Aware of this,

ET selected well-educated, competent people to train. Although ET's salary costs were higher, it was able to provide American- and European-quality service in India. By hiring foreigners and Indians on the same professional level as European or U.S. employees, ET produced the same or better quality of work as a premier travel company located in Munich or New York City. And it was able to deliver that quality from Bangalore and Delhi.

Because ET was passionate about personally experiencing, testing, and validating all hotels and restaurants that it recommended to its clients, it also tracked feedback about every hotel in its portfolio. ET invested a lot of time and money in test trips to build a destination from the ground up because the possible bias of trip advisors and independent rating agencies made it important to verify that a destination was a tailor-made travel experience. This extensive, time-consuming quality control process made expansion to a new destination a major research project. Nonetheless, ET preferred to take this slower approach to growth to make sure that its system was in sync with its promise to give guests a trip to remember.

Pricing. Laxminarayan gave all the credit for the success of the ET pricing model to the absence of middlemen. He considered it "the most innovative factor of our pricing model." Explaining why ET was not completely positioned as a luxury travel company, Laxminarayan said:

We are not as expensive as Abercrombie and Kent, the world's leading luxury travel company but neither are we as cheap as a regular tour operator. We are somewhere between those two in terms of our price positioning. We believe we offer amazing quality at a price-competitive proposition. But obviously in order to deliver that quality, we can't be playing with very small margins, which is very risky.

How to Continue Scaling?
Sowing the early seeds of Enchanting Asia, which would initially comprise Bhutan, Myanmar, Sri Lanka, and Nepal, and then slowly include Vietnam, Cambodia, Laos, and eventually reach the Chinese borders, was ET's main focus for 2010. Also in 2010, ET planned on growing Enchanting South America to harness the potential for Argentina and Chile and in a year

or so expanding to Peru and Brazil. The focus in India was to scale up by exploring avenues for new marketing channels. Laxminarayan explained:

of our big questions going forward is how to do China? We don't have the same comfort level as we would have in South America. In China, we are daunted by the challenge of what it would take to actually run an operation with Chinese managers or even with western managers. We need to figure out the massive potentially viable business opportunity that China presents. Would we pull that off using Africa's [joint-ownership] model or along the lines of the South American [solely owned] model?

In Laxminarayan's opinion, "One of the big challenges going forward is how to get the managers to drive growth and independently manage initiatives as opposed to me having to spend several months setting up a new operation as I did with Enchanting South America in Argentina." He concluded:

Whether we can become the Google of the travel world (at a relatively smaller scale given our industry of course) is a question that will hopefully be answered in the coming years, but I am hoping that we at least emerge as the world's leading company for high-end tailor-made travels to exotic destinations with a global reach in terms of markets and destinations.

LESSONS FROM ENCHANTING TRAVELS

1. Scaling a personal service business depends on having good hiring and training processes and low employee turnover.

2. Scaling a personal service business successfully requires extensive quality controls processes that can mitigate bad customer experiences quickly.

3. Scaling this business required variance feedback immediately and processes to remedy the bad experience or problem quickly.

4. Scaling sales required technology to reach and serve global customers.

5. Enchanting Travels' growth model is two-fold: first, continuous acquisition of new customers and, second, selling more trips to different geographies to existing customers.

Enchanting Travels' scaling challenge, like most service companies, is a people, execution processes, and quality controls challenge. Its challenge now is to build a cadre of managers that view Enchanting Travels as a meaningful career with a financial incentive to act like "owners."

SAMMY SNACKS[3]

Sammy Snacks presents a story of the scaling of a product business with two parts: one scaling failure and one scaling success.

Sammy Snacks opened its first retail store in Charlottesville, Virginia in 2003. Its Founder, Pamela Peterson, loved her dog Sammy, a Labrador retriever. She, being concerned about his nutrition, started baking him dog treats using ingredients that she used in baking her breads and desserts. Sammy loved them. Peterson, like Susan Feller of 3 Fellers Bakery, leveraged a personal need into a business by sharing her dog treats first with friends, then selling them at farmers' markets till she had a customer base large enough to open a retail store in Charlottesville. This was classic formula for starting a business.

That store was successful in generating a large customer base. Peterson's strengths were her love of dogs, passion for her products, sales, marketing, and public relations. Unfortunately, she was weak at managing operations, accounting, and finance. Her weaknesses necessitated that she seek bank financing to keep her business running and eventually to bring in a sophisticated investor in 2004, who invested in her business on the condition that she aggressively grow to 10 stores by the end of 2007 and 20 stores by 2010.

Premature Geographical Expansion

Those aggressive growth goals propelled Peterson to expand geographically before she had figured out how to operate her Charlottesville store profitably. In April 2005, a time when the retail market was hot, Peterson expanded by opening a second store in Richmond. She took on the responsibility of operating it on a daily basis, commuting to and from Richmond every day.

The Richmond store never achieved profitability, in spite of investments in excess of $200,000. The store's fixed occupancy (rent) cost was $8,000 a month, but the business was never able to sell more than $9,000 worth of products a month, at a gross margin of nearly 50%, before closing in 2006. Opening the second store had diverted Peterson's time and focus, as well as the resources from the Charlottesville store, which operated at a loss for 2006. Operating losses for 2006 were funded by the investors and the bank line of credit.

The Charlottesville store was located in the Barracks Road Shopping Center, an area with a high traffic count. Sammy Snacks Treats for dogs and cats were created and baked right in the store. These small treats were not only nutritious and wholesome for animals but also for humans—giving Sammy Snacks product differentiation. In 2006, in addition to Peterson, the Charlottesville store employed a full-time manager and accountant, a part-time retail sales person and warehouse worker, and a baker who worked two-thirds of the time. The store's primary product was dry dog food, which included chicken and lamb flavors for variety.

Peterson's love for her product did not diminish in spite of the store's dismal financial situation in 2006. She still wanted to reach more pet owners and to deliver the highest-quality nutritional dry dog food possible. She continued to outsource manufacturing to a Texas company, and she continued to build a Charlottesville client list of over 2,000 customers.

Concerned Investors
In January 2007, faced with these disappointing results, the increasingly impatient investors, who by now had over $400,000 invested in Sammy Snacks, brought in a consultant, Matthew Frey. His job was to analyze Sammy Snacks' costs and operations in an attempt to discover why the business was losing money.

Consultant's Recommendations
Frey spent the months of January and February 2007 reviewing the accounting records of Sammy Snacks, interviewing the employees, studying the premium-natural-dog-food market, and then submitting a plan to

turn the business around by reducing warehousing costs, shipping costs from the manufacturer, and personnel, and increasing revenue through the wholesaling of Sammy Snacks–branded products. Frey prepared three PowerPoint presentations: "Costs Analysis," Inventory Analysis," and "Going Forward." He made the following recommendations:

1. Reduce head count in the Charlottesville store by curtailing the hours of the full-time CPA and reduce retail staff.

2. Store dry-dog-food inventory at the store rather than off-site.

3. Reduce shipping costs per bag by ordering in larger quantities.

4. Reduce out-of-stock incidents and lost sales by better inventory management.

5. Grow the wholesale business as its net margins were significantly higher than retail net margins.

6. Do not open more stores.

CEO.   It was understandable that the current management did not take kindly to this outside critique. Frey's report also brought to light inventory-management issues and cash-flow problems. In March, in a move to help Frey execute his plan, the investors hired him as president and CEO. Based on the 2006 results and Frey's report, the investors requested that Peterson resign as CEO. The new president invested cash in the company, received a stock-incentive grant, and bought the company. Peterson resigned her officer position but remained a major stockholder and board member.

One of the first things the new CEO did was to meet with the baker. Frey knew he needed her to stay as she was a hard worker and the mainstay of the branded product. He also thought the dog-treat business could be increased by 50 percent very quickly. He was frank with her about the distressing state of the business and asked her to give him a chance. To show his respect for her abilities, he increased her responsibilities, hours, and hourly pay by more than 30 percent. Frey could afford these costs as he had terminated the full-time CFO, eliminated third-party warehouse costs, and reduced the number of retail employees to one.

Results

By the summer of 2007, Sammy Snacks had regained a positive monthly cash flow. Major factors that contributed to this result were a reduced annual employee cost of approximately $30,000, a reduced annual off-site warehousing cost of $14,000, a reduced shipping cost of $8,000, an increase in the sales of dog treats, and the wholesaling of Sammy Snacks–branded dry dog food to six stores in Richmond.

Serendipitous Chinese Recall

At the time, sales were also helped significantly by the recall of dog-food products made or manufactured in China, resulting in the heightened sensitivity and demand for quality U.S.-manufactured dog food. This increased demand strained the Sammy Snacks supply chain and cash reserves.

In the three months of the last quarter of 2007, the business sold $45,000, $48,000, and $60,000 of retail and wholesale products. Approximate retail net margin was 18 percent, and the wholesale net margin was 33 percent but on a much lower sales price. Cash flow reduced payables and lowered the line of credit needed to buy inventory. The highest fixed cost was the approximately $4,700 a month in rent that Sammy Snacks paid for its store space in the Barracks Road Shopping Center.

The business finished 2007 with strong last-quarter results, including a net profit of $21,000 after a first-quarter loss of $38,000. If the business continued to operate at this financial level, it would show a net profit in 2008 of $100,000. At that rate it would take five years to pay back the investors invested capital excluding interest. For 2007, approximately 20 percent of Sammy's revenue had been from the wholesaling of product.

Growth Realities

During 2007, the CEO worked from 70 to 80 hours a week. The CEO believed the Charlottesville store was operating at its gross-income capacity, with little room to cut costs further. The company could redo its Web site to make it a channel of distribution, but the fact remained that the market for high-end premium dog food was limited and there were many competitors, including the two big natural brands with significant marketing clout: California Natural and Wellness.

The CEO knew that the retail pet-store business, in general, was dominated by three large national chains, but he also knew that the market did accommodate a large number of mom-and-pop retail outlets, run primarily by animal lovers who were not business lovers. With the president and shareholders—who had invested more than $500,000—looking at him to grow Sammy Snacks in order for them to realize a return on their investment, the CEO knew he had to consider his growth options.

Scaling Distribution

Opening more retail stores was capital intensive and would require the hiring and training of more people. Frey did not think that was a viable option. He decided that for 2008 he would focus on expanding the wholesale business by personally calling on other privately owned boutique dog stores in Virginia. This strategy of wholesaling the firm's dog foods and snacks resulted in a six-fold increase in net profits and increased its wholesale sales from 10 to 17 percent of the revenues.

In December of 2008, the Sammy Snacks board met and proposed that Frey hire a salesperson to focus full-time on wholesale sales to individual retail stores.

Frey estimated the cost of a salesperson for a year would be $120,000 dollars, which included salary, bonus, car allowance, employee benefits, and travel expenses; however, that estimated cost exceeded not only the net profit for 2008 but also the projected net profit for 2009. Frey responded that he had planned on using the projected net profit from 2007 and 2008 to build a new Sammy Website to increase on-line sales, to increase Sammy's advertising, and to purchase a delivery truck.

The Board told Frey that it wanted to grow the business faster and if he did not want to hire a full-time salesperson to call on the boutique retail stores, then he should come back in January with a strategic plan on how to grow the business quickly.

2009

Frey rejected the Board's suggestion that he hire a full-time salesperson because he was concerned about spending more than two years of projected net profit ahead of earning it. He began 2009 by continuing to personally call on more retail stores and sign them up to buy his products wholesale. By midyear, he had signed up twelve new stores in northern Virginia and seven grocery and convenience stores in Charlottesville.

Another Recall Propels Sammy

Frey also signed up Sammy Snacks with an on-line virtual wholesaler, WholesalePet.com, which sold pet supplies for 120 vendors. Then, in early 2009, one of Sammy's competitors experienced a recall. This created an opportunity: A large distributor that sold to dog stores in five states approached Sammy about becoming its exclusive distributor in those states. The distributor would buy two to four truckloads of Sammy's products a month. This would increase Sammy's annual revenue by 90 percent. But with this opportunity to sign on with a five-state regional distributor came several challenges.

The Costs of Growth

Wholesaling to big regional distributors would be a big step for Sammy. Yes, it would increase sales, but selling through distributors instead of directly to stores would reduce Sammy's profit per bag of dog food by more than 30 percent. Furthermore, each regional distributor would require Sammy to hire a regional salesperson at a cost of approximately $90,000 to work with that distributor educating its retail store customers about the products, design marketing programs, and setting up store displays.

Wholesaling would also require Sammy to invest $90,000 in preprinting the labels on the dog-treat bags at the manufacturing plant for these big distributors rather than its usual practice of affixing the labels manually in the store after it received shipments from its manufacturer in Texas. This cost would have to be paid before the dog food was manufactured. Although distributors generally paid for purchases 30 days after delivery, Sammy paid its manufacturer COD.

Wholesaling created another challenge for the business. Sammy now baked its dog treats in its Charlottesville store, where its manufacturing capacity was 400 pounds a day. A regional distributor would buy 5,000 pounds of dog treats per week. Outsourcing the production of the dog treats created quality control issues and, more important, required Sammy to disclose for the first time its proprietary dog-treat recipe. The dog treats could only be manufactured in a facility that met human standards because the market differentiator for Sammy's Treats was that they were so good that they were edible by humans. And I know that is true from personal experience—tasting them myself. They are good.

As expected, Sammy's Board was gung-ho to sign on with the five-state regional distributor because its members thought this was a good way to grow the business. But Frey had several management challenges to overcome to make this opportunity work.

Frey and the largest investor convinced their bank to loan them the $90,000 for the labels and Frey convinced the distributor to delay the customer service rep requirement and Frey signed on the regional distributor.

Frey smartly changed his sales efforts from single retail stores to calling on large regional wholesale distributors. . Frey's goal by the end of 2010 was to have regional distributors selling Sammy Snacks dry packaged food plus Sammy's proprietary treats in every state East of the Mississippi River plus Texas.

With the new distribution strategy Frey was able to finance expanding the Charlottesville treat baking operation to a different industrial space. The impact by August 2010 was phenomenal in that Sammy Snack's revenue for the month of August exceeded its annual revenue for 2009.

Quality Controls Are Critical

Frey was a good entrepreneur in that he took no big risks while he learned by iterating how he was going to scale sales and distribution. A recall of Chinese and U.S. of dog food created opportunities for him that, because he focused on quality controls and natural ingredients in all his products, has kept Sammy's so far above the recall fray.

LESSONS FROM SAMMY SNACKS

1. Peterson's story is inspiring in how she created a business and a world-class product. But her story is also sad because she lost control of her business and dream by agreeing to her investor's aggressive growth goals, for which she was not prepared or qualified to make happen.

2. Opening a second store in Richmond prematurely and having Peterson commute every day to run it exacerbated the problems of managing Sammy's and made Charlottesville a money loser, too. Opening a second store when the business model was not that profitable was high risk. Another entrepreneur in my study made the same mistake by expanding to two other states before she had her operational model down pat. Growing too quickly can be deadly. Taking on investors whose goals maybe different than yours is a recipe for disaster.

3. Sammy Snacks tried to scale through geographical expansion by opening more stores. This strategy failed the first time, and by that time the investors had little appetite for another try. Then Frey personally started selling wholesale to other Virginia retailers and that got the business profitable. Frey planned to continue scaling the business by selling individually to geographically proximate retailers and ultimately hiring a sales person. But a product recall by a domestic large producer created the opportunity for Sammy's to scale more efficiently and faster by selling to large regional wholesale distributors. While they purchased in large volumes, Sammy's sales priced decreased by 30 percent and its profits decreased—but that was the cost of increasing sales twelvefold in one swoop. Notice how Sammy's iterated through the sales scaling alternatives: retail sales, more retail locations, wholesaling to individual retailers, Internet sales, and selling to large wholesale distributors.

4. Frey ended up where some other entrepreneurs did in my study. Dennis Lee built Octane Fitness into a market leader outsourcing manufacturing to the Far East and scaling sales by only selling to large retail chains. Another entrepreneur scaled production by manufacturing in India and Vietnam and scaled sales by selling to only three large national big box retailers. In both of those cases, the entrepreneurs had substantial experience in their industry with manufacturing and customer relationships prior to starting their business. Frey had to learn as he went along what they already knew when they started.

5. Frey was able to take advantage of the quality problems that other dog food producers experienced because he had patient investors and he knew that he had to have the best quality product or he had no chance to win in the marketplace.

CHAPTER 5 TAKEAWAYS

1. Growing a business is primarily a challenge of scaling. How do you do very well a lot more of what you are already doing successfully? Scaling a business requires you to figure out how to scale sales, production, distribution, and people.

2. Scaling requires you to decide what parts of the customer value chain you must keep control of and what parts you can outsource to limit your financial investment costs.

3. Successful businesses are execution champions that constantly improve every day. As important as improving your products or services is improving how you do business. Improvements are the "bread and butter" of a business. You must become better, faster, and cheaper than the competition to "outrun the bear."

4. Scaling a business is dependent on planning, prioritizing, and processes. You cannot effectively scale without processes because scaling increases your risks. Processes help manage quality and financial risks.

5. Scaling usually requires more people and that means hiring and training processes. More people means you need more structure—some people besides yourself managing other people.

6. Scaling and improvements are not an *either–or* alternative. Think of constant improvements as a given. Scaling is how you accelerate growth.

6

CREATING THREE

GROWTH PLANS

This chapter involves a workshop exercise using the concepts discussed in Chapters 2 through 5 as well as the lessons learned from the Eyebobs, 3 Fellers Bakery, Global Medical Imaging, Enchanting Travels, and Sammy Snacks stories.

First, you will be given some background information on C. R. Barger & Sons, Inc. and asked to create a growth plan for the business. After you formulate your plan, you will be provided with details of the strategies that the company put into place and the results so that you can gauge the merit of your recommendations.

Then, you will be given the story of Hass Shoes, a business that needs your guidance in improving its stagnant sales. You will create a growth plan for Hass Shoes while specifically weighing the challenges that growth places on people, processes, and controls.

Last, using the Growth Planning Template introduced in Chapter 4 plus the four ways to grow a business, you will be asked to create a list of growth ideas for your business.

C. R. BARGER & SONS, INC.[1]

Eric Barger took over a subsidiary of a family business that sold a commoditized product and was in decline. Commoditization occurs when the only differentiation between products or services offered by different companies is price, and usually the lowest cost provider prevails. Unfortunately, for smaller businesses, the lowest cost provider is often the biggest, most well-capitalized competitor.

I call commoditization the cancer of business because the lack of a differentiated product or service will kill an entrepreneurial business unless radical treatment occurs.

Your task is to read Barger's story and, using the concepts of growing through improvements, innovations, scaling, and acquisitions, create a plan to reignite growth in this business. Approach this workshop not only from a strategy perspective but also from the perspectives of marketing, new customer acquisition, and creating a differentiating customer value proposition.

Background

Headquartered in Harriman, Tennessee, C. R. Barger & Sons, Inc. (Barger) operated two businesses. The first was the installation of gas, water, and sewer-lines and the second was the manufacture and sale of precast-concrete septic tanks and grease interceptors. In 2002, after 35 years as a local supplier of septic tanks, that part of the business had reached a plateau. Not only did Barger not have a distinctive brand or product, its sales were limited primarily to East Tennessee.

In early 2004, Eric Barger, the founders' grandson, assumed leadership of Precast Concrete Operations (PCO). Barger was on the verge of closing down the septic tank subsidiary of its business. Though still in his 20s, Eric had worked in the family business since he was a teenager and continued after getting a civil engineering degree from Tennessee Technological University. Now the challenge Eric faced was how to take the precast septic tank, a non-distinctive commodity-priced product, and grow it into a viable growth business.

History

In 1967, Eric's grandparents, Charles (C. R.) and Mary Barger, started C. R. Barger & Sons, Inc. Straight out of high school, C. R. initially worked as a warehouse stock boy and then transitioned to plumbing work and building houses. In 1959, he purchased his grandfather's country store, Barger Groceries but, as a side business, continued plumbing and building houses, and also started installing septic tanks and field lines. C. R. ordered his septic tanks from third parties and often had problems receiving shipments on time, which frustrated his customers. One day, C. R. drove to a septic tank manufacturing plant in Georgia and observed how tanks were made and shipped. After the trip, he decided to make his own septic tanks to solve his supply-chain delivery problem.

C. R. and Mary made their first precast-concrete septic tanks in a small tin shed behind Barger Groceries. Together, they handcrafted the tanks with trowels, using a simple metal form. At that time, 750-gallon and 1,000-gallon tanks already were available on the market. The Bargers started by making only the 1,000-gallon tanks and, because the cement for each tank had to be individually mixed by hand with a shovel, only one tank per day was cast.

After two months without making a sale, C. R. and Mary sold their first tank to a local resident. This single sale helped spread the word that there was a new family business in town, and soon the phone started ringing with customers asking for their handmade tanks. At a time when the concept of marketing was practically nonexistent in the industry, the Bargers' septic tank side business grew into an eastern Tennessee precast-concrete-tank success story over the next three decades.[2] Mickey, one of C. R.'s sons, joined Barger's after obtaining a degree in business and helped to further grow the company.

Family Ties and Company Tradition

In January 2004, Mickey Barger passed the precast-division reins on to his 26-year-old son, Eric, although he retained management control of the utility division. The precast division was usually staffed with five employees, and the other divisions were made up of about 40 employees. Eric took great pride in the family heritage and the traditions of his company. He considered his floor workers' and delivery drivers' positions to be as strategic as those of a winning Super Bowl football team. "The guys who make the tanks are critical—they're our offensive linemen. And the drivers are similar to quarterbacks—everyone knows who they are; they're the first contact with clients . . . a lot of the pressure is riding on them."[3]

The Business

When Eric took over PCO in early 2004, the division had two production employees, two delivery drivers, and a company secretary, who divided her time between the three divisions within the company. Eric had limited time to oversee his division because he was also heavily involved with the utility division.

Back in 2003, sales of precast-concrete products—primarily residential septic tanks and commercial grease interceptors—had reflected a 24 percent reduction over the previous business year and represented only $135,000 per full-time-equivalent employee. Word of mouth and an existing customer base drove precast sales.

The entire customer base of the company was located in Tennessee. About 30 percent of its business came from residential homebuilders and contractors and 70 percent came from the commercial and industrial segment. The 70 percent broke down further into 60 percent from utility districts and 10 percent from storm shelters and grease interceptors. The Barger market share of precast-concrete products, although believed to be small, was unknown. The Barger name was recognized by, at best, 20 percent of the licensed installers in the area, and the company's presence in the residential market segment was negligible.

Industry Character

The septic tank manufacturing industry was mostly made up of small mom-and-pop businesses. As in any other industry, differentiating the products from those of other manufacturers was perceived to be essential to growing business. Because septic tanks were buried in the ground, however, they did not capture much attention. Usually, homeowners made decisions based on their contractor's advice without knowing much about the septic tanks they purchased.

In addition, contractors relied on price alone when recommending specific tanks to their customers. And because little information on the merits of different precast-concrete products was available to contractors, many believed all septic tanks functioned equally. Showing that one manufacturer's tanks were better than another's was difficult.

Eric's Goals

Although Eric knew his family was considering shutting down the septic tank end of the business, he was determined to try to make it a success. So he set some audacious goals:

1. Increase sales by a factor of three within four years to reestablish PCO as a viable, sustainable business entity;

2. Build the highest-quality precast-concrete products in the area; and

3. Establish a reputation as the premier source for precast-concrete-tank information and products.

Because this future scenario would be very different for the business, the question for Eric was how to accomplish those goals.

WORKSHOP #4: HOW CAN BARGER GROW?

What actions should Eric take to accomplish his goals? Think about having four arrows in your quiver: improvements, innovations, scaling, and acquisitions. Also, remember that growth can come from both top-line, revenue-generating initiatives as well as from bottom-line efficiencies and productivities that reduce costs. Prepare your list of action items, including marketing, branding, and advertising ideas.

Helpful hints: This activity should take you over 90 minutes. There are over 25 different things that Eric can and did do. Create your list of actions or steps that Eric can do under the headings of (1) *Improvements* (products, service, inventory control, productivity, and business processes), (2) *Innovations* (doing something new), (3) *Scaling* (sales, production), (4) *Acquisitions*, (5) *Marketing and Brand Awareness*, and (6) *Creating Differentiators*.

BREAK FOR YOUR WORK

Do not read ahead until you have completed your list of growth initiatives. Two blank pages follow.

WHAT ERIC BARGER DID: THE RESULTS

Now as you read what Eric did please make a list using the same six headings you used to make your list and catalog all the things Eric did. This will allow you to compare your list to his actions. Understand that you may have had different ideas than Eric, but the purpose of this is to teach you to think granularly about what creates growth and all the different ways growth can occur.

It had been almost four years since Eric Barger became president of the PCO division of Barger. At the time he took over the position, the company was considering shutting down this business because of its persistently stagnant revenues. But Eric had decided to give the PCO division his best shot.

Eric's best shot was effective. By the end of 2007, Eric had turned the PCO division around and had grown it into a leader in the precast-concrete industry by implementing a multifaceted strategy. Eric accomplished this by differentiating the product and incorporating technology into the manufacturing process for higher quality and efficiency. He also expanded Barger's customer base geographically and added new customer segments after launching an aggressive Internet branding program and educational effort.

2004 Growth Strategy

When Eric took over the PCO division in 2004, Barger could not differentiate its precast-concrete tanks from those of other manufacturers in the area, in spite of having been in the business since 1967. Basically, Barger sold a commodity product that had little market or brand recognition.

Eric's revitalization strategy included seven goals:

1. Create product differentiators;

2. Increase manufacturing efficiency;

3. Create brand awareness;

4. Create new customers by expanding geographically;

5. Create new customer segments;

6. Be a first-mover, incorporating new national standards; and

7. Make service a differentiator.

Creating Product Differentiators

Water-tight traffic rated.   Part of the PCO product line was crafting precast grease interceptors for commercial and utilities operations. For public highway or utilities, grease interceptors collect grease and oil that might otherwise clog municipal water systems. As a major step in promoting this business, in September 2004, the company got its grease interceptors H20-highway-traffic-rated to accommodate the Knoxville Utility Board's request.

The H20-highway-traffic rating standards were applied in high-traffic areas as defined by the American Association of State Highway and Transportation Officials. Owing to these rigorous standards, Barger's new line of H20-rated products had price tags much higher than those of existing product lines. For instance, a 1,000-gallon non-traffic-rated grease interceptor cost about $400, but if it were H20 traffic-rated, it cost $2,500.

Barger became the only east Tennessee precast-concrete tank manufacturer offering watertight, traffic-rated grease interceptors, grit traps, and septic tanks. The company manufactured watertight 40 to 6,800 gallon tanks, including ones traffic-rated for H20 loadings and deep-burial applications.

The use of watertight, traffic-rated grease interceptors maximized tank performance and useful life, thereby enabling utility districts to effectively combat the problem of grease clogging municipal wastewater systems.

Baffle walls.   Another new critical design feature that further differentiated Barger products was its use of monolithic baffle walls that enhanced structural integrity, thereby eliminating premature failures.

Independent manufacturing certifications.   Eric also introduced the most rigorous industry standards into the company's manufacturing processes, which further enhanced product quality and further differentiated its products. In October 2005, the company was certified by the industry's leading trade association, the National Precast Concrete Association (NPCA), and became the only NPCA-certified plant in east Tennessee specializing in tank manufacturing.

The NPCA Plant Certification Program was a challenging test of the plant's ability to produce quality precast-concrete products. The program was administered by a world-renowned engineering and materials science firm. Assigned inspectors comprehensively assessed all aspects of precast-concrete production at a plant. To be certified, plants have to meet high standards in all areas of production, safety, delivery of products, and information management.

Certification processes.   Achieving the NPCA certification meant that Eric had to make the company's manufacturing process more disciplined. He maintained comprehensive manufacturing records and obtained required industry certification for those employees performing the concrete testing.[4] According to Ty Gable, president of NPCA, Barger had proven its commitment to manufacturing the highest quality of precast products by joining this elite group of precasters.

Using technology.   As part of the NPCA certification process, Eric introduced innovative technology solutions and extended the company's computer network to include the manufacturing plant. The production side of technology solutions included the use of more precise concrete forms and the application of technically superior concrete, adhesives, and ASTM-compliant, chemical-resistant sealants.[5]

Operations Management

Inventory.   Concurrently, Eric developed and implemented two software systems that streamlined operations management. The first system, called PreCast-IT! is an inventory-management software system designed specifically for manufacturing, delivering, and maintaining records for precast-concrete products. PreCast-IT! uses barcodes and portable data terminals to maintain a complete history of each product manufactured and delivered to a customer, eliminating the time-consuming and error-prone manual data-entry method.

Supplies/production schedules.   A second software system, Produce-IT!, provided detailed requirements for the materials for any selected time period based on the schedules, product structure, and bill-of-materials maintained in the system. Produce-IT! allowed manufacturing planners to easily schedule product pours and automatically generated a complete list of production-material requirements. The system allowed the user a five-day window into production schedules. The schedule for a specific concrete form could easily be shifted forward or backward in time to accommodate unforeseen demand or outages. Because Produce-IT! maintained complete product structure and bill-of-material records, it could generate a summary report on material requirements across any desired time period and facilitate efficient ordering of production materials.

Customer-Service Enhancement

Eric communicated Barger's commitment to providing excellent service both to his employees and to all customers. He wanted all employees to embrace the notion that excellence in service was not just an idea but also a way of life at Barger. He wanted all employees who came into contact with customers to be effective representatives of the quality of the company's product and guaranteed maintenance service. So, as part of customer-service enhancement, Eric demanded well-trained personnel for everything the company did and encouraged all employees to be certified in their relevant domains.

Eric also led by example. For instance, he was dedicated to answering questions from customers and judiciously followed up on these inquiries by contacting them and/or sending AutoCad computerized tank drawings and other relevant product information on the same day he received their inquiries.

On-time delivery guarantees.   On-time deliveries, which were rare in the industry, became the company's signature service, saving contractors the cost of having crews on standby for several hours waiting for a delivery. Not satisfied with this significant improvement, Eric pushed on-site delivery service to a different level as proclaimed on the Barger Web site:

Delivery drivers are first-class people, willing to go the extra step it takes to ensure you are happy with your order. That includes handling the tank in a fashion that is safe and courteous, being on time for deliveries, and maintaining a good relationship with each customer. The drivers are just an extension of the business and the biggest representative that contacts the customer. Being able to make decisions on the job site, scheduling future deliveries and making sure that the customer has not ordered too much or forgotten a small item they may need.[6]

Additionally, both Barger's and Eric's personal expertise in utility operations helped enhance customer service in a way that other precast-concrete manufacturers could not. For example, Eric and several other employees held Water Treatment Plant and Licensed Distribution certifications and could assemble water-meter vaults. To simplify the on-site tank-installation process, Barger started selling preassembled vaults to utility districts that were ready to be set in the holes and hooked up to the tanks.

Branding

Eric wanted to establish Barger as *the* underground-tank authority and to promote it as representing values that brought "old-school thought and 21st century marketing together."[7] Barger's marketing strategy encompassed various forms of awareness campaigns and education on product-design features unique to its products. This strategy was targeted toward all potential customers (i.e., individual homeowners, building contractors, engineers, architects, utility districts, and state and municipal regulators) who influenced the market.

Awareness campaign. To raise awareness among prospective customers, Barger adopted the theme, "We're Number One in the Number Two Business," which was carried throughout all PCO advertising. Because he did not have an expert marketing team on board at the time, Eric himself developed brochures, T-shirts, hats, and even pocket knives sporting the company logo.

Advertising. Eric filled a billboard with a display of the major Barger products and corporate theme and then had it placed strategically on Interstate 40. The company advertised on the two Knoxville talk radio stations at a cost of $50,000 per year per station. Radio advertising by commercial voice-overs by well-known personalities helped inform Barger's target market about important product features and company attributes. It also hosted a four-hour radio show that ran five days a week on one of the stations whose radio waves reached five different states. The radio show's host became an advocate for Barger.

Trade associations. Some of Barger's employees, including Eric and his father, Mickey, belonged to relevant industry associations and actively participated in trade associations and industry-standards groups. Eric served and networked with others in the industry as a member of the NPCA Quality Assurance Committee, as the director of the NPCA Educational Foundation, and as a member of ASTM Committee, C27, Precast Concrete Products. While widely networking in the industry, Eric simultaneously pursued various opportunities for the company to be featured in articles in industry publications.

Educating influencers.   Community outreach was also expanded to sponsor direct delivery of industry trade-magazine subscriptions free-of-charge to decision-makers, engineers, and utility owners. Barger also sponsored free technical classes where engineers and architects earned continuing education credits.

Internet marketing.   To promote education among prospective customers, a new Web site was designed without an emphasis on sales. The new site accommodated prospective customers' varying needs and interests. Anyone who visited the Web site was given unlimited access to detailed plans, design specifications and drawings, white papers, and published articles to use when designing and developing project specifications.

For nontechnical homeowners, the Web site also offered a list of frequently asked questions and provided information on how to best use and maintain a septic tank. This was different from the traditional way septic systems had been sold in the past when homeowners were seldom involved until the bill was presented to them. Eric's hope was that educating homeowners about residential septic systems would enable them to play a significant role in their purchase, a decision usually made by their contractors.

In designing the new Web site, Eric carefully chose metatags (keywords) embedded in each of the company's Web pages, so even with a quick search using a Web browser, Barger popped up on a computer screen for anyone looking for watertight concrete septic tanks, grease interceptors, and storm shelters.

The Results

Expanded customer base.   Shortly after launching the new marketing strategy, Eric started getting phone and Web site orders from Georgia,

Virginia, and Kentucky. When the company received sales inquiries from a new state, it quickly familiarized itself with that state's regulations governing its business to become compliant with relevant regulations. At the end of 2007, Barger had expanded its customer base from its home state of Tennessee to 12 more states, including Arkansas, North Carolina, South Carolina, Illinois, Mississippi, West Virginia, Ohio, and New York.

Thanks to its open-source Web site and customer-centered philosophy, Barger's quality products generated some unusual requests. For example, Eric received a call from a wildlife conservationist in San Juan, Puerto Rico, asking about a 5,000-gallon grease interceptor. This government official, who was responsible for the preservation of one of the most endangered birds in the world, had found Barger on the Internet. Situated in a remote location of the Caribbean National Forest, Luquillo Aviary was a captive breeding sanctuary for the Puerto Rican parrot. The sanctuary needed a cistern as part of the government's 19-year-old formal recovery plan for the parrot. The sanctuary bought Barger's grease interceptor as a rainwater storage tank to provide chemical-free drinking and bathing water for the birds. To ensure proper installation on-site, Eric filmed and narrated an instructional DVD that was shipped with the interceptor.

Now because of the order from Puerto Rico, Barger was advertised as a "parrot's best friend" in NPCA's industry magazine, *Precast Solutions Magazine*, in the spring of 2006.[8] Other media exposure included a feature article about the company, one about the lessons learned from the company's Web experience, and a technical feature presenting the results of a study on inflow and infiltration from unsealed septic tank access ports. Eric's Web-savvy marketing also led to negotiations with American contractors in the Middle East.

By providing various technical white papers and personalized services to his customers, Eric built buy-in for high-priced, H20-highway-traffic-rated product lines. In 2006, Barger sold 60 percent more H20-rated products than products without the rating to both its commercial and industrial customers. H20-rated products buffered liability concerns customers had and helped them promote safe, ecologically friendly tanks.

Almost daily, new customers called or e-mailed. But attracting new customers was secondary to keeping existing business relationships thriving.

At the end of 2007, Barger's customer base was 40 percent homebuilders, (a 10 percent increase from the previous four years) and 60 percent commercial/industrial customers. This 60 percent broke down further to 40 percent utility districts and 20 percent grease interceptors.

Bottom-Line Efficiencies & Productivity

The two software systems Barger developed to improve its production and management processes turned out to be great investments. Produce-IT! reduced the time required to develop pour schedules by 90 percent. In addition to saving several hours of effort per week developing pour schedules, Produce-IT! reduced the company's material supply stock by 50 percent.

Barger received the NPCA's Award of Excellence in 2007. It was one of only three plants in the United States to receive it. The award was based on scores from an independent, unannounced audit of the manufacturing plant, its processes, procedures, and employee qualifications. In 2007, Barger also received the Pinnacle Award, presented after a competition for the leading innovations, inventions, and ideas throughout the precast-cement industry. The award specifically recognized the PreCast-IT! inventory-management software as the most innovative industry development for 2007.

By charting and implementing a pathway to excellence, Barger's PCO reached a position of market dominance and preeminence in its field in four years. Gross sales for the 2007 fiscal business year exceeded 2003 sales by 400 percent and topped the goal established in 2004—these results reflected an average annual sales growth of 42 percent over the four-year period. The sales per full-time-equivalent (FTE) employee in 2007 were $202,000, reflecting an increase of 50 percent over 2003 figures. The number of FTE employees in the division alone grew from 4.5 in 2004 to 15 at the end of 2007.

When compared with the modest growth in construction in the area, Barger's 400 percent increase in sales suggested that some amount of business was taken away from competitors.

LESSONS FROM C. R. BARGER & SONS

1. Eric approached growth by figuring out how to improve his business and how to create differentiators for his products. Eric understood

that he needed to create differentiators that both were important and valuable to his customers and that were different from his competitors' offerings.

2. Eric then approached creating differentiators in his product design, how he produced the product, and how he delivered and serviced the product. He used on-time delivery guarantees and his engineering expertise as differentiators.

3. Eric positioned himself and his company as the "expert" on the best and most environmentally friendly septic tank and storm drain products. He wrote articles and participated in industry trade associations to create the validation for his expertise.

4. Eric helped create industry standards that he could meet but that most of his competitors could not meet, which was a key differentiator.

5. Eric created software to manage his raw materials needs, inventory, and his production process.

6. Eric changed the role of his employees into business ambassadors and engaged team members through education, culture, and making their jobs more meaningful and respectful.

What did Eric do that surprised you? What can you apply to your business? Take some time to think about how Eric transformed his little business unit into a better, more defensible, high-performance business and how you can make your business better and more defensible from competition.

HASS SHOES

The next exercise involves a situation where the entrepreneur needs to take steps to create growth. Unlike Eric Barger's story, this scenario describes a retail business in which the entrepreneur does not manufacture his own product. As such, it gives you the learning opportunity to think about growth from a different perspective.

THE HASS SHOES STORY[9]

Hass Shoes, an independent shoe retailer located in Charlottesville, Virginia, had been in business for more than 15 years. In its freestanding store,

Hass primarily carried quality shoes for men and women and accessories such as socks and hosiery. The store provided parking for its customers and, to better serve its working customers, was open from 12 p.m. until 8 p.m. on Monday through Friday, 9 a.m. until 6 p.m. on Saturday, and 12 p.m. until 6 p.m. on Sunday.

Conscious of its membership in the community, Hass contributed to local charities and belonged to several civic and business clubs. In 2008, Hass joined the National Shoe Retailers Association (NSRA) and had been using the Association's benchmarking process to track products, services, expenses, and inventory turns of its current performance against past performance and other best practices. Hass now operated above NSRA averages.

From its approximately 10,000 transactions per year, Hass grossed $800,000, averaging $80 per sale. The business turned its inventory 2.7 times a year and, after paying its owner's salary, netted a 7 percent before-tax profit. Hass did not try to compete on price but focused instead on service, selection of shoes, and maintaining a stock of hard-to-find sizes; however, Hass did not collect the usual data on individual customers such as number of visits, number of purchases, or the total average cost of purchases per year.

Hass had weathered the 2007 recession well, but its business had basically been flat since 2001. Now the shoe retailer wanted to grow its revenue by at least 10 percent per year and increase its net margin.

Business Advice

To get started on a plan to grow the business, Hass sought advice from professors at the Darden School of Business in Charlottesville. From them, the retailer learned about the two basic business models: the niche-value-added and the high-volume, low cost. Hass also received the following suggestions for retail business growth:

1. Increase the number of buying customers by either generating new buyers or by converting more existing shoppers into buyers;

2. Increase the number of purchases per year per customer;

3. Increase the average purchase amount per customer;

4. Add high-margin, complementary products to inventory;

5. Add high-margin, related services to its offerings;

6. Add a new customer segment;

7. Bundle offerings; and

8. Increase reasons for customers to buy.

Role Models

Hass wanted to learn from other best-of-class retailers not part of the shoe or clothing sector and, to this end, studied the growth of Best Buy and Tiffany & Co. Back in 2005, Best Buy had changed its business model from a product-centric focus to a customer-centric one and to do so had conducted an in-depth study to identify its best customers, why they shopped, and when they shopped. Best Buy found that 80 percent of its profits came from 20 percent of its customers.

Hass also found that Best Buy grew its business by expanding its product offerings; selling more complementary products (e.g., accessories), adding services, selling warranties, and stocking such frequently sought products as CDs and DVDs in order to bring shoppers into the store more often. Lastly, to attract more shoppers and drive volume, Best Buy started to carry certain brands (e.g., Apple) that had broad appeal and captured more profit from the value chain.

Although Tiffany & Co. was mostly known as a top-of-the-line jewelry retailer, the store still sold sterling silver to many customer segments. At first, Tiffany customers typically bought for special occasions such as weddings, birthdays, anniversaries, graduations, and especially for the special holidays: Valentine's Day, Mother's Day, and Christmas. Then Tiffany increased its sales, by suggesting other reasons for celebration to shoppers beyond the special holidays, such as a good report card, a new home, or a business accomplishment.

Weighing Alternatives

Hass first considered offering women's handbags and scarves to match its shoes and adding men's belts to its inventory until other NSRA members described the high probability of risk involved in trying to match accessories with shoe purchases. Hass next thought about offering men's

EEE- and EEEE-width shoes as a wholesaler to other shoe retailers in Virginia.

In the end, Hass decided it needed to learn more by finding the answers to some questions: How could it make shopping more fun and entertaining the way Sam Walton did in his early days of retailing at Wal-Mart? What could it do to attract customers without a specific need and then generate spontaneous buys? How could Hass make shopping more of a Starbucks experience, so the emotion of shopping at Hass would add 5 percent more margin? Could Hass produce an increase in purchases with a customer loyalty program such as airlines used? Could teaming with local Avon saleswomen increase sales? Should Hass buy a van and set up a booth at flea or farmers' markets? Should Hass sponsor community education on foot health? Should Hass go into the shoe-repair business?

WORKSHOP #5: HOW CAN HASS SHOES GROW?

Hass seeks your advice. What growth initiatives would you recommend? Create a list of things that Hass can try, taking into account costs, risks, and ease of experimentation. What can Hass do to increase the number of new customers? What can it do to increase the amount that existing customers spend? What can Hass do to increase the frequency of existing customers' purchases? How can Hass make buying shoes from it a different experience than buying from the competitor? How can Hass become the shoe expert?

WORKSHOP #6: YOUR GROWTH IDEAS PORTFOLIO

Now you are ready to spend some time creating your list of ideas of how you can grow your business. Think about what you can improve and what you can scale. This exercise is idea generation. Of course, before doing anything, you must use the concepts of Chapters 2 through 4: the Growth Decision Template, the Risks of Growth Audit, and the Growth Planning Template to properly plan and pace your growth.

This exercise is a brainstorming exercise to get you to think granularly about business process improvements, differentiators, better customer service, and, as in Hass Shoes, how you sell more to existing customers or get new customers.

CHAPTER 6 TAKEAWAYS

1. Entrepreneurial businesses grow primarily through improvements and scaling.

2. Compelling customer differentiators are critical.

3. To be a differentiator, what you do must be valued by the customer and different from what the competition does.

4. Differentiators can be differences in how you do business—how you service and care for customers.

5. Growth can come from adding complementary products and services that your existing customers need to your offering.

6. C. R. Barger undertook a comprehensive improvement, branding, and advertising program to reignite growth.

7. C. R. Barger utilized technology to improve productivity, manage supplies more cost effectively, and increase on-time delivery.

8. Growth should be customer-centric. What do your customers need that you can deliver? Growth does not come from trying to sell customers what they do not think they need. Listening to customers is key. Be customer-centric not product-centric.

9. You cannot listen to customers and talk at the same time.

10. Sell after you listen.

PART III GROWTH REQUIRES THE RIGHT LEADERSHIP, CULTURE, AND PEOPLE

GROWTH IS MUCH MORE THAN A STRATEGY[1]

BUILDING A GROWTH SYSTEM

We know that business growth depends on excellent and consistent execution. Growth requires consistently delivering more products or services to more customers, on-time, 99 percent defect free with caring service. Growth results from the actions and behaviors of employees. Businesses must have the right strategies, processes, and controls as well as pace their growth so that it does not overwhelm the business. While necessary, these steps are insufficient. Without consistent execution of the strategies and processes, a business will not have satisfied customers.

How does a business create the environment where that consistent execution is more likely to happen? Even better, how can you create an environment where employees are engaged in the daily pursuit of excellence?

Alignment: Consistency and Self-Reinforcing

Part of the answer lies in alignment. That is, creating an internal system designed to send consistent messages to employees about the business's goals and objectives. These messages must also concretely state what actions are necessary to reach those goals and the rewards associated with reaching them.

Alignment means consistency, seamless and self-reinforcing messages, policies, measurements, and rewards. The opposite of alignment is the hypocrisy that results from inconsistent messages and from entrepreneurs not "walking the talk."

Behaviors Produce Financial Results

My research and consulting have shown me that to create alignment and successful business growth, it is important to focus on behaviors. What specific behaviors drive value creation in your business? In focusing on behaviors, define them as granularly as possible because you want employees to model their behaviors in ways that will result in success for both the business and them.

After you define key behaviors, you will need to develop the means to motivate employees to exhibit those behaviors and develop tools to measure whether employees exhibit them.

Finally, of course, to embed the desired behaviors into the business culture, you must reward employees who consistently exhibit these behaviors. Defining good behaviors is not enough. It is also important to define the behaviors that are unacceptable. Unacceptable behaviors cannot be tolerated and must be corrected.

Aligning employee behaviors with the business mission and goals sounds elementary, but my experience shows that it is very difficult. Much of my work with public companies with revenues between $2B and $6B involves helping them to define those behaviors and to create a growth-enabling system to foster those behaviors. It is easy to talk about your products or services, the competition, or potential new customers. It is much more challenging to drill down and isolate the exact behaviors along the value chain that are critical to the business's success.

Creating the Right Internal Environment

In this chapter, my objective is to explain the concept of an internal-enabling growth system. Later, in Chapters 8 through 10, I will focus on three critical findings of my private growth company research that involve (1) how the entrepreneur can personally grow to become a better enabler of growth, (2) how successful entrepreneurs learned to create such a growth system, and (3) the difficulties entrepreneurs had in building an aligned management team.

I first encountered the growth system concept in my high-growth public company research. Six research studies, including mine, have found that less than 10 percent of the public companies studied were able to grow above industry or gross domestic product averages for four years or more. When you extend the time frame to seven years or more, the percentage drops to below 4 percent.[2]

In my research, I looked at some exceptional companies that were able to sustain prolonged growth.[3] I took twenty-two public companies that were able to grow above industry averages for seven years or more and examined how they were able to do what 96 percent of other public companies could not do. My research findings were surprising and contradicted many theories espoused in the business press and by management consulting firms.

I called these successful companies high organic growth companies (HOGs). Among consistent HOGs, growth is more than just strategy: it is an internal seamless linked self-reinforcing system that links strategy, structure, culture, execution processes, human resources policies, measurements, and rewards to drive behaviors that result in growth.

THE DNA OF SUCCESSFUL HOGS[4]

My research hypotheses in studying the HOGs were based on my professional experiences as an investment banker and as a strategy consultant. They were that (1) these companies produced unique products and services; (2) they had visionary, charismatic leaders; (3) they had a diversified portfolio of strategies; (4) they had outsourced or off-shored all noncore activities; (5) they had the best talent; and (6) they were the most innovative in their industry. My hypotheses were neither unique nor original but reflected the views espoused by many academics and management consulting firms.

Surprisingly, my research on HOGs found that none of these hypotheses was necessary to produce consistent high organic growth. Instead, I found that HOGS had the following attributes:

1. They had simple, easy-to-understand, and focused strategies.

2. Their leaders were not visionaries but were humble, passionate operators who grew up in the business and were focused on the details of the business.

3. Most did not offshore or outsource.

4. They did not necessarily have the best talent, as defined by top-flight MBAs, but they got the most out of their talent by achieving high employee engagement.

5. They were technology-enabled execution champions.

6. They acted with a small company "soul" in a large company body.

7. No company had unique products or services.

8. Most companies were not the most innovative in their fields but they had a constant improvement, "be better" DNA.

In addition, HOGs proactively and simultaneously managed a portfolio of growth initiatives. Underlying most of these initiatives was an iterative, incremental improvement mentality—not the search for or creation of big "wow" innovations. Every HOG had an underlying "be better" DNA. This "be better" focus was the underpinning of every growth initiative whether it was top-line, bottom-line, or developing new concepts.

The HOGs' growth systems had two overriding objectives: (1) to create new income streams that could be scaled across a large distribution or customer base and (2) to leverage core operating competencies into new income streams or new cost efficiencies.

Notably, many research findings from my *public* company research are consistent with my *private* growth company research findings discussed in this book (see Exhibit 7.1).

Many of the public companies I studied (e.g., Sysco, UPS, Best Buy, Tiffany & Co., Outback Steakhouses, PACCAR, Walgreens, Wal-Mart, American Eagle Outfitters, Stryker, and TSYS), as well as some of the private companies shared one commonality: they iterated until they had a growth system that consistently, seamlessly, and in a self-reinforcing manner linked strategy, structure, culture, leadership philosophy, employee policies, measurements, and rewards to drive desired behaviors.

EXHIBIT 7.1

Successful public and private companies have focused strategies, high employee engagement, a small company feel, a DNA of constant improvement, and they execute better than the competition. Interestingly, their CEOs are humble, passionate operators who understand that line employees are the people who make success happen.

CREATING A GROWTH SYSTEM

The creation of a growth system is both science and an art. The science part is drilling down to identify the specific employee behaviors that create value and then creating consistent policies, measurements, and rewards to drive those desired behaviors. The art of creating a growth system is managing the inherent tensions, such as the tension between needing both centralized controls and decentralized entrepreneurial activities and the tension between achieving high employee accountability and a high employee engagement, "family" environment.

To be successful, these holistic growth systems require (1) a near maniacal sensitivity to inconsistencies of messages and unintended consequences and (2) a heightened vigilance against complacency, hypocrisy, and hubris. These growth systems are challenging to build, need constant adjustment, and require constant vigilance to identify and ward off inconsistencies. Many public companies that I studied that have iterated a successful growth system believe that, because it is so difficult to build and maintain, their growth system is their differentiating competitive advantage.

It is important to emphasize that the focus of growth systems is on behaviors and that the right behaviors will produce growth and value creation. This focus on concrete behaviors is in contrast to the approach of those CEOs who put tremendous emphasis on growth and pressure their people to just hit financial metrics.

HOGs with successful growth systems focused on creating the right environment to enable and encourage the right behaviors on a daily basis. That environment can result from seamless, consistent, and self-reinforcing messages in a company's culture, measurement, reward, and promotion policies. These companies stood back and constantly asked whether individual policies, changes, or memos were sending a message that was consistent with the defined objectives.

Implementation of successful growth systems requires effective communications within the business about its goals and the necessary behaviors to achieve those goals. Communications must be concise, clear, and capable of being understood and internalized by line employees.

In the companies that I studied, communications about the required behaviors and the rewards for achieving them were clearly articulated. As a result, employees focused daily on improvement because they knew that if they performed well, they would be rewarded and have the opportunity to advance. Employees also knew that they would get feedback about mistakes or behaviors that needed improving.

Other interesting consistencies across these successful public companies about their growth systems include the following:

1. HOGs focused on measuring behaviors and not just financial results.

2. They had high employee engagement, retention, productivity, and stock ownership.

3. They emphasized a promotion-from-within policy.

4. They had relatively stable and highly transparent measurement and reward policies, which engendered trust in the system.

5. They had one set of rules for both management and employees with the devaluation of elitist perks.

6. They worked to implement and maintain positive learning environments instead of environments of fear, vicious politics, or autocratic management.

Not all companies that I studied started out with a vision for a growth system. Rather, a frequent pattern was that this view evolved and, at some point and for varying reasons, the companies began to focus on aligning culture, measurements, and rewards.

What was interesting about my research with successful high-growth private companies was that so many were trying to create such an aligned internal system. Because of resource constraints, such systems were not as detailed or sophisticated as ones in large public companies. But, nonetheless, the key concepts were the same. Examples in this book are found in the stories of Room & Board; Defender Direct, Inc; Trilogy Health Services, LLC; Leaders Bank; SecureWorks; and Enchanting Travels.

ROOM & BOARD[5]

One example of a successfully aligned internal system is the unique growth system that John Gabbert built at Room & Board.

In the fall of 2007, while reading *Business Week* magazine, I came across an article that caught my attention: "Room & Board Plays Impossible to Get—Private Equity Sees Growth for the Retailer but Founder John Gabbert Prefers His Own Pace."[6] The reporter, Jena McGregor, wrote; "By all conventional standards, Room & Board should be bigger than it is."[7] Given my interest in business growth, I was intrigued by the story, which illuminated a contrarian view. I wrote to John Gabbert and asked if I could do a case study on Room & Board. He graciously agreed and the Room & Board story follows.

Room & Board is a privately owned home-furnishings retailer, offering products that combined classic, simple design with exceptional quality. Over $250 million of revenue a year was generated through Room & Board's fully integrated and multichannel sales approach, consisting of its eleven national retail stores, an annual catalog, and its Web site.

Based in Minneapolis, Minnesota, Room & Board's story was one of contrarian success as a company that had abandoned the standard retail-industry business model, disavowed debt and equity-growth financing, and embraced a unique multiple-stakeholder model that valued quality and relationships ahead of the bottom line while producing stellar financial results.

That the company had achieved consistency and harmony between its values and actions also added to its uniqueness. Its culture supported an energized, positive growth environment for its employees that fostered high employee engagement and, in turn, high customer engagement.

Room & Board was wholly owned by John Gabbert, who had created it more than 25 years earlier.

History

Gabbert grew up working in a family retail business that sold traditional home furnishings, and at the age of 24 succeeded his father as the CEO. Family dynamics proved challenging, so when he was 33, he left the family furniture business to pursue his own business model, initially basing his furniture company on IKEA's business model. He also diversified into other businesses, but by the late 1980s, feeling overextended and unfulfilled, he decided to focus all his energy on building a business with people he liked and on a model that represented quality. All this drew him into the design aspect of the furniture business.

Quality Relationships

To Gabbert, quality relationships were just as important as quality home furnishings. This belief had helped shape Room & Board into a business focused on creating long-lasting relationships with customers, vendors, and employees, who were all fully integrated into the model of selling quality furnishings. At Room & Board, quality was also about providing value.

That value was inherent in its products, which lasted and whose style and design were timeless—furniture that customers could count on enjoying for many years. But Room & Board went further by believing that a customer's home should be a favorite place where a customer should be able to create a meaningful special environment. This customization was made attractive by offering customers a multitude of special-order products, ranging from fabric choices on throw pillows to customer-designed solid-wood storage pieces.

Supply Chain

The retail-furniture industry was generally controlled by large manufacturers that dictated style, product availability, and price, and that made many products overseas with cheaper labor than could be found in the United States.

Room & Board decided early on that it did not want to play that game, so the company created its own supply chain of approximately 40 different vendors, nearly all privately owned family businesses, many having grown alongside Room & Board over the years.

More than 85 percent of the company's products were made in the United States—in places like Newton, North Carolina; Martinsville, Virginia; Minneapolis, Minnesota; Grand Forks, North Dakota; Shell Lake, Wisconsin; and Albany, Oregon—by craftsmen and artisans using hardwoods, granite, and steel of high quality. Most of these products were made exclusively for Room & Board, and more than 50 percent of the products were manufactured by 12 of its key vendors. Room & Board met with its vendors frequently to plan growth, discuss needs, and share financials to ensure that everyone was making a fair living while creating high-quality, well-designed products.

These vendor relationships evolved over the years into true partnerships, which allowed Room & Board to set an annual goal of having 85 percent of its products in stock at all times, contributing to quick deliveries. Special-order products were programmed ahead of normal production with the aim of delivering the product as fast as possible to the customer.

Under this model, Room & Board was more in control of its destiny; it had control over product quality, inventory availability, and the risk of supply-chain disruptions. This unique model carried its own risk, however, as almost all of Room & Board's suppliers were private, family businesses that shared the company's challenge of growing at a rate that sustained their economic health.

Culture

Room & Board had rejected common attributes of private-company culture: hierarchy, command and control from the top, information on a need-to-know basis, and, in the retail industry, high turnover resulting in customer-service challenges.

Its culture was based on the principles of trust, respect, relationships, transparency, entrepreneurial ownership of one's job and career, and the importance of a balanced life. Room & Board eschewed rules, lengthy policy manuals, and elitism. Rather, it believed individuals thrived in an environment where they were empowered to make decisions, and everyone's view was heard and respected. These core beliefs were outlined in its *Guiding Principles*, partially based on the following expectation:

At Room & Board we hope you find meaning in your work. There is both tremendous productivity for the company and personal fulfillment for each staff member when someone finds their life's work. It's a wonderful circle of success.

Room & Board tried to achieve this "circle of success" by creating an environment of collaboration and engagement. This engagement was evidenced by deep relationships with customers, fellow employees, and suppliers. Respect for different views, openness to feedback, and responsibility for one's actions all drove the staff's behavior.

What worked for Room & Board as it tried to achieve balance was defined by Gandhi: Harmony exists when what you feel, what you think, and what you do are consistent. Many businesses talked a good game, but Room & Board actually tried to "walk the talk." In the resulting company environment, there was a heightened sensitivity regarding the impact of actions across functions and an awareness of the real message being communicated.

Room & Board believed that success was rooted in shared accountability; therefore, there were no rules for personal leave or sick pay. All 670 employees were shown the company's annual strategy priorities and a complete detailed financial package every month, so everyone could understand the goals and the business. All financial and operating numbers were transparent to encourage responsibility for owning and, in turn, effecting Room & Board's success. In discussing the company's normal eight-hour day, Gabbert stated:

I learned a long time ago that most people only have so many productive hours a day—it is the number of productive hours that count, not the number of hours at work. We strive to have an environment which results in energy and productivity. That is why we have a full physical-fitness facility with classes going on during the workday, a masseuse, as well as a great kitchen for employees to prepare healthy lunches.

Room & Board also operated on the principle that people who have a balanced life, with a life outside work, were happier and dealt well with customers and with each other. Gabbert, who understood that what set his company apart was its engaged employees, who tried to make every customer experience special, said:

I never wanted to be the biggest. I never thought about size. I just wanted to be the best and to spend my time at work with good people doing something more meaningful than just making money or keeping score.

Employees

The retail industry was generally known for its high employee turnover, with many part-time employees to keep expenditures on employee benefits low and commission-based compensation to lower fixed costs. But Room & Board was proof that a very profitable, quality business could be built by not following any of those common retail practices.

Instead, Room & Board had very low employee turnover, mostly full-time employees, and full benefits for part-time employees, and paid its retail sales staff on a salary basis rather than on individual sales. The rejection of a commission-based structure, together with its integrated and multichannel purchasing options, allowed Room & Board customers to shop and purchase in the manner that made the most sense to them. "We want customers to rely on us for the best advice and to trust that we have their best interests in mind—sales commissions run against that type of trust," said Gabbert. Room & Board employed over 670 staff members, including 237 store personnel; 220 delivery personnel; 62 store and delivery leadership team members; and 100 central office staff.

Room & Board stores more than five years old had average employee tenure of over five years, which was very high for the retail industry. Delivery and warehouse personnel in delivery centers open for more than four years had an average tenure of five years. Employee tenure was 5.7 years for the central office, and total employee tenure for the company averaged nearly five years.

Room & Board also took a different approach to measuring employee satisfaction: by tracking how many employees referred family and friends for jobs and how many employees participated in the company's 401(k) program. Room & Board believed that these measures truly contributed to long-term employee engagement.

Following the philosophy that employees needed good physical, mental, and financial health, Room & Board offered an extensive physical-fitness facility, a healthy-lunch program, and personal financial-planning services and 401(k) investment advice from an outside financial consulting firm at no cost. In addition, all employees could buy Room & Board products at a substantial discount.

LEADERSHIP TEAM

Room & Board was led by a six-member advisory board made up of John Gabbert and five other senior level managers. The leadership team was incentivized by a generous bonus program if key company objectives were met.

Key Expectations for Employees and Leaders

Room & Board's *Guiding Principles* was the foundation for the company's expectations and also served as a tool to help employees understand their connection to the business. The document, which spoke primarily to respect, individual accountability, and engaging the business, included the following statements:

- Respect is foundational to our work environment. Everyone is expected to build relationships based upon mutual respect and collaboration.

- Use good judgment when making decisions and apply principle, not rules, to each situation.

- The more you seek to understand how your role is related to our business objectives and tied to the broader success of the company, the more rewarding, enjoyable, and challenging the effort.

Just as all employees were expected to understand and embrace the core beliefs outlined in *Guiding Principles*, leaders were expected to adhere to their own additional roadmap. Room & Board set forth a number of leadership objectives for its central office, store, and delivery/distribution leadership team, including the following:

- You take ownership for your business—you're independent and therefore do not wait to be told what to do.
- You lead less with rules and rely more on principles.
- You value building relationships; collaboration is much more important to you than competition.
- You appreciate and desire longevity within your role. You do not seek to move from location to location or from department to department to get ahead; your growth occurs from richer experiences within your current role.

Delivery Centers

Another point of differentiation from other retailers was Room & Board's philosophy regarding deliveries. Many furniture chains outsourced their deliveries. Room & Board did not, operating its own delivery centers staffed by full-time Room & Board professionals. These teams delivered all the local products. For national deliveries, Room & Board had an exclusive relationship with a Minneapolis company. To ensure ongoing collaboration, a few employees from the national shipping company's office worked out of Room & Board's central location.

In addition, the company had dedicated delivery teams for just Room & Board products. It was not unusual for customers to assume that these delivery professionals were Room & Board employees, not just because of their Room & Board uniforms, but also because they adhered to the same principles that all Room & Board employees followed: namely, that the customer experience during every step of the process was hassle-free and treated as an opportunity to create long-lasting relationships. The individuals who had the last interaction with customers about purchases were viewed as brand ambassadors and acted as such.

Room & Board's goal of providing a great customer experience at every step of the buying-and-receiving process required delivery personnel to deliver and set up the product and leave the customer happy. Delivery times were scheduled to allow time for customer interaction, discussions, and the proper placement of the new purchases.

If there was a problem, delivery personnel were empowered to solve it on the spot because they were trained to "leave the customer in a good place." The focus on interaction with the customer, from the beginning of the experience to the end, drove customer satisfaction, in terms of loyalty and referrals, to a rate of more than 95 percent.

Real Estate

To avoid the high rent typical in retail malls, Room & Board owned most of its locations, and searched out freestanding sites with ample parking and easy access for customers. The company often chose to renovate an existing location, blending its store in with a particular environment rather than building a new one. This practice served as inspiration to customers who dealt with similar challenges when designing and furnishing their own spaces.

Moreover, the practice prevented Room & Board from adopting a "cookie cutter" image for its stores and fostered the company's philosophy of unique design. The central-office facility was furnished with Room & Board products, so even employees who were not in customer-facing roles understood what the company sold, its quality, and its lasting design.

Pricing Model

Room & Board's pricing model was simple: no sales, no volume discounts, and no discounts for interior designers. Everyone paid the same price. As John Gabbert put it:

Nothing makes me madder than to buy something and then see it go on sale. I feel taken advantage of. That is why we have no sales, and we guarantee all prices for a year after purchase for each calendar year. If we sell a product within a year of your purchase for less than you paid, we will refund the difference.

LESSONS FROM ROOM & BOARD

Room & Board had achieved the enviable market position of managing its growth and avoiding the capital market pressures produced by both debt financing and equity partners and being a public company. It had built a loyal and highly engaged work force, dedicated to its way of doing things, and managed to be a model of productivity and engagement without sacrificing quality. The company did not strive for the lowest operational costs but, instead, embraced a vertically integrated business model and earned good net margins.

The beauty of the Room & Board success story is how it created a consistent, seamless, self-reinforcing system that cut across culture, structure, execution philosophy, employee hiring, and benefits. The result was a company with a high-performance environment that manufactured 85 percent of its products in the United States, paid its people well, sold quality products, and made good profits.

Room & Board adhered to a multiple-stakeholder philosophy of capitalism, much like the European model and less like the sole-stakeholder model more common in the United States. It believed that it would do well if its customers, employees, and suppliers did well.

LEADERS BANK[8]

The Leaders Bank story is another high-performance private company that built an internal system to enable its service business—a community banking business.

Leaders Bank, headquartered in Oak Brook, Illinois, provided commercial, industrial, and real-estate lending, as well as treasury-management and retail-banking services for privately held businesses and their owners. The bank was founded in 2000 by five industry veterans—Patrick Kelly, James Lynch, Steven Schuster, Laura McGrath, and Gordon Fitzsimmons—whose vision was to create a personalized banking experience for entrepreneurs and small businesses.

In an industry fraught with mergers and acquisitions and the resulting depersonalization of service, Leaders offered a refreshing alternative. As its name implied, the bank treated its customers and employees as leaders, focusing on their strengths and professional competencies and on developing long-term relationships based on communication and trust.

The bank's officers were given the authority to take risks and make au-
tonomous decisions, which resulted in the customized solutions and fast
responses that business owners valued.

In addition, because of a workplace culture centered on respect, Leaders kept its employee turnover rate close to zero; consequently, its clients
were able to work with the same banking professionals, who understood
their businesses and goals. Therefore, it was not surprisingly that in a
2005 independent customer survey, Leaders received an overall satisfaction rating of 94 percent—no small feat considering that few financial
institutions could claim a client satisfaction rating above the 75 percent
industry average, reported by the American Customer Satisfaction Index.[9]

With CEO Lynch at the helm, the number of Leaders' employees grew
within eight years from 9 to 72, and three new banking centers were established in the Chicago area. Revenues grew 85 percent in three years,
reaching $30.5 million by 2007. The bank's holding company, Leaders
Group, Inc., saw its assets balloon from $37 million in 2000 to $646 million in 2008.

In 2008, during the most challenging economic environment in decades, *Entrepreneur* Magazine ranked Leaders number 51 on its list of
the Hot 100 Fast-Growth Businesses in the United States.[10] The company
also won Chicago's 101 Best and Brightest Companies To Work For award
three years in a row and was a finalist on the *Wall Street Journal*'s 2008
Top Small Workplaces list.

By building a strong culture that fostered high employee engagement
and loyalty, the bank was able to thrive in good times and weather the
bad ones. Reflecting on the bank's success, Lynch said:

[We've] stuck to our model, communicated effectively, and made Leaders Bank a
great place to work every day . . . We put our employees in a position where they
can utilize their strengths, and we make sure they are supported well. This approach nurtures personal job satisfaction, which translates to low turnover and
high levels of employee and customer satisfaction.[11]

Starting Out
The founding of Leaders coincided with a slowing of the U.S. economy in
the second half of 2000 that ended the banking industry's string of eight

consecutive years of record annual earnings. When Leaders opened its doors in 2001, the economy was showing signs of the first recession in a decade. Then came the terrorist attack on 9/11, and the stock market plummeted. The Federal Reserve feverishly slashed short-term interest rates to the lowest level in four decades.

Reflecting on the bank's early days, Steve Ritter, senior vice president and director of human resources, thought that market conditions had always been among the biggest challenges facing the company. Ritter said, "Certainly, in the first few years of our operation—2001 and 2002—there were a number of Fed rate reductions similar to what we've experienced in 2008." Ritter continued:

But because we are focused on the low end of the middle market our typical customer is an entrepreneur, a small business owner; that's a customer who often doesn't make the radar of a big bank anyway. In some ways, this economy makes our niche customer the perfect customer, because these are folks who are being challenged to grow their businesses as well. So there we were in 2000, a de novo bank with a vision of treating employees well and treating customers well. And there were businesses out there, looking for someone just like us.

Building a Strong Foundation with a Common Thread

James Lynch had wanted to build a bank around a culture with the vital elements of respect, leadership, quality, partnership, communication, and integrity. Ritter emphasized that Lynch started to lay the foundations for that culture long before his bank opened its doors in 2001. Ritter explained:

When Jim began looking for investors to start the bank, he was selling that vision about the way you treat others with respect as part of what he wanted people to understand would grow. Similarly, when he started looking for partners for the executive leadership team, he looked for people who got it. Respect, transparency, communication, partnership, and integrity were the values that people had to live and embrace on a day-to-day basis. And as diverse as our team was, Jim's vision resonated with all of us—it was our common thread.

Because the modus operandi at Leaders had always been inclusion and participation, the defining elements of the workplace culture were fine-tuned by the employees themselves, mostly during leadership retreats

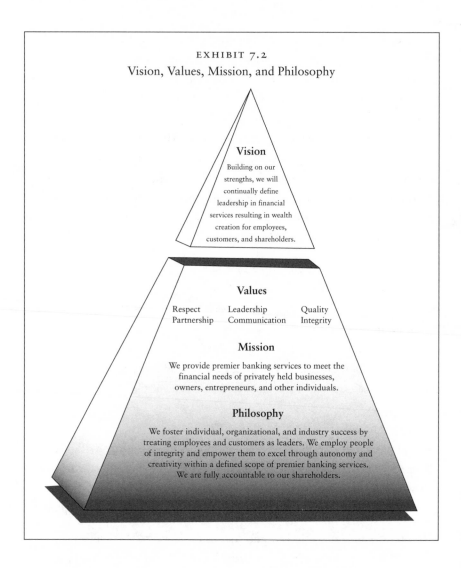

EXHIBIT 7.2
Vision, Values, Mission, and Philosophy

Vision

Building on our
strengths, we will
continually define
leadership in financial
services resulting in wealth
creation for employees,
customers, and shareholders.

Values

| Respect | Leadership | Quality |
| Partnership | Communication | Integrity |

Mission

We provide premier banking services to meet the
financial needs of privately held businesses,
owners, entrepreneurs, and other individuals.

Philosophy

We foster individual, organizational, and industry success by
treating employees and customers as leaders. We employ people
of integrity and empower them to excel through autonomy and
creativity within a defined scope of premier banking services.
We are fully accountable to our shareholders.

conducted and described by Ritter: "We sat in retreat session after retreat session and hammered out the mission and the philosophy and the values." Ritter continued:

The rule was to challenge every word, and we did not move forward on the definition of these things until everyone in the room was comfortable that "this is what we live" and "this is the way we behave." So there's a real values-in-action model to what we do because when that is what defines your culture, then any kind of its violation stands out in a big way.

To ensure that the human factor did not get pushed to the sidelines and the culture did not get diluted as the organization grew, Lynch invited Ritter to join the company's senior leadership team, whose members, besides Lynch, included the chief financial officer and chief credit officer. Since the company's inception, Ritter had conducted leadership retreats, team-building workshops, and career-path coaching sessions to help employees discover their strengths; he was also responsible for the most of the company's recruitment efforts, in addition to presiding over a three-person HR group.

A Culture of Respect

In an effort to recruit and retain top talent, Lynch and other Leaders executives worked hard to foster a corporate culture in which employees felt appreciated and were rewarded for exceptional performance. Lynch remarked "employees need to believe they are valued and that the quality of the work they do makes a difference." He continued:

Those who don't feel valued or respected are more likely to go off and seek greener pastures . . . A sincere compliment for extra effort or a job well done takes nothing away from the bottom line and pays big dividends, especially for smaller companies, which are generally less able to afford the time and cost of hiring and then losing an employee. It's also important to routinely acknowledge workers as individuals with a smile, a handshake, a pleasant comment. And we always make a point to remember their birthdays.[12]

Viewing Employees as Leaders

Lynch attributed his company's success in large part to its unique philosophy of treating employees and customers as leaders. "Because we view our employees as being leaders themselves," Lynch said, "we give them the authority to make decisions without always having to check with their superiors. In staff meetings, we consider all ideas good ideas."[13]

Maintaining a healthy equilibrium between employee empowerment and internal controls can be a tough balancing act for many companies.

While Leaders' employees were encouraged to take risks on behalf of their customers and were empowered to make their own—sometimes fast—decisions, the company's top management ensured that controls were in place, but that they did not stifle employee decision making or entrepreneurial spirit. According to Ritter, "The balancing factor is a sense of shared accountability." Ritter continued:

If somebody wants to bend the rules on behalf of the customer, they know how far they can go. The underpinning of everything we do is the credit quality, so there are parameters that people don't spread beyond. They hear what kinds of deals are being negotiated in the pipeline meetings every week, and they understand what our norms are. The fact that our CEO has a strong lending background and is involved in every deal establishes an unspoken set of parameters based on loan policy.

To encourage employee commitment to the success of the business even more, top management implemented a Leaders' stock-purchase plan so that 75 to 80 percent of the employees had ownership in the organization through stock ownership. "We want everyone to function like an owner of the organization," Ritter said.

Open Communication
An important factor in employee empowerment was communication, which Lynch described as an "open, two-way street." Because he believed that some of the best ideas for improving operations, cutting costs, and gaining efficiencies came from front-line employees, he stressed the importance of soliciting their continuous feedback in meetings and with company-wide surveys. Lynch also valued employee feedback about organizational health and culture and suggested asking employees: "What can be done to make this a better place to work?" He gave employees the option of making suggestions anonymously and advised implementing the best ideas immediately. "Employees will notice and appreciate a sincere, ongoing effort to improve the work environment,"[14] he said.

Leaders' employees participated in a confidential survey twice a year. "It is designed to measure the kind of distress that you would expect to see in organizations that are growing and changing," Ritter said, and explained that the survey asked for feedback in the areas of leadership, vision, collaboration, communication, commitment to excellence, morale, learning, and how well the company managed change.

The top management at Leaders treated employee feedback as a call for immediate action. "Whenever the aggregate data rises above even the smallest measurable level of distress, we get together as a group and plan around that," Ritter said. He remembered the time, when the company experienced an intense growth spurt, going from 33 to 47 employees in six months, and survey data indicated concern about company-wide communication. Ritter continued:

We added dinners with the CEO, breakfast with the board of directors, an employee newsletter, and a couple of different summer events, and the number went down to nearly zero within six months. We're proactive about getting folks' opinion about the strength of the organization, and then we address these things before they have a chance to take root and influence our culture.Part of the company's open-communication policy involved financial transparency. The details of the company's financial performance were shared with all employees on a monthly basis during staff meetings. In addition, "the company newsletter has a performance dashboard in the corner that shows what our gross level is, what the return on equity is, tracking the major financials month to month," Ritter said. "So that's as open-book management as we can get." As Ritter explained, the data on how individual lenders were doing relative to their targets was not available to all employees, but individual contributions were transparent within each team.

On those rare occasions when employees did not live up to the company's high expectations in terms of performance or upholding its cultural values, they were asked to leave. However, the terminations did not have a negative effect on employee morale precisely because of the company's emphasis on open communication. Leaders' management worked hard to convey what was expected of its employees and made sure they understood how their individual contributions affected overall company performance. Ritter explained:

Whether you're a bank teller or a chief credit officer, you know what it is about your work each day that moves the needle of the organization in some way. And everyone experiences a collective responsibility for linking all those strengths and talents together to achieve successful results. When someone isn't holding up their end of that shared responsibility, everyone understands that it's costing the rest of us money.

Recruiting—The Culture Fit

Lynch gave Ritter a mandate to screen out prospective hires who did not share the company's values. From the beginning, "Jim wanted to have a threshold of culture evaluations on the front end of every interview," Ritter said, admitting that some of that evaluation was subjective. "We talk about what's important, the way we treat people, and what our values are, and we see pretty quickly whether people get that or not." Nevertheless, whether a job candidate realized it or not could make or break an interview. Ritter explained:

While there is a technical aspect of evaluating a prospective employee, there has been a culture-fit evaluation on every single hire from top to bottom, including very experienced, high-level people. And if I give the culture a "thumbs down" that decision will be respected. It has only happened a handful of times, but when we miss the mark on the subject of culture in the recruitment process and the person gets on board after having had a good interview but they don't fit, it becomes evident to everyone in a short time. And, generally, Jim will stand up as the CEO and apologize to the entire organization for missing that one.

A typical interview process for a midlevel job candidate started with a culture-fit screening with Ritter, followed by an interview with the leader and select members of the team that had the job opening. Ritter described the second interview as "a team screening for technical ability and fit with the team." The last leg of the recruiting process involved a leadership interview with a member of the executive team—often the CEO—"to kind of embrace the fit," Ritter said.

Leaders viewed the job interview as an opportunity to present the best features of the company to a candidate. For that reason, Ritter and the HR team tried to ensure potential hires had a chance to meet Lynch. Ritter said:

We really want people to hear the Leaders Bank story from Jim's perspective since he started it. So to the extent that we are measuring the candidate, we know that the candidate is measuring us, too, and we want them to know fully what the culture is about and what's expected of someone who works here. And Jim does a wonderful job relating that. He also has a real good assessment competency for understanding whether people fit our culture or not.

Benefits Package

To attract and retain talent, Leaders offered its employees an attractive benefits and compensation package. "We are very attentive to the compensation surveys for our industry and our geographic area, and we pay people competitively," said Ritter. He added that the company offered a "better-than-competitive" benefits package with medical and dental coverage. "We've got a very strong 401(k) with an employer match. But all that is typical," Ritter said.

Less typical were other job perks—such as the ability to adjust hours—designed to cultivate healthier work and home environments for the staff. "A corporate culture of respect means also helping workers succeed as individuals in their private lives," said Lynch.[15]

He acknowledged that because Leaders was aware that the number of employees taking care of elderly family members or small children had increased, it encouraged flexibility in scheduling whenever possible. "It is not difficult to accommodate an employee who has a family emergency or occasional daytime appointment, and we've found that the modest inconvenience is greatly offset by the loyalty and goodwill such gestures tend to generate,"[16] Lynch said. The company was particularly attuned to the needs of Leaders employees who were single parents.

The Wellness Program

A fringe benefit that attracted the attention of the Society for Human Resources Management, which listed it among its best practices in January 2007, was the company-sponsored wellness program. Every year, Leaders designated a pool of money—$1,500 per employee—to encourage its workforce to make healthy lifestyle choices. Ritter explained how the program worked:

You can earn these dollars by lifestyle changes, such as quitting smoking or losing weight. You can earn these dollars by getting your annual physicals, your dental cleanings, or through fitness/health related things. People are getting immediate financial rewards for their choices to be healthy, and then they can cash in the money they make on a monthly basis for any numbers of things. They can hire personal trainers, buy exercise equipment, get wellness coaching, health club memberships, or nutritional consultations. They can even buy things like musical equipment or iPods to help them relax.

Since being implemented in 2005, the wellness program had shown measurable return on investment. In 2007, Leaders' employees used only 31 percent of their available sick-leave time. "Basically, they're leaving seven out of ten days on the table each year," Ritter said. But he added that the program also had less tangible benefits. "There're some obvious positive things that have happened in terms of morale and things like that," Ritter said.

Part of the wellness program included an annual health-risk assessment for everyone, which Ritter credited with detecting potentially serious medical problems facing two Leaders employees early on. "In addition to gathering aggregate return on investment data from better wellness, we've had a couple of good catches with folks who were closer to major medical issues than they thought they were," Ritter said, referring to the health-risk assessment. "Their participation in the wellness program saved them a lot of medical trouble."

Training and Education
Aware of the high cost of recruitment and training, Leaders took great care in finding the right person for the job in the first place and then spared no effort to engender employee loyalty. According to Lynch, one of the best ways to ensure that the most talented and valuable employees stayed with the company was to offer them the kind of support that helped them succeed in their jobs. "We are always inviting people to sit down and have discussions about how their natural strengths fit their career path, and how we can grow and develop them," said Ritter.

Leaders' employees received training not only at the beginning of their employment when they developed an annual training plan with their supervisors. In addition, they learned new skills by attending conferences, seminars and workshops, or took advantage of a tuition reimbursement program to take courses that increased their professional capabilities.

Focus on Individual Strengths

Lynch believed that the key to unlocking employee potential was to see them as individuals with unique strengths and weaknesses. All senior staff at Leaders was required to read the management book *First, Break All the Rules*,[17] which recommends that companies take advantage of people's strengths by placing them in areas where they could succeed, instead of merely identifying their weaknesses and working to overcome them. Lynch elaborated:

Take, for example, someone good at organization but lacking interpersonal skills. We would not expect that person to do well in sales; we would place the individual in an operational support position, where he or she would have the opportunity to excel, and provide one-on-one support to mitigate weaknesses.[18]

Employees at Leaders used the Gallup Organization's Web-based StrengthsFinder Instrument to pinpoint their five signature strengths, which were then analyzed during so-called strength sessions, which were part of the performance-evaluation process. "We look at the StrengthsFinder results, and we tie it to people's career-path plans," said Ritter. "We make sure that we grow and develop people in a way that's aligned with their natural strengths and competencies."

Performance Evaluation

The performance evaluation process at Leaders ensured that all employees got the training they needed to improve their performance. Even though official performance reviews at Leaders took place once a year, in many cases performance evaluation was a year-round process. "Often, the learning goals that come out of the evaluations are things that you follow up on an ongoing basis," said Ritter.

To get a comprehensive look at how its officers and executives were performing, the company implemented the 360-degree feedback review, which included feedback from three co-workers—one selected by the individual's supervisors and two selected by the employee being evaluated. In addition, an employee was evaluated by his or her supervisor and also submitted a self-evaluation. "All that feedback becomes a written document, and then we associate a merit increase with that depending on the performance," explained Ritter, adding, "We track it throughout the year to make sure that we're moving in the ways that we agreed to move."

Leaders also used the 360-degree feedback system, part of a leadership competency tool developed by Lominger International, to evaluate its executive team. "It's a three-year cycle where we all get 360-degree evaluations through Lominger," said Ritter. "We all receive executive coaching on a monthly basis. And then the cycle ends with another 360-degree to measure our growth."

Monthly executive coaching was a huge cost commitment, and Leaders decided to implement a more cost-efficient model by investing in the training and certification of a team of internal coaches who would provide professional coaching to everyone in the organization. "The research supports the fact that your return on investment is much greater when you can get coaching into the organization internally as opposed to hoping that coaching of the executives will trickle down," Ritter said.

Celebrating Success

While Leaders understood that one of the ways to keep the enthusiasm and emotional engagement of its employees consistently high was to honor their achievements, "the fact that we've been the recipient of a sequence of awards also helps," said Ritter. "Recognitions have been coming in regularly enough that it gives us reason to stop and celebrate."

Keeping the morale high and energy up was a day-to-day effort that Leaders' management took very seriously. When the bank surpassed $500 million in assets in early 2008, Leaders' top management decided to treat its entire workforce to a White Sox game, renting a luxury skybox at U.S. Cellular Field. "Putting everyone in one bus and driving downtown together, singing karaoke, and going to a ball game was a nice way to celebrate that. We try to recognize, acknowledge, and celebrate whenever we can."

Investing in Workplace Culture and Measuring ROI

Such fringe benefits as the wellness program, various companywide initiatives, and dinners with the CEO were designed to create a strong workplace culture at Leaders, but they were not cheap. To justify the expense to the board of directors, Ritter and his team demonstrated the impact of workplace culture and retention on Leaders' bottom line. "When we took the subjective, soft, philosophical approach to culture and translated that into metrics and numbers that affected shareholder value by virtue of retention, the light bulb went on and the board understood it," said Ritter.

Ritter and his team first looked at the data from a companywide employee survey conducted by the Best Places to Work organization. Most Leaders employees (97 percent) had responded in the affirmative to such statements as: "I would invest my own money in this organization"; "Senior leadership models the organization's values"; and "I know how my job contributes to the organization's success." Next, Ritter's group identified the concrete, measurable results of having a strong workplace culture: a 4 percent turnover rate in 2006 versus a 30 percent industry benchmark and the 30 percent of unused available sick days. "Then, we did a little exercise," said Ritter. He explained:

If you look at 4 percent retention in an industry that experiences 30 percent, if half of those people were business developers, what would be the cost to an organization and what would be the impact on shareholder value? We made an assumption that the average business developer is making $120,000 and he's got a $12 million annual loan target, and we lose 4 percent of those versus the industry's 30 percent, and there's a vacancy rate of 90 days to get them replaced. And so we calculated a little bit of recruitment expense and then we looked at the opportunity costs that that person is not making 25 percent of their target because they were gone for three months and you can multiply that by a 2.48 percent average yield on a current loan. The opportunity cost is about $75,000, and there's another 30-odd thousand dollars in recruitment and training expense. And so we calculated the turnover costs conservatively at $111,000. Now the ROI Institute says that a business developer's turnover cost is about 125 percent of annual salary. So we're going slightly under—about 95 percent of annual salary. We said,

"Leaders Bank's losing two business developers at a 4 percent turnover costs the bank $222,000." And if it were six business developers and a 30 percent impact, that would end up costing $445,000, and saving nearly $300,000. If you multiply our earnings, our number of shares, it ends up being nearly $3 a share that it earned the shareholders by virtue of maintaining good, solid retention and low turnover.

Managing Growth

With the opening of three new banking centers in the Chicago area in 2008, the company started experiencing the challenges associated with organizational growth. However the Leaders executive team and the HR group worked to identify and address problems before they grew roots. To ensure that the culture was strong in all of Leaders' locations, "we are trying to have as much leadership team visibility in all locations as is humanly possible," Ritter said. He and his vice president of HR visited all bank centers regularly. Each location had an HR person, a compliance person, trainers, and access to the leadership team. In addition, instead of having one companywide staff meeting every month, each location had its own with an agenda especially tailored to each group.

Ensuring that the bank's employees had access to the members of the leadership team was particularly important because as Ritter said, "We are modeling the culture from the top down." He continued:

We know that our behavior has to model mutual trust, inclusion, ways to take risks, conflicts being invited and addressed rather than avoided, accountability, inviting and welcoming feedback, direct communication, group interest versus individual interest. We know that if we take care of those things and model it from the top, that's the way the teams will behave as well.

LESSONS FROM LEADERS BANK

Let's engage in another learning-by-doing exercise. I want you to reread this story and, as you do, make a list of everything Leaders Bank did to align in a consistent manner its policies, culture, processes, measurements, benefits, and rewards to recruit, hire, train, develop, and retain leaders as well as create the environment and culture that enabled and reinforced the right employee behaviors and attitudes.

CHAPTER 7 TAKEAWAYS

1. Growth is much more than a strategy—it is an internal enabling system that links in a consistent, seamless, and self-reinforcing manner a business's strategy, structure, culture, leadership philosophy, human resources policies, execution processes, measurements, and reward policies to drive desired behaviors that result in differentiating value creation.

2. These systems focus on behaviors, defining what behaviors are critical to the business's success and what behaviors are not acceptable from our business "family" members.

3. How do we want to treat each other, and how do we want to treat our customers?

4. How do we want to do our jobs? Do we want to be part of a high-performance environment that results in daily excellence? If the answer is yes, then what behaviors are necessary to produce that result and what behaviors inhibit or negate that result?

5. Does our culture promote those right behaviors?

6. Do we measure those right behaviors?

7. Do we reward those right behaviors?

8. Do we teach those right behaviors?

9. Do we discuss those right behaviors in our recruiting?

10. Do we celebrate those right behaviors?

11. Are we vigilant about complacency and self-satisfaction?

12. Are we paranoid about inconsistencies between what we say and how we act?

8 THE ENTREPRENEUR MUST GROW, TOO!

CEO QUOTES

- "If the business makes it three or four years, it hits a ceiling. Not a business or opportunity ceiling but an entrepreneur ceiling."

- "A lot of entrepreneurs get trapped in the 'well, I will just do it myself' syndrome."

- "My biggest struggle was reinventing myself to the business."

- "Ego fails. Control freaks fail. Listen till it hurts."

- "Delegation is not a natural human characteristic."

- "Delegation is the most difficult management skill to learn."

- "My biggest struggle has been constantly reinventing my relationship to the business. You go from a business that's in an extra bedroom to 200 employees nationwide, $150 million in sales, and that is a huge challenge in itself, both in terms of process, skill, and psychologically. Every year I say to my wife that I have to reinvent my relationship to the business."

GROWTH IS CHANGE, EVOLUTION, AND LEARNING

In Chapters 1 and 2, I outlined a unifying theme of this book: that growth is change, evolution, and learning. Nowhere is this theme more definitive than in how entrepreneurs themselves must change and evolve as the business grows.

This chapter focuses on how the growth of a business changes the entrepreneur and how, for the business to grow successfully, the entrepreneur must change. As a business grows, an entrepreneur must change not only the content of what he or she does, but also how he or she interacts with employees and outside entities. In addition, these shifting roles and responsibilities are not one-time events. As the business continues to grow, the entrepreneur must continue to adapt and evolve with the business's changing needs.

Growth changes both what the entrepreneur does and how he or she does it. Growth requires the entrepreneur to continuously redefine his or her relationship to the business and to its employees. Because growth changes what the entrepreneur does each day, his or her focus necessarily will change. The continuing change in focus requires that the entrepreneur develop new skills, which are often quite different from those entrepreneurial skills that made the business successful in the first place.

THREE-DIMENSIONAL CHANGES

This redefinition of the entrepreneur's role as the business grows can be viewed along three dimensions:

1. The movement from a hands-on doer, to a manager, to a leader, and ultimately to a coach/mentor of others;

2. From a functional specialist to a general manager, back to a functional specialist, and ultimately to a strategy and culture "conductor;" and

3. From having a passionate belief in the primacy of oneself, to having a belief in others, and finally to having a belief in the importance of working toward something more than just the financial rewards of the business.

At each change point along any of the three dimensions, the entrepreneur may need to realize, often with difficulty, that he or she may not be the right person to be the CEO of the growing business. In such cases, the entrepreneur has the choice of bringing in a CEO with the appropriate skill sets or deciding that the business has reached a comfortable size that he or she can continue to manage and additional growth is no longer the goal. Even if the entrepreneur chooses the latter, steady-state option, the business goal must change from growth to continuously improving the customer value proposition and defeating the competition.

DELEGATING: LEARNING TO MANAGE

Entrepreneurs who reach the stage of focusing on business growth have successfully traversed the start-up challenge—a victory in and of itself. They generally struggled, adapted, and iterated while being passionately consumed with the business, working long hours, and doing anything that needed to be done. In the best cases, this success at building a business builds self-confidence; in the worst cases, it builds arrogance and/or hubris.

Many entrepreneurs who withstand the start-up challenge develop a style of management that is top–down—a "my way or the highway" approach. Although that management style does not translate well when business growth is the target, many entrepreneurs have difficulty in moving toward more of a partneurial style with managers because of the initial success of the autocratic style.

A successful serial entrepreneur stated it this way: "[We] entrepreneurs tend to think we know everything. And the quicker we recognize that we don't and we open up our ears and eyes instead of just our mouth, things start going well."

Many entrepreneurs learn to delegate only when forced to. At some point they cannot physically do all of the tasks the business needs: finding, selling, and servicing customers; delivering the products or services; and tending to the myriad of administrative tasks. So, entrepreneurs are forced to change and to delegate. Few do this willingly or easily.

The threshold questions entrepreneurs face when growing their businesses are: What tasks do I delegate? To whom? The next logical question is: How do I delegate?

How to Delegate

A thoughtful, successful entrepreneur talked about delegation this way:

I don't think that learning to delegate is a linear process. You have to delegate. Then you do delegate and you find that some things fall apart. Then you gather them up, pull them back in towards you and fix them and then start the process all over again.

It is difficult for many entrepreneurs to accept that others may get the job done differently than they would have. Part of accepting the need for delegation is acknowledging that what comes naturally to you may have to be learned by others who will make mistakes.

Part of learning how to delegate involves learning that someone else may do a good job while doing the task differently than the entrepreneur. How one reacts to these inevitable mistakes or differences will either enable future learning and employee growth or it will hinder it by making people timid about trying new approaches or making decisions.

Delegating involves patience, teaching, correcting, and trusting others. Another entrepreneur who built a successful service company stated: "It (delegation) is baptism by fire. You start looking at the fact that if you don't let go, you will lose."

Delegation transforms an entrepreneur into a manager. Successful entrepreneurs have made this transition by learning to "trust but verify"— having daily team meetings to set daily priorities and a short team meeting each day to teach a key point.

Successful delegation is directly related to having processes in place for others to follow. In addition, successful delegation requires implementing a system of measurements for important activities of the business to serve as an early warning system. The right metrics expose defects, variances, and discrepancies. Learning how to delegate and implementing the appropriate processes and measurements are all necessary for an entrepreneur to evolve from doer to manager.

For the initial step in this delegation process, some entrepreneurs chose an outstanding employee to promote to team leader or manager position. They engaged the employee in writing the key steps, instructions, and tasks necessary to accomplish the job that the employee was going now to be responsible for. Next, they gave the employee responsibility for the task of communicating that to other employees. Then, they frequently checked on the progress until they were convinced that the employee could execute the task appropriately and consistently. Frequent checking was then reduced to sporadic checking as the employee earned the trust of the entrepreneur.

What Tasks Do You Delegate First?
What tasks do you choose to delegate first? That depends on the business. Because successful delegation involves an appropriate level of knowledge and trust, one should start with easy, noncritical tasks and work toward delegating more complex, higher-level tasks. Some general observations were that entrepreneurs kept control over finances, quality, and customer relationships until they had to delegate them. Even after they were forced to delegate, they maintained rigorous oversight over those three critical areas.

When Do You Start Delegating?
Although it is hard to come up with consistent rules of thumb about when entrepreneurs should delegate substantive tasks to other managers, the magic number seems to be around ten employees. Even before that point, some general delegation occurs. As a business grows, delegation involves more differentiated tasks and the entrepreneur losing physical oversight of the tasks being done. At around ten employees, an entrepreneur needs to designate a person or persons as manager(s), which creates structure.

Learning to Lead: Managing Managers
After learning to delegate, the next big transition for entrepreneurs is learning how to manage the managers chosen to help run the business. Managing managers means the entrepreneur is evolving into a leader. Most entrepreneurs in my study had between four and eight direct reports. Learning how to manage these people individually and as a team required most entrepreneurs to learn new skills and become more emotionally intelligent.

This process of learning to lead changes both the "what" and "how" of what entrepreneurs do daily. Much more time is spent relating to, listening to, and engaging direct reports in meaningful conversations, including getting buy-in to both short-term and long-term goals. It also required teaching, correcting, giving feedback, and sometimes having difficult conversations. This new menu of work is challenging for many entrepreneurs because it takes emotional engagement, self-management, patience, and a lot of time.

This People Stuff Is Hard

Many entrepreneurs found this "people stuff" much harder and more emotionally taxing than their past activities of selling products or services to customers, making the products, or delivering the services. The people stuff does not come naturally to many business people. One entrepreneur described the change in focus this way:

As you push decisions down you have to spend more time in alignment and prioritization making sure people are focused on the right thing, that they are communicating well and getting along, and that they've got the requisite skill sets to do what needs to be done.

Many entrepreneurs told me the need for this "emotional" people-focused management was the reason why so many entrepreneurs fail as leaders and must step aside so the business can continue to grow. This transition to becoming a leader who manages managers creates questions of how involved the entrepreneur should be in the details of the growing business.

How do you verify and check on your managers without conveying to employees that you do not trust them? When and how do you disagree with a manager's actions? How do you prioritize or decide where you will give managers leeway? What elements of the business are non-negotiable? How does an entrepreneur discover the optimal way to train and communicate with each manager?

These management-related questions are qualitatively different than the business questions concerning quality, financial metrics, logistics, sales, and production. As the entrepreneur's role changes with business growth, many miss the daily direct customer contact and practicing their craft. In fact, many became entrepreneurs because they did not want to be managers, removed from customer contact. Growth can create a major tension for such entrepreneurs. How can an entrepreneur continue doing what he or she enjoys doing when growth requires a shift to managing people and processes and implementing controls?

Remember in the Global Medical Imaging story discussed in chapter 4, Scott Ray, one of the founders, learned that he added more value to the business not by managing sales but by being a superstar salesman. It takes emotional maturity and a manageable ego to take that step.

The people part of building a business is a significant and essential part of business growth. Learning and developing one's teaching, managing, and leadership skills emerges as mission-critical needs to continue growth.

These transitions from manager to leader were summarized by a serial entrepreneur this way: "It takes one set of skills to run (manage) a company and it takes an entirely different set of skills to grow (lead) a company."

These personal transitions present to many entrepreneurs a big personal growth challenge. It should be clear by now that as one entrepreneur so aptly stated, "Businesses don't grow, people do."

Effectively, to grow a business, the entrepreneur has two choices. The entrepreneur must either be a good enough manager and leader to inspire and receive high performance from his or her employees, or the entrepreneur must remain a functional specialist and find someone else to manage the people.

From Leader to Coach/Mentor

As the entrepreneur learns to lead, teach, and build managers, he or she will have learned that each manager is a unique individual with strengths and weaknesses, needing an individualized approach to foster his or her personal growth. In other words, the leader must develop a repertoire of skills to be able to communicate with and teach each manager individually to be most effective.

As managers develop and learn, they each will begin their individual journey from manager to leader. As the business grows, each entrepreneur will have an increasing number of direct reports to manage and to develop into leaders. These managers will need to learn to be leaders. These cascading personal transitions will continue as growth continues.

Nurturing the transitions of the managers to increasingly responsible roles requires the entrepreneur to adopt a new way of interacting with his or her direct reports. At this stage, what is required is to be a personal mentor and coach for each direct report. Entrepreneurs must learn to maintain high accountability for results while, at the same time, serving as a trusted advisor and helping the direct reports deal with their leadership challenges.

This mentoring role requires a deeper emotional engagement characterized by emotional vulnerability and honesty to ensure the trust of the developing manager that the mentor truly has the manager's best interests at heart. The quandary here is that although developing a trusted mentoring relationship is important, it is complicated by the fact that the entrepreneur mentor can fire the mentee. The entrepreneur must continue to do what is right for the business. Understanding and acknowledging this tension is critical to an effective coaching relationship.

PSYCHOLOGIST OR BUSINESS BUILDER?

One entrepreneur told me that he thinks many companies quit growing not because of the challenges of financing growth but because entrepreneurs often lack the skills and tire of addressing the personal needs in mentoring members of the management team. He stated, "No one told me I'd be more a psychologist than a businessman!"

Evolution to a coaching/mentoring role requires the entrepreneur to move toward becoming a leader whose mission is to help others to be all they can be. As an entrepreneur told me, "When I started four years ago, I did everything. Literally, I touched it, did it, wrote it, fixed it. And now I do nothing like that. Today I have to learn how to be the CEO of a sixty-five-person organization." To do this, he spends every Monday and Tuesday in meetings with his direct reports individually and, when needed, as a group. In addition, he noted: "I have to constantly educate myself and reinvent myself to keep up with the business."

One entrepreneur in my study talked about coaching this way:

My challenge as a leader was to transform away from performance management and metrics management to this more intangible thing of *leadership*, trying to increase people's capacities, or else they've got to "get off the bus," to quote Jim Collins.

SPECIALIST TO GENERAL MANAGER BACK TO SPECIALIST

Another transition an entrepreneur makes as the business grows is related to what business functional areas (sales, marketing, finance, human resources, or operations) the entrepreneur opts to focus on. During the start-up, infancy, and adolescent stages of business growth, the solo entrepreneur acted as a general manager who is involved in all functional areas whether or not he or she had experience in those areas. Why? Out of necessity. When more than one entrepreneur was involved in the start-up, they may or may not have overlapped in the tasks they performed.

In either case, as the business grows and good management teams are built, many entrepreneurs can choose to spend more time in the functional area that they enjoy in addition to their leadership role. The trajectory for those entrepreneurs is from specialist to generalist and back to a specialist over the different business growth phases. This transition back to specialist generally happens after the "doer to manager" and "manager to leader" transitions. As the business growth continues, the entrepreneur either evolves into a coach/mentor, focuses on strategy, or installs someone else in that role and returns to being a specialist in the functional area he or she excels in.

THE FINAL JOURNEY: FROM "ME" TO "THEM"

Concurrent with the role transitions is another major transition that happens with some entrepreneurs as their business grows. They find a new meaning in the business other than financial reward. For many entrepreneurs, growth for financial gain is no longer reason enough to deal with the challenges of continuing to grow. They find a new meaning in coming to work every day.

Motivated by the new meaning, they either focus on culture, building leaders by giving employees opportunities and education, or aligning the business with a community or charitable mission. Notice that this development is shown in several stories in this book, notably Defender Direct, Room & Board, Leaders Bank, and Trilogy Health Services.

As an example, Dave Lindsey of Defender Direct described his personal transition this way:

It's been a humbling learning [experience] for me as a business owner. It's not about having a better plan or a widget. It's about helping your employees, because every time they grow, I grow. And that's what keeps me going, that's my calling in life—to build and develop leaders . . . We don't want to be in the business of buying and selling businesses. We want to be in the business of growing and developing leaders. We have a platform to do that. So that's what my goal is.

VOLUNTARILY STEPPING ASIDE AS CEO

In a few businesses in my study, the entrepreneur realized that he or she had neither the skills nor the emotional makeup to take the business to the next level of growth. In all of those cases, they brought in an outsider to run the company. The entrepreneur then either became the CEO in name only, returning to working as a functional specialist, or they became the chairperson/CEO with a president or chief operating officer reporting to them. The latter occurred in about 15 percent of the companies studied.

DEFENDER DIRECT, INC.[1]

Defender Direct is a good example of how an entrepreneur grew as his company grew. As you read the Defender Direct Inc. story, focus on how Dave Lindsey's role changed as the company grew and how he evolved as a leader. Also, notice how Defender Direct reinforces many of the points made in the previous chapters:

- "Businesses don't grow, people do."
- "Build a culture on purpose, not by accident."
- "Build a business that could be 'McDonaldized.'"
- "Focus equals growth."

Defender Direct, Inc., headquartered in Indianapolis, Indiana, is a privately held company that sells and installs ADT security systems and Dish Network Satellite TV to homeowners in the United States. President and Chief Executive Officer Dave Lindsey started the business out of his home in 1998, making the transition to entrepreneur from new-product development at Medeco Security Locks, Inc. He used $30,000 of his and his wife's personal savings to fund the start-up, which he called Defender Security Co.

From its humble beginnings in the Lindsey's spare bedroom, Defender became one of the largest security and satellite dealers in the Midwest, experiencing an average annual growth rate of 60 percent over 10 years.

In 2008, Defender generated $150 million in revenues and ranked 387th on the *Inc.* 500 list of America's Fastest-Growing Companies. With 1,500 employees, the company had a national footprint of 120 offices in 40 states.

Defender's stellar growth was fueled by an aggressive direct-marketing focus and national expansion, but Lindsey credited the Defender culture, which fostered continuous employee development. He elaborated:

Defender has grown faster than its peers not because we are better at selling and installing security systems but because our people have grown. Our sales have doubled because the capacity and talents of our leaders have doubled. A few years ago, we stopped trying to double our business and realized the way to grow was to double our team members' enthusiasm, optimism, and skills. Send people to seminars, leadership conferences, and self-help programs. Build a culture on purpose, not by accident.[2]

The Founder

Lindsey was born in 1969 and grew up in the Midwest. He graduated with honors from Indiana University with a BS degree in Business Finance and an MBA in Marketing and Finance. After graduation, he worked for various companies in the lock and door hardware industry and became interested in security systems. A turning point for Lindsey came when he was passed over for a promotion while working for Medeco Security Locks, Inc., in Salem, Virginia. "We're going to start a business," he said to his wife, "because I don't want to ever be in this spot again, where it's office politics controlling my career."

At Medeco, Lindsey had been involved in a program called "Medeco Business Advantage"—a 2X Strategy to Grow Your Business, a set of business processes inspired by Michael Gerber's bestselling book *The E-Myth: Why Most Businesses Don't Work and What to Do About It.*[3] According to Lindsey, "It was a way for a mostly traditional type of locksmith to double their business, using the 2X process and then up-selling. We would teach it to our locksmith dealers, and I saw it work and decided, 'I've always wanted to own my own business, why not buy a locksmith shop, double it, and create value?'"

Opportunity Knocks

Lindsey and his wife started looking for a locksmith business to buy, but after finding none at a price they were willing to pay, they moved to Indianapolis. "That's where my family was and my support structure, and where I really wanted to be permanently," said Lindsey. He reflected on his days as a freelance locksmith:

I began changing locks and installing deadbolts, which was pretty horrible because every psychological test I've ever taken says that me and a power drill should stay as far apart as possible. I have some great stories about taking out my friends' locks and not being able to put them back on . . . So that's how I began, pretty ugly, and my intention was to never do installation, because I'm not technical. But I had to get out and learn.

While his wife took over the role of a family breadwinner, Lindsey researched the security industry. "I was, like, if someone needs a lock, maybe they want an alarm system? And in the mid-90s the alarm industry really exploded." Lindsey jumped at the opportunity when ADT Security Systems and other brands began offering $99 start-up packages for homeowners, making home-security systems more affordable to a wide group of consumers. "We wrote a business plan, got ADT to take a chance on us, and began as an ADT Authorized Dealer. We never looked back. I never did another lock job once we signed our ADT contract."

Learning the Ropes

For his first three months as an ADT Authorized Dealer, Lindsey focused on meeting the sales quota. Failure to sell 15 systems per month not only could lead to problems for the business but also could result in a financial penalty, which would have swallowed much of the Lindseys' start-up capital. A devotee of the principles Gerber laid out in *The E-Myth*, Lindsey said he "was looking for that Gerber-type of repeatable system, something that could be McDonaldized."

Lindsey took advantage of a sales-training program offered by ADT. "The Dealer Program I came into was 90 percent door-to-door sales," he said. "ADT was teaching us to knock on doors. They threw me in a van with a bunch of other guys and put me on the street, and I'd sell ADT systems door-to-door."

The day that Lindsey, who had never sold an ADT system before, made his first sale within a couple of hours, he "saw it work." He immediately called his wife to tell her he was going to buy a 15-passenger van. He recalled:

I had seen a repeatable process, which involved a van; when you go door-to-door you have to have that team environment—when you drive together in one car, you've got to pick the people up so they can't leave, until they get a sale. When everybody drives individually, they end up getting back in their cars and leaving.

During the first month of knocking on doors, Lindsey sold six security systems and fifteen during the second month, with the help of a friend. It was cause for celebration because they had met ADT's monthly quota. The third month was even better; with first hires onboard, Lindsey and his team sold 30 systems.

The ADT Sales Contest

By September 1998, Lindsey had assembled a team of 10 salespeople. "I really wanted to start the team out with a bang," he said. "I needed a catalyst, a point of focus." ADT's sales contest with its $15,000 prize was exactly what Lindsey needed to fire up his team. "Each dealer's quota was based on the previous three months' sales," he said. "I believed we had a great opportunity to win since our previous three months' quota would be only 17 units." The team launched a sales blitzkrieg. As Lindsey recalled:

My living room was converted into our Sales Meeting War Room. My artwork was covered up with a makeshift sales board, and my entertainment center became an employee mailbox system. Administrative paperwork was handled from my back bedroom, complete with a board stretched out on the bed to form a desk, a computer, and a borrowed fax machine. Side meetings and training sessions were held on the front lawn. We were entrepreneurs, making the rules up as we went. We had no fear and knew we had a great product and wanted to meet as many people as possible. We went out together each day, feeding off each other's energy.[4]

One day in mid-September, while his sales team was gathered in his living-room, Lindsey went to the back bedroom to call ADT's headquarters to find out how his team ranked among other ADT Authorized Dealers. His surprise turned to shock when he learned that, as a new ADT Authorized Dealer, Defender had its sales quota increased from 17 to 45. Shaken, Lindsey weighed his options.

What happened next was what Lindsey referred to as "an inflection point in the company" and "the moment of truth" for him as a leader. He took a few minutes to compose himself and went back to the living room to face his sales team. He candidly related the news about the quota and then spent a few minutes rallying his troops. "We're going to blow through this," he said.

With 45 sales already under its belt and two more weeks to go, Defender still had a shot at winning the contest. "We took it up a notch or two during those last two weeks and worked long hard days," Lindsey said. Defender's installation crew tripled its capacity to make sure every system Defender sold got installed the next day. By the end of September, with 142 systems sold and installed, Lindsey's sales team was 316 percent above its quota and 835 percent above its three-month historical average.[5]

In snatching the top prize in the sales contest, the upstart company had defeated hundreds of other ADT Authorized Dealers from across the United States. "September was crazy," Lindsey said. "After four months of knocking on doors, we had a system, and we knew what we were doing. Soon after, we sold 200, 300 systems, and we ran pretty quickly to the 600-range a month. And it kind of skyrocketed from there." Dave had something scalable.

The Entrepreneurial Mindset

During its first few months of operation, Defender subcontracted all systems' installations. "You know the old adage, nothing happens until a sale happens," Lindsey said. "So we focused on creating demand." In September, when sales numbered 142 systems, however, Lindsey hired his first installation technician. At the beginning, Defender hired technicians with minimal industry experience, who were able to handle a wireless alarm system that was relatively easy to install.

At approximately the same time, Lindsey hired his first sales manager, who took over driving the van with the sales team, freeing up Lindsey to "get the paperwork done to support this," as he put it. "I was able to stop and go back and put some processes in place." He reflected on the early building of the business:

We kept in mind Gerber's three roles in a business: the entrepreneur's job is to create the process, the manager's job is to assure the process is used, and the technician's job is to follow the process and use it. And that has dominated my thoughts for the past 10 years. Every time we're trying to grow something, we are very clear about who is playing these roles, and we make sure somebody's doing each of these. In the beginning, I played all those different roles, but I was conscious that I was ultimately the entrepreneur, and for the first three our four years all I did was build processes.

Thinking Big—With a Clear Focus

In November 1998, Defender opened a second office and sold 125 systems the first month. Lindsey's sales team pledged to open a new office every 90 days, and Defender ended its first year of operation with four offices. As Lindsey said, "We lived, and still do, by Gerber's tenet—'big business is just a small business that thought big.' And we wanted to be much bigger. In those days we'd always remind ourselves that it's not okay to put a mom-and-pop system in place, because that's just going to keep us small forever." Dave needed processes that would be scalable.

Looking for ways to grow his business, Lindsey considered expanding into the commercial security market, but after some thought, he decided that the residential market would be Defender's staple. "We weren't so much a security company as a home market and installation company," Lindsey said. "We found another product that could be marketed in a mass way and be installed in homes."[6] That product was satellite TV, which Defender added to its offerings in 2001 and with it quickly became one of the top Dish Network dealers. Dave defined his business to installing products in the home. Simple and focused.

Since making the decision to concentrate on the residential market, Lindsey stayed on course and steered his company away from potential distractions. "We have a saying posted all over our offices—Focus Equals Growth." He elaborated:

Today we still only have 13 part numbers in our inventory room, the same 13 we had 10 years ago. We have not added things. We keep doing more of the same better, trying to McDonaldize it. We understood focus as the goal early on, constantly using an ABC format to prioritize. I coach all of our new leaders, "We don't pay you to get everything done—we pay you to get the most important things done."

Defender's "Hedgehog Statement"

For help in knowing on what to focus each day, Defender employees turned to what the company called its Hedgehog Statement—"We are best in the world at customer acquisition for top brand-name products and services that target homeowners."[7] The Hedgehog Concept was one of the principles of greatness outlined in Jim Collins's 2001 bestseller *Good to Great*.[8] As Collins's research indicated, great companies refused to do anything that did not fit with their Hedgehog Concept, and they made as much use of stop-doing lists as to-do lists.

Lindsey cited Collins as one of his biggest influences and made his employees read his book. They even read whole chapters out loud in the office. Having spent five years discovering its Hedgehog Concept, Defender leadership used it as a frame of reference for all its decisions. As Lindsey said, "We really pride ourselves not on our to-do list but on our not-to-do list. And we have found that the more we say 'no' to things, the more we grow."

Defender's "Circle of Life"

Another practical tool, which Lindsey and his leadership team used on a weekly basis, was the so-called "Circle of Life" (see Exhibit 8.1). It was a visual representation of their understanding of how the business worked. "Imagine a clock face," Lindsey said. "Twelve o'clock is marketing, three o'clock is sales, six o'clock is installation, and nine o'clock is admin and finance. It used to be just sales, door-to-door, but it all starts with marketing. So I spent my energy on really ramping it up over the last five years."

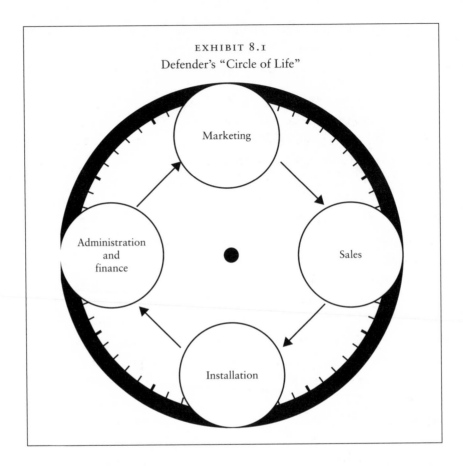

EXHIBIT 8.1
Defender's "Circle of Life"

Whenever Lindsey noticed a bottleneck in any of the four areas of the circle of life, he would focus his full attention on that particular spot to alleviate the bottleneck. He elaborated:

First, I'd work with marketing until we had enough leads. But we didn't have enough salespeople, so I'd jump over to sales, and make sure we close all the leads until we didn't have enough technicians. Then, I'd go down to installation and make sure we're getting all the systems installed, and it would flow back up, and then we'd have a paperwork backup, so I'd make sure ADT was paying us. And then as soon as that is all released, we say that the money flows around that. Marketing takes a dollar and starts at 12 o'clock, and you hope that two dollars come up when you spin around the circle. So then I'd go back to marketing and say, "Okay, we've got some more marketing programs: let's go. And I just kept running around that circle. The faster you spin the circle, the faster we grow.

I've had my direct reports say to me, "You're focusing on my part of the circle right now. You've been to my office every day this week," and I'm, "Yeah, I'm going to be in your part of the circle until our install rate or our backlog is down." Today, I'm backing up from that a little bit as I'm changing my role.

To keep a close eye on his business's financial performance, Lindsey used a scorecard, which he had introduced a year after starting Defender. "It's a concise Excel spreadsheet," said Lindsey, "with weeks' and months' worth of history and then this week's numbers, like, what's the close rate? We want to get that scorecard more automated, and we want that to be a live dashboard." Lindsey held weekly Friday meetings with his direct reports, during which they thoroughly reviewed all metrics on the scorecard. The meetings started in the afternoon and lasted more than four hours.

Financing Growth

All entrepreneurs know that funding growth is an expensive proposition and that access to capital is one of the biggest challenges facing start-ups. Defender had an advantage in that area because of its business model, which involved acquiring new customers and then "selling" them to ADT and Dish. "They cash us out upfront," said Lindsey. "We sell the contract, which is a three-year agreement that has a value, just like a bank sells a loan. It has always kept us cash rich, and we've been able to fund all this growth without any debt." In addition, Defender pulled in regular revenue from installation and monthly monitoring services.

But the company experienced its share of bumps in the road. About a year into his entrepreneurial journey, Lindsey struggled to make payroll. At a family dinner, he wanted to forget about work but could not stop thinking about it. "I remember my dad and I made eye contact," Lindsey said. "I just broke down crying, telling him how stressed out I was. So that's early on, just cash flow and understanding. You've got all these people believing in you, and you're trying to have that initial confidence just to get the ball to roll." Lindsey elaborated:

It got really ugly, and that led us to getting into Dish Network Satellite TV in addition to ADT. So, luckily, things righted there. But that was huge; we had one year of negative growth in 10 years, and that was that year. It was really just about holding things together. I remember I had everybody in the company on speakerphones, giving them a speech, "We're going to get through this, and these are the three or four things we're going to do." That was probably the biggest time I felt like a general of an army.

Dave survived a supplier concentration risk and diversified his products.

The Evolution of the Business Model

For the first three years, Defender's sales force consisted of "full-commission door-knockers," as Lindsey put it. "It was a great way to start, because there's no marketing, and you're only paying someone when the sale is made. Then we realized we could set appointments instead of knocking on doors, and we became 100 percent telemarketing-based."

Around the time Defender was transitioning to telemarketing, an acquaintance of Lindsey's introduced him to Marcia Raab, owner of a small call center in Indiana. Defender soon became Raab's exclusive customer. "She did a great job, was such a servant to our business—she really did it at an exchange rate with us," said Lindsey. "Terrific marketing and sales person. She grew the 20-person call center to 200 people in two centers, and she owned that."

Defender eventually bought Raab's call centers and Raab became Defender's vice president of sales and marketing. "She was an absolute dynamo," said Lindsey. "She started coming to our staff meetings, when she was our outsource partner with her own call centers, which she ran like a division of ours. And then we formalized it and put her in the VP spot."

The telemarketing operation had to be scrapped in 2001, with the introduction of the "no-call list hit," as Lindsey named it, allowed consumers to put a stop to unwanted telemarketing pitches. "So, we reinvented the business for the third time," Lindsey said. "Now it's 100 percent direct mail and the Internet, so our call centers handle only incoming calls."

Defender's call center kept growing, reaching more than 400 sales and customer-service agents in five contact centers located in Indiana and Ohio. The sales agents handled inbound calls from potential customers, who responded to Defender's newspaper ads, pitches on the Internet, or direct-mail offers, while customer-service agents handled the calls from existing customers seeking support. "The inbound agents who are taking calls from prospective customers are paid minimum wage plus heavy commission," said Lindsey. "And with those people we have a fairly high turnover. You have to hire four or five to get one who's good."

Lindsey's Biggest Challenges

From the time Lindsey launched his own business, he had been challenged to continually evolve his relationship with the company, transforming himself from a door-to-door salesman to sales manager to controller to regional manager to president and CEO in 10 years. As he reflected on his changing role,

My biggest struggle has been constantly reinventing my relationship to the business. You go from a business that's in an extra bedroom to 200 employees nationwide, $150 million in sales, and that is a huge challenge in itself, both in terms of process, skill, and psychologically. Every year I say to my wife that I have to reinvent my relationship to the business. It started with hiring the first sales manger to go take these guys to knock on doors for me, to then jumping to be an admin lead and putting someone else in my place. I feel like I kept filling a hole and then leaving somebody behind. Then taking it from being in Indianapolis to being a regional presence and all the skills it takes. And today I'm evolving even more into being—I think of it as a chairman, a shareholder, investor, as well as business strategy and new products.

Managing People

As Lindsey's relationship to his business evolved, so did his management philosophy. At first, he found it hard to delegate. "It was hard to release control," he admitted. "At one time I thought I could do it better than anybody else. All it took was to hire a couple of people and understand they could do it better than me."

After six months of driving a van with his door-to-door sales team, Lindsey found a sales manager he trusted who eventually became the number one ADT sales rep in the country and rose through the ranks to become vice president of sales. Similarly, the first installation technician Lindsey hired grew to become Defender's vice president of installation. When Defender was generating $20 million in revenue, he was in charge of installation for the whole company. "When the job started to outstrip him, he was put into a regional role, which was still almost a $10-million region," said Lindsey. "I always say to people whose jobs outstrip them, 'You still have the same level of responsibility or more.'"

As a manager who never had much tolerance for mistakes, Lindsey described himself as a proponent of tough love. "I kind of manage with a Bobby Knight-type[9] of mentality with my direct reports," Lindsey said. "I've always said I need people with thick skin who themselves do not tolerate mistakes."

By 2010, Lindsey had four direct reports: chief operations officer (COO), chief marketing officer (CMO), chief information officer (CIO), and chief financial officer (CFO).

COO John Corliss, whom Lindsey had met at Medeco, came on board in January 2006 as Defender's CFO, a position he held for a year. As the COO, Corliss was responsible for the company's customer service, human resources, and installations departments. Installations included all field installation technicians, who were full-time Defender employees working in 120 installation locations around the country. In 2008, Lindsey made him partner in the business.

Marcia Raab, a Defender employee since 2001, was promoted from vice president of sales and marketing to CMO and in 2008 became a partner. She was responsible for managing the planning and purchasing of all Defender marketing programs as well as overseeing the operations of Defender call centers. Lindsey said, "Marcia is the drumbeat of the organization, and as fast as she beats that drum, the rest of us dance." In the spring of 2010 Dave promoted her to president of the company.

Bart Shroyer, the CFO, came onboard in 2007. He was responsible for all accounting, funding, and financial management for Defender. Shroyer, who had a breakout year in 2008, was made partner in 2009.

Gregg Albacete, the CIO, joined Defender in 2007. He was responsible for building and maintaining systems, databases, and the IT infrastructure that supported and extended Defender's business model.

Finding the Right CFO

Among the many challenges Lindsey faced while growing his business, one of the toughest was filling the CFO position. At first, Lindsey "gave a box of receipts to an accountant," as he described it, but nine months into his contract with ADT, Lindsey's wife took over the accounting function of the business. A few months later, with the help of QuickBooks accounting software, Lindsey said, "She came on full-blown," and continued in the CFO role for five years, until the arrival of the Lindseys' third child when she became a full-time stay-at-home mom. Then, her assistant, who "grew up in the business," took over.

Lindsey admitted that he has had "four to five people" in the CFO position since he started Defender. "It was the hardest job to fill," he said. He elaborated:

Our average growth rate was 60 percent a year for the last 10 years. So you hire a bookkeeper, then you need an accountant, and then you need a controller. I didn't shoot far enough ahead. The problem was, when I tried to shoot ahead, I got real schmoheads. CFOs are all by nature pretty conservative people. They are sharp guys, not looking for a $10-million business to work in. The only person who wants to be CFO in a $10-million business says, "Well, I'll just start my own business. I'm not going to work for this guy, take on his risk." So I got a couple of screwballs who didn't seem that way when I interviewed them. Once we got to $50 million plus, it was a lot easier to attract people.

Defender's Culture

Lindsey attributed Defender's success to its culture, which he built around each employee's personal growth (see Exhibit 8.2). Describing it further, he said, "Another word is 'terrific.' We talk about being terrific every day, and we choose to be that way."

Lindsey was continuously learning and growing, and he encouraged his employees to do the same, sending them to various self-improvement seminars, such as Dale Carnegie Training and Ed Foreman's Successful Life Course. "We coined a saying, 'Businesses don't grow, people do,'" said Lindsey. "I don't want this to become a cliché around Defender because it's been our secret sauce. All of us had to grow. We've accomplished this reinvention through good books and good tapes and networking with good people."

Dave Grew and Defender Grew

Over the course of 10 years, Lindsey reinvented Defender's business model three times, reinvented himself and his role, but, most important,

EXHIBIT 8.2
Defender's Culture

At **Defender Direct, we are about being the best!** We have founded ourselves on the principle that we can be the best in the world at customer acquisition for top brand-name products and services that target homeowners. It doesn't stop there. It has infiltrated throughout our entire company.

We have the best employees! We have the kind of employees that are constantly working on themselves and building themselves into leaders. At Defender Direct, you will find people that are always striving to set and meet new goals. That is why we are always promoting people from within. Our four passions act as a roadmap for making our people the best they can be, and they really take it to heart.

We work with the best products! As a Dish Network dealer, we are one of the top-five dealers in the country. For ADT, we are also a top dealer. How do we do that? By working with the best products in the industry and products we believe in. Our employees are some of our best customers! At Defender Direct, customers will find that we do our best so we can be the best! We strive for excellence and that is what customers get each time.

Defender Direct is the best in the world at customer acquisition for top brand-name products and services that target homeowners

Rewards and Recognition
- **Annual Superstar Celebration.** Every year we celebrate our employees' accomplishments by taking them on an annual trip. For 2008, we took 278 employees and their guests to Cancun, Mexico. Past trips have included trips to Jamaica and the Bahamas. Our superstars are what make us what we are, and we want to celebrate that with a trip that lets them know how much we appreciate their dedication and commitment to achieving their goals.
- **Defender Family Day.** Each Labor Day, we invite our employees and their families to spend time with us for some fun and sun, our treat! Past events have taken us to Indiana Beach and Six Flags Kentucky Kingdom. It's a great way to celebrate the last hurray of summer.
- **Sales Contests.** We understand that our sales team is a key driver for our success. We have weekly contests and awards for our sales team to keep them working on hitting and breaking new records. This year we even gave away a car!

(continued)

EXHIBIT 8.2 *(continued)*

- This is just a small list of the many things we do to reward and recognize our employees' dedication and hard work. We are always coming up with new ways to reward them for all they contribute. We put this as a high priority on our to-do list.

Training
- Every technician we hire attends Defender University, a complete training program that gets them ready to be successful in the field. We have had some of the top techs in the industry come out of Defender University, and we continue to expand the size of our classes every month.
- We are always looking for opportunities to send our employees to training and seminars, so that they are continuously developing and working on themselves. Programs include the Dale Carnegie Training Program, Ed Foreman's Successful Life Course and much more. We believe in self-improvement, and we are always looking for ways to help employees do just that.

Additional Perks
- Extensive library with books from great authors such as John Maxwell, Jim Collins and Jack Welch.
- Corporate-sponsored Weight Watchers program to help employees achieve personal weight-loss goals.
- Corporate chaplains
- Much more!

---

he redefined the purpose of his business, which had evolved from making money to growing people. "Our growth plan is that you have to reinvent yourself this year," Lindsey told 1,500 Defender employees at its annual Self-Improvement Day, held in April in Indianapolis. This companywide commitment to personal growth and continuous reinvention was the linchpin of Defender's corporate culture, and Self-Improvement Day provided an opportunity for reaffirmation every year.

Lindsey was particularly proud of Defender Advantage, the company's four-year initiation program into the Defender culture, during which employees received leadership training, participated in the company's book club, and traveled with their families on mission trips abroad to work as volunteers.[10]

In addition, newly hired installation technicians attended Defender University, a complete training program that prepared them to be successful in the field. Part of the Defender University's curriculum was Corporate Culture Day, during which all new hires listened to Defender's senior managers, including Lindsey, via satellite. The main purpose of Culture Day was to drive the following message: "We are asking you to work harder on yourself than on your job." On Culture Day all new hires were also given the Defender Leadership Advantage Board, which charted the path of their growth.

Besides focus and drive, Lindsey listed forgiveness as one of his greatest strengths as a leader. As he told his staff, he believed that their "ability to forgive each other really built a culture around here. It's the glue that allows us to stay at this breakneck speed." Lindsey, who described himself as a "student of leadership," stressed that his "basic belief in forgiveness comes from [his] faith and having learned from Jesus, who was a servant leader." Still, when reflecting on his entrepreneurial journey, Lindsey always emphasized the lesson of continuous employee development:

It's been a humbling learning [experience] for me as a business owner. It's not about having a better plan or a widget. It's about helping your employees, because every time they grow, I grow. And that's what keeps me going, that's my calling in life—to build and develop leaders . . . We don't want to be in the business of buying and selling businesses. We want to be in the business of growing and developing leaders. We have a platform to do that. So that's what my goal is.

LESSONS FROM DEFENDER DIRECT

Defender Direct is a good summary of many of the key points made in this book: the power of culture; the necessity of processes and evolving the business model; the transitions the entrepreneur must make from doer to manager to leader; the creating of an internal system to drive self-improvement that results in the business constantly improving; the power of scaling; how growth is change; learning; and the difficulty of building a management team that works well together.

CHAPTER 8 TAKEAWAYS

1. For the business to grow successfully, the entrepreneur must change.

2. Growth changes both what the entrepreneur does and how he or she does it.

3. Growth requires the entrepreneur to continuously redefine his or her relationship to the business and to its employees.

4. Delegating involves patience, teaching, correcting, and trusting others.

5. Delegation transforms an entrepreneur into a manager. Learning how to delegate and implementing the appropriate processes and measurements are all necessary for an entrepreneur to evolve from doer to manager.

6. Learning how to manage people individually and as a team required most entrepreneurs to learn new skills and become more emotionally intelligent.

7. As you push decisions down, you must spend more time in alignment and prioritization, making sure people are focused on the right thing, that they are communicating well and getting along, and that they've got the requisite skill sets to do what needs to be done.

8. Learning and developing one's teaching, managing, and leadership skills emerges as mission-critical to continuing growth.

9

THE SILVER BULLET
Highly Engaged Employees

CEO QUOTES

- "You can build a star system or a team system."
- "If you are in it just for the money, you'll never succeed."
- "If growth is the primary objective, it is going to be very hard to keep people aligned and motivated."
- "But being a great place to work takes work—it takes positive effort to keep it going."
- "The big danger as you grow is how do you keep true to who you were."

HIGH EMPLOYEE ENGAGEMENT

In Chapter 7, we examined my public company growth research, which showed that high organic growth companies (HOGs) generally had highly engaged employees who were dedicated to constant improvement. Other significant academic research supports the finding that highly engaged, satisfied employees have a positive impact on customer satisfaction.[1] Employees' happiness and belief in the business is transmitted to customers and can result in high customer satisfaction.

Previous chapters have documented that business growth requires change in a wide range of parameters. Growth alters the number and, often, types of employees. It necessitates an increased number of rules, controls, and processes. Growth adds managers and functional specialists. In addition, growth requires entrepreneurs to grow personally and professionally. These growth-related changes evolve as the business grows and new employees join and others leave the business.

As the business continues to grow, different people, processes, and infrastructure are needed to support that growth. Often, both additional managers and qualitatively different types of managers are needed to manage the evolving needs of the growing business. The changes in personnel, processes, and infrastructure all contribute to major shifts in the interpersonal dynamics of the business. These changes are always challenging, sometimes tumultuous, and can be catastrophic if not handled well.

THE GLUE IS NECESSARY

What binds people together during the continuous changes that mark a company's growth? What is the glue? What business environments inspire employees to work hard and continuously improve rather than view their jobs as merely a means to a paycheck? What employee behaviors does an inspiring business environment encourage or discourage? What behaviors should be encouraged or discouraged? What are the rules of interpersonal engagement in the workplace?

One of the answers is fostering the right business culture to support the growth of the business as well as the people within it. Culture encompasses the written and unwritten rules, beliefs, and values that a business aspires to and actually embodies in the daily behaviors of its employees with each other, suppliers, customers, and the community.

Culture is not a neutral concept. Some business cultures foster high employee engagement and high performance, while others can be corrosive to the very aims a business hopes to achieve. Good cultures do not just happen; they take constant work and upkeep. A business cultures reflects the founder. As examples, consider how the Eyebobs' culture, described in Chapter 2, reflects Julie Allinson's personality. Think about how John Gabbert, described in Chapter 7, built a Room & Board culture that reflected his passion for quality and the importance of relationships. Think about how the Defender Direct culture, described in Chapter 8, evidenced Dave Lindsey's belief in learning and becoming better.

CULTURE DRIVES HIGH PERFORMANCE

What is the relationship between culture and high performance? The research on high performance organizations has consistently linked high employee engagement to high performance. High employee engagement generally results from employees having an emotional attachment to the organization that is more meaningful than simply having a job. Creating an emotional engagement between employees and a business can result in high performance, loyalty, and productivity.

These are all drivers of excellent execution that translate into satisfied customers and business success. But high-performance business cultures and the results they generate do not happen in a vacuum. They occur when organizations have meaningful purposes, with values articulated by leaders who "walk the talk." High-performance organizations consistently promote and teach the values of business excellence. They also measure and reward behaviors demonstrating those values and penalize behaviors that violate those values.

High performance organizations do not just happen. They must be built, nurtured, and constantly lived.

IT IS NOT ABOUT THE ENTREPRENEUR

My research documented that, in growing their businesses, many entrepreneurs had to shift their perspective about the business. This shift was from a largely self-focused perspective to one that encompassed a broader view, including recognition of the importance of developing the skills and engagement of the people making that growth possible—the employees.

The original motivations for the entrepreneur may not have been entirely altruistic and likely included a drive to make money, build a business, or be successful. However, at some point the entrepreneur realizes that it is essential to attract and retain high-quality employees who will work hard to grow the business. How do you build a great place to work? How do you create a work environment that inspires excellence and high performance? How do you make the work or mission of the business meaningful for nonowners?

THE AWAKENING: THE "AHA!"

Many entrepreneurs are passionate, driven people, comfortable in knowing that they can get the job done. As the business grows beyond the size that an entrepreneur directly controls everything, however, he or she realizes that continued success depends increasingly on others. Often, that realization comes only after some bumps in the road, or even catastrophes, related to finding, hiring, training, and retaining good employees and managers.

The realization of the critical importance of committed employees in growing the business transforms the entrepreneur's perspective. Employees become the necessary "end" rather than simply the "means" to an end.

WHAT DO ENTREPRENEURS WANT?

Why do entrepreneurs start businesses? What do they want? The reasons are varied and personal, but there are some commonly expressed reasons:

- Some entrepreneurs, like John Gabbert of Room & Board, start a business because they want more control over their destiny or they are tired of conforming to someone else's business plan.

- Others saw an opportunity to launch a different way of doing business and were not able to sell their employers on that vision. Entrepreneurs with a different business vision include the founders of Wal-Mart, Home Depot, and the company formerly known as EDS.

- Some entrepreneurs, like Dave Lindsey of Defender Direct, burn out on the dynamics of big company politics.

- Others are forced to become entrepreneurs out of necessity after getting laid off.

- Some, like Julie Allinson of Eyebobs, identify a customer need and ask, "Why not me?"

Whatever the initial incentive for starting a business, most entrepreneurs have the goal of earning a living doing something they enjoy and that provides personal validation and rewards. Many want the opportunity to flourish on their merits and not be impeded by inept bosses or corporate politics.

WHAT DO EMPLOYEES WANT?

In many ways, employees do not differ from entrepreneurs in what they want from their jobs. Many want to be associated with a "good" business—a business that produces good products and services that meet a valued customer need and a business that treats people fairly and honestly.

In addition, given that employees necessarily have bosses, research shows that employees want to be respected and listened to by their bosses. They want to have some control over the content and execution of their jobs, the opportunity to excel, and to do work they feel good about and want to share with their family.[2]

A consistent finding is that money is not enough to motivate employees or to get them fully engaged in the business culture. High employee engagement cannot be purchased or dictated. Likewise, employee engagement cannot be promoted simply by aiming at the target of growth for growth's sake. One entrepreneur expressed that point this way: "Growth is not good enough. We are actually doing something that is right. There is a mission behind it. There is value—something we care about that drives us." Another stated:

If you are in it for just the money, you will never succeed. But if you are in it because you love your product and you love your customer and you love what you do and you want to make them happy, you will never have to worry about wealth.

ENABLING A POSITIVE BUSINESS CULTURE
AND EMPLOYEE ENGAGEMENT

So, if financial incentives and business goals of growth are inadequate to foster a positive business culture and employee engagement, what variables are important? There are several.

The Manager's Behavior Is Key

First, employee satisfaction translates directly to employee loyalty, productivity, and customer satisfaction. Business research tells us is that the

EXHIBIT 9.1

Many entrepreneurs learned the fundamental lesson that if you treat employees well, they will treat customers well.

number one determinant of employee satisfaction and engagement in a job is how the manager treats the employee. Does an employee's manager treat the employee with respect? Listen to the employee? Teach the employee? Care about the employee as a person? Help the employee advance? Review the employee's performance frequently and fairly?

Not surprisingly, managers are more likely to act in those positive, enhancing manners if the entrepreneur treats the manager in the same manner. Building a business culture that promotes employee satisfaction is essential because as a business grows most customers have direct contact with line employees, not with the entrepreneur.

CHARACTERISTICS OF HIGH-PERFORMANCE CULTURES

The challenge for the entrepreneur and his or her managers is how to create the right business culture to produce high employee satisfaction and engagement. My high organic growth company research found that the following characteristics helped create a positive business culture:

1. "ownership;"

2. promotion-from-within policies;

3. education and training opportunities;

4. creating a "family" atmosphere;

5. constant communication about the key values of the business;

6. the celebration of successes;

7. consistent and fair reward and promotion policies;

8. information transparency;

9. living the values; and

10. hiring for "cultural fit."

The Room & Board, Trilogy Health Services, and Leaders Bank stories in this book illustrate these points.

Research Findings on High-Performance Cultures
My findings about the importance of fostering a positive business culture are consistent with the findings of Collins and Porras discussed in *Built to Last*.[3] In fact, their twelve myth-shattering findings provide a good roadmap for any entrepreneur who is trying to build a business that can endure.[4] Consistent with my research findings regarding high organic growth public companies, Collins and Porras reported preserving many aspects of a small company soul in a large company body. Collins and Porras also found that successful growth was often accomplished by having highly engaged employees led by humble, passionate, home-grown leaders who, in many cases, were neither charismatic nor visionary.

It is important to note that building the right cultural environment is not a one-time accomplishment. Because business growth itself is a dynamic enterprise, crafting a positive business culture requires constant adjustments.

As one entrepreneur stated: "But being a great place to work takes work. It's like being a homeowner. If you do not do anything to your house, it will fall apart. It actually takes positive effort to keep it going."

MISSION, VALUES, AND CULTURE
Entrepreneurs try to create meaning and employee engagement by focusing on questions like:

- "Why do we exist?"
- "What do we do that is important?"
- "What do we stand for?"
- "How should we behave?"
- "How are we helping our customers and employees?"
- "How do we create a place that good people want to be part of?"
- "What behaviors can we not tolerate?"

As discussed in Chapter 7, growth is more than an overarching business strategy. Successful growth requires an internal system that links consistently, seamlessly, and in a self-reinforcing manner a business's culture, structure, leadership model, human resources policies, measurements, and rewards to drive desired behaviors that answer questions such as those just posed.

Promoting a positive-growth business culture cannot simply be an abstract goal. Businesses and their leaders must lead by example and, yes, walk the talk. Modeling the business culture is easier said than done.

Many business people think that implementing high employee engagement policies necessarily requires that you be soft on employee accountability and performance. This is not so—you can have both. Look at the Room & Board, Defender Direct, Inc., Enchanting Travels, Trilogy Health Services, SecureWorks, and Leaders Bank stories for examples of high performance, accountability, and a positive, engaging work environment.

MEANING, FUN, AND EMOTIONAL REWARDS

My research found three consistent areas that entrepreneurs focused on in building positive growth company cultures:

1. meaning;

2. fun; and

3. emotional rewards.

Meaning: The "Why" This Business Exists

For several businesses in my study, indentifying the meaning of the enterprise translated into finding a purpose in the business beyond making money. Nonfinancial elements of meaning included helping people, saving lives, making the world a better place because your product contributes to a healthy life, providing care to the sick, providing financial services to growing companies, or providing healthy and delicious foods to people with allergies. Meaning in the workplace also included nonemployment-related activities such as collaborating in doing charitable projects with the company organizing and/or supporting such efforts.

Fun: Celebrate Learning

Incorporating fun into the business culture translated to the celebration of individual and group successes in business and life outside of work as well as big events such as birthdays, anniversaries, and births. Such celebrations were found to build bonds among employees similar to the celebration of such events within a family. In addition, many companies also supported spontaneously ordering pizza or ice cream or holding barbecues and other get-togethers with employees and their families.

Emotional Rewards: Money Is Not Enough

You cannot buy emotional engagement. Money is not enough to generate a high-performance environment. The research shows that the positive impact of salary raises or bonus payments decreases substantially after a few weeks because they become part of the baseline for employees. Successful business builders learned this and changed their methods accordingly.

The importance of emotional rewards in the business culture was evidenced by the efforts to showcase individual and group successes. This included formal recognitions for performance; being acknowledged as contributing to an effort; giving awards, gifts, and trips for jobs well done; providing education opportunities and promotions; and in giving small gifts that said "thank you" and "we care about you." Some entrepreneurs evidently learned from their elementary school teachers the importance of gold stars in promoting performance!

Taking "Ownership"

To attain high employee engagement, employees need to feel like they "own" their job in that they have input into how it is done and some stake in the outcome. This feeling of ownership also has two corollaries. Employees want some control over their destiny in that if they work hard and perform according to the rules, they want to be evaluated and rewarded fairly.

This feeling of ownership can be actual, through stock ownership or incentive compensation, or virtual, through emotional rewards evidenced by awards, trips, education opportunities, and promotion opportunities.

Several entrepreneurs believed strongly that "if you want people to act like owners, then make them actual owners" of the business through the distribution of stock. A few companies I studied gave stock ownership to 100 percent of the employees. Others gave an ownership stake to all managers. Others limited stock ownership to just a few people.

Those that did not spread stock ownership broadly used virtual "ownership" mechanisms to make people feel like appreciated and valued members of the company. Some of these mechanisms included annual rewards for achieving specific targets, or semi-annual firm-wide holidays with spouses at a grand vacation destination. Others built internal training and education programs and designed career paths for employees, showing them how they could progress to more responsibility and more compensation.

HIRING FOR "CULTURAL FIT"

As companies grew and maintenance of the positive business culture became a priority, many entrepreneurs formalized a process to hire for "cultural fit." The mechanism for assessing "cultural fit" varied, but some created a cultural scorecard or required top management, who served as protectors of the culture, to approve all hires. Others tried to limit new hires to those recommended and vouched for by current employees.

Even with such efforts aimed at ensuring a "cultural fit," hiring mistakes sometimes occurred. Entrepreneurs often learned the hard way that employees that do not fit culturally can rarely be retrofitted and that the best course is to recognize the bad choice and rectify it quickly.

The importance of identifying and remedying a poor employee choice quickly should be emphasized, and business policies should be tailored to ensure this happens. In fast-growing companies, some entrepreneurs graded managers on employee satisfaction and retention, which were viewed as critical to promoting a positive business culture. However, if employees were terminated within six months of hiring, suggesting the recognition of a poor "cultural fit," those terminations did not count against the manager's employee retention numbers. Thus, the adage: "Hire slowly and fire quickly."

MEASURE POSITIVE BEHAVIORS

Measurements of employee performance are critical but challenging for entrepreneurs in growing companies. Entrepreneurs must continually define and redefine what behaviors are desired to drive value and make the business a great place to work. Then they must craft useful measures of those behaviors and provide feedback and rewards to employees. This is an iterative process of trying to be more and more granular in promoting the specific elements of employee performance.

Not only must the entrepreneur and his or her management team be able to identify and reward employee behaviors, it is important that the basis for identifying good and bad performance as well as the standards for promotion, awards, and bonuses be clearly defined and transparent to employees and both fairly and consistently applied.

INFORMATION TRANSPARENCY AND TRUST

Many companies routinely practiced full disclosure to all employees of the business strategy, annual goals, and financial results. The belief behind this disclosure is that greater employee engagement is attained when employees are equipped with a better understanding of why their job is important and how it fits into the business strategy.

Building employees' trust can take the form of meaningful feedback; training and education opportunities designed to help employees advance; and transparent, consistent, and fairly applied performance measures. This trust is reinforced by constant, honest communications—keeping employees informed of the business's successes, challenges, and failures.

SERVICE COMPANIES

While having a positive business culture is important in all businesses, it is particularly critical in service businesses because success is usually dependent on employees' direct, one-on-one interactions with customers. What we do know is that satisfied employees make for satisfied customers. This result is understandable because people who are satisfied in their jobs project that to others. It leads to better performance and to customers who enjoy doing business with you.

Because the information is more easily available, most examples of culture that lead to high employee engagement, loyalty, and productivity are public companies. Companies such as Southwest Airlines, Costco, Starbucks, Whole Foods, Levy Restaurants, Best Buy, UPS, and Sysco have different forms of high-performance-enabling cultures.

The lack of private company information does not lessen the importance of building a private company culture that generates high employee performance. The private organizations that I studied, including SAS, Chik-fil-A, Patagonia, Room & Board, San Antonio Spurs, and the United States Marine Corps, also have high-performance-enabling cultures.

BEHAVIOR IS KEY

Entrepreneurs learn that, to grow their business successfully, they need to enlist others in their journey. Eventually, they also realize that money is not enough. A business needs a "soul" in that it needs to be a meaningful organization. Culture helps define that meaning and sets boundaries for behavior. But words alone are not enough. The entrepreneur must exhibit behaviors on a daily basis that reinforce the values and meaning that he or she wants to create. Employees watch the manager, leader, and entrepreneur as role models. Granular behaviors send messages, both good and bad.

Entrepreneurs must become very sensitive to the impact that they have on others and on the emotional environment daily. One entrepreneur told me that every day is "show time;" in that he learned that he was on stage every day and he needed to behave accordingly. This takes self-discipline, self-management, and sensitivity. Again, people skills are critical to growth.

TRILOGY HEALTH SERVICES, LLC[5]

Randy Bufford is the leader who built Trilogy Health Services into a high-performance service company in a very difficult industry—providing residential health care to an aging population. Health service is a difficult job that has intrinsic meaning but, like public school teaching, is not usually a high-paying job. How did Bufford overcome these difficulties to build something successful and special?

History

Trilogy Health Services, LLC is a privately held senior-living-services company with headquarters in Louisville, Kentucky. It was launched in December 1997, by Randall J. Bufford, Trilogy's president and chief executive officer, whose vision was to create "health campuses" that provided a continuum of personalized care for older adults—from independent and assisted living to skilled nursing and rehabilitative service.

Under Bufford's leadership, Trilogy grew to 17 facilities in seven years. In 2004, Frontenac, a Chicago-based private-equity firm, bought the company with the intention of further expanding its network of facilities. Three years later, when Trilogy had 44 health campuses, another private-equity firm, Swiss-based Lydian Capital, bought it for $350 million.

With Bufford still at the helm, Trilogy continued to grow, maintaining its focus on under-served, nonurban communities in the Midwest. Rising demand for Trilogy's services, fueled by an increasingly large senior population, allowed its facilities to operate at nearly full capacity—just above 90 percent.[6] Trilogy's revenues hit $257.8 million in 2007, having shot up 200.4 percent from its revenues in 2004, just enough for the company to be ranked 1,871 on *Inc.*'s list of the 5,000 fastest growing private companies in the United States in 2008. In addition to earning top ratings in customer-satisfaction surveys, Trilogy was voted the Best Place to Work in Kentucky by its employees two years in a row, not a small feat in an industry where turnover rates were as high as 150 percent.

Culture Is the Competitive Edge
By 2009, Trilogy operated 56 health campuses in Kentucky, Indiana, Ohio, Michigan, and Illinois, all based on a culture of compassionate service. Bufford firmly believed that it was Trilogy's culture—with its emphasis on people and service before earnings—that formed the company's competitive edge.

"We have a simple philosophy," Bufford said. "If we take great care of our employees, they take great care of our customers, and we have a bottom line. Our challenge as we grow is to make sure that we keep the culture high and don't lose sight of our mission."

The Founder
Bufford was born in the Midwest. His father was a career military man in the U.S. Air Force, and Bufford grew up on bases across the country. After graduating from the University of Louisville with a bachelor's degree in accounting in 1981, he started his career as auditor with the accounting firm of Arthur Young & Company. Then he held various positions at the Cardinal Group, a Louisville, Kentucky-based nursing home company, where he rose to the position of chief financial officer.

In 1993, Bufford started Transitional Health Services, a senior-care company in Louisville, and, in a management-led buyout, acquired selected assets of the Cardinal Group. He served as the company's general manager and CEO until it merged with Centennial HealthCare Corporation.

During his tenure at Centennial, Bufford was the executive vice president of business development. He oversaw the operations of Centennial's ancillary service companies, participated in the 1997 IPO, and played a role in the company's acquisition efforts.

Trilogy Health Services: A Cash-Starved Start-Up

As Bufford rolled out Trilogy's first 10 health campuses in 1997, the business community was in the midst of the Internet bubble, and one of the biggest challenges his company faced was access to capital. "We're a very capital-intensive sector," Bufford said and added that, at a time when his business was in need of funding, "there was no capital—zero—being given to any organizations."

Bufford and his management had been aware that the Balanced Budget Act of 1997 was going to affect nursing homes, and they planned accordingly when making their financial projections. What Bufford and his executives did not realize, however, was the effect the Balanced Budget Act would have on Trilogy's peers, and "how that would ripple down into lack of investor confidence in the sector as far as making investments," Bufford said. He continued, "Seven out of the top nine public companies in the senior-living-services sector went bankrupt. We could not convince people that we were a viable model."

To fund the start-up, Bufford said:

We primarily relied on management's capital and then some of the real estate investment trusts; we partnered with them for bridge loans. I had one debt piece. Our new CFO looked at it and said, "Is that right? Is that 22 percent interest?" I'm, like, yes sir, it is, but it kept us out of bankruptcy.

To make matters worse, "While we were starting our business, we went through a very difficult time in our sector as far as reimbursement," Bufford said. To ward off failure and avoid sharing the fate of many of Trilogy's peers, "We had to do a good bit of juggling and emptying our own piggybank to make sure we had sufficient resources to run the company on a day-to-day basis." And, Bufford continued:

We stretched our vendors pretty thin. But we did that with good communications; we had one-on-one meetings with all of our major vendors, our top 20 that get 80 percent of our vendor dollars. We never stretched the little guys, who are probably not as well capitalized, and they're in our local community. So we pushed our top 20 vendors hard.

The Trilogy Health Campus

Before Bufford launched Trilogy, he canvassed potential customers and used their feedback to put together a business plan for a group of nursing facilities in Kentucky. He learned that the elderly preferred to stay at home and receive any needed health care services in the least-restrictive setting and were willing to pay for such services. Based on his research on the evolving needs of older adults, Bufford developed an innovative senior-care model, which offered a continuum of services on one health campus: adult day care, assisted living, and skilled nursing. According to Bufford, the services were affordable to middle-income seniors.

Trilogy's prototypical campus covered approximately 48,000 square feet, and was built on a "town-square" model. Residents usually lived in private rooms configured in "neighborhoods" that surrounded a town square. Each neighborhood had a small, one-person nursing station instead of the more common large central one. To encourage consistent and personalized care, caregivers were assigned to only six or seven residents in a neighborhood. Bufford thought "the neighborhood concept lends itself to person-centered care."[7]

A 60-bed skilled-nursing facility and an assisted-living facility with 35 apartments were separate buildings located on opposite sides of the campus. Each had its own parking, entrances, dining room, and common-space areas but shared infrastructure, which contributed to operating efficiency. On most campuses, the assisted-living operation consisted of 23 traditional units and a separate, secure wing with 12 apartments for elderly residents who suffered from dementia.

Trilogy management took great care to ensure that senior-living centers they operated had state-of-the-art facilities. In some markets, Trilogy established independent living villas and patio homes surrounding its health campuses. Overall, Trilogy buildings had a less institutional feel than older facilities found in many senior-living communities.

A Culture of Compassionate Service

Having attractive facilities certainly enhanced the environment in which Trilogy residents lived, but it was Trilogy's culture of compassionate service that convinced many visiting seniors to stay. "We've tried very hard to ensure that we have high standards at each of our communities," Bufford said, adding that one of the vital elements of Trilogy's culture was an understanding that growth in earnings was an outcome of great customer service, not the other way around, and that focusing on financial returns ahead of service almost always guaranteed failure. Bufford emphasized that Trilogy's commitment to providing exceptional customer service was what differentiated his company from its peers:

I can assure you that our financial results are not what we think about first thing in the morning. It's important that we keep track of those and make capital investments in our information systems, but those don't ensure success. In fact, if you're not doing well, all those will do for you is tell you how bad you're doing. We're in a business that's all about service and all about taking great care of people. And that's one key ingredient that's often missing.

Creating the Best Place to Work

Bufford asserted that the best way to ensure customer satisfaction was to create a nurturing environment for Trilogy's front-line employees—the caregivers, nursing assistants, nurses, and others. "I want them to say that this is the best place they've ever worked," Bufford admitted, emphasizing that "if we take great care of our employees, then they'll take great care of our customers." He and his management team worked hard to promote "the kind of culture where our employees feel supported by a culture that says, 'No person is any more important than others.'" (See Exhibit 9.2.) Bufford thought that the right attitude at the top was essential to unlocking the potential of front-line employees:

It starts with a culture of management where we are leading our employees, not directing them. We have executive directors, and I've even pondered whether that

EXHIBIT 9.2
Our Culture: E's to Successful Customer Service

Expectations
- We have high expectations of Excellence in customer service for our residents.
  - Zero tolerance for failure to execute our Trilogy Service Standards.
  - Zero tolerance for failure to have prompt response and resolution of customer needs and concerns.
- We have high expectations for employee conduct.
  - Zero tolerance for patient abuse.
  - Zero tolerance for harassment of any type.
  - Zero tolerance for ethical misconduct.
- Set high expectations for yourself . . . you'll be surprised at what you achieve.
- Campus leaders have the responsibility to communicate our company's expectations to their staff! We take very seriously our leadership of high expectations! You cannot ask someone to do something you will not do yourself!

Excellence
- We should strive to exceed our Customer's Expectations at all times. Our focus is Customer Service Excellence!
- Excellence is achieved by having compassion for our residents. You have to love the elderly to work for this company!
- Small things are what create excellence:
  - Everyone does the basics.
  - Pay attention to details as they are the ingredients to Excellence.
  - Excellence is created by the execution of our Trilogy Service Standards.
  - Go out of your way to help our customers or another employee . . . your efforts will return dividends to you.

Employees
- The Right Employees make the difference!
  - Great Physical Plant + Average Employees = Average Facility
  - Average Physical Plant + Great Employees = Great Facility

(continued)

- The Right Employees have the following attributes:
  - Compassion for service to others.
  - Willingness to support the team ahead of themselves.
  - Understanding of the importance of details in achieving service Excellence.
  - Readily embrace hard work as a key to success.
  - Willingness to be an example and leader for others.
- Employees must work as a team.
  - Everyone pulls on same rope . . . customer service.
  - To get everyone on the same rope—communicate!
    - Communication must be effective and often.
    - Communication goes both ways . . . input and feedback are EXPECTED!
- When employees are treated like royalty, they will treat our customers like royalty.

Empowerment

- Every employee is empowered to improve our services for our customers.
  - Empowerment means saying yes first and then figuring out how to meet the objectives.
  - We have to be solution oriented to have Empowerment in Customer Service.
- Leadership and Education unlock the empowerment door.
- Employees need training on Customer Service . . . it is an absolute must to create Empowerment!
- Entrepreneurial spirit means the most important people in the organization are the people closest to our customers . . . our caregivers!

Education

- Education and Training are Customer Service Separators.
  - Employee orientation, in-service and seminars is an essential part of employee retention and customer service success.
  - The most effective education is done by Example. We teach and train best by being role models of our culture, customer service, operating procedures, etc.
  - Training is a personal responsibility that runs on a two-way street.

EXHIBIT 9.2 *(continued)*

- There is no better way to show your commitment and caring to an Employee than through Education and Training.
- Education is the best investment our company makes!

Earnings
- We have a responsibility to our shareholders to achieve a return on their investment.
  - Positive financial returns will allow for re-investment in improving our services and campus environment.
  - Earnings generated in the local market can be returned to the community through taxes and charitable contributions or services.
  - We should seek out ways to be a partner to our community, both on a financial and service approach.
- Improvements in service lead to growth in earnings, which allows the company to invest in more ways to improve service. This is known as the Flywheel to Success!
- Focusing on Earnings ahead of Service is a start to the "Doom Loop." We understand that financial returns follow great customer service and not vice versa!

Execution
- Now all we have to do is execute.
- Execution does not happen by accident. Leadership is required to spur along the right combination of execution ingredients.
  - Hard work
  - Teamwork
  - Compassionate commitment
  - Communication
  - Trilogy Service Standards
- Execution success requires connecting the values of the company to what the task at hand involves!

is the right title because we don't direct anybody to do anything. As soon as you start ordering people around, you get the bare minimum performance.

Bufford and his executives devoted a lot of time to coaching Trilogy's midlevel managers, encouraging them to read and educate themselves to become better leaders. "We read books as a company," Bufford said, citing Ken Blanchard's *Know Can Do!* as one of the reading assignments.[8] "We took some thoughts from it to help [our managers] understand how to lead our people into wanting to have the right performance and creating an environment where they'll do the right thing without thinking about it," Bufford said.

We Work Hard on Humility
In his coaching efforts, Bufford stressed that leadership was not an innate gift that some had and others lacked. "We tell our managers that leadership is a learned business skill," Bufford said. "It starts with somebody who's willing to humble themselves for the benefit of others. We work hard on humility."

Even Trilogy's mission statement, which was printed on the back of everyone's name badge, addressed the issue of humility (see Exhibit 9.3). Promoting humility companywide went hand-in-hand with fighting arrogance. "Overall, we've got a good culture of not having arrogance,"

EXHIBIT 9.3
Trilogy's Mission Statement

- We are committed to exceeding our customer's expectations.
Excellence is achieved by execution of our Trilogy Service Standards.
- The right employees make the difference.
Communication and training are the keys to success.
- The team approach works best.
Let everyone contribute to his or her fullest potential.
- Pay attention to the details.
The details separate the winners from the losers.
- Take what the company is doing very seriously but not yourself.
Our company has zero tolerance for egos or politics.

Bufford said. "And when I see it, I really emphasize that it can tear you down pretty quickly."

Walking the Talk

In addition to offering a competitive benefits package for its employees, Trilogy put in place a number of policies and programs to help retain and motivate them. "We walk our talk, and we back it up with tangible things. We have employee retention programs into which we pour literally seven figures every year," Bufford said and added that in 2008 when gasoline prices were rising, every full-time employee who had been with Trilogy six months or longer was eligible for a $30-a-month subsidy to cover increasing commuting costs. "Whether they're line staff or managers, everybody in the company gets it, except for ownership," Bufford said. He continued:

Once a month we do a recognition party; we call it the ER3 party. If it's your six-month anniversary—you get recognized. If you have perfect attendance—you get recognized. If you had a baby or your daughter-in-law had a baby, we give you a Trilogy baby onesie. All those things create an environment where it's going to be a little easier not to get burned out.

Employee Training and Education

At Bufford's direction, Trilogy emphasized employee education and training early on. "We've always understood that we're a service business, and we've invested heavily in training our staff," Bufford said. "There's no better way to show employees that you care about them than investing in them."

For Trilogy's new hires, learning started on their first day of work with a 30-minute customer-service training program, followed by two hours of in-service training. Adhering to the principle of always putting residents and their needs first was at the core of Trilogy's training program and an important part of what differentiated the facility.

Making Work Fun

In an effort to make the training program engaging, Trilogy tried to mix in elements that were fun. For example, one year's theme was "A Race to Customer Service," and the winner received tickets to the Indy 500 and an overnight hotel stay. The program also covered such customer-service basics as speaking to anyone within close proximity (10 feet), regardless of whether that person was a patient, family member, co-worker, or vendor; making eye contact; speaking clearly; displaying good body language, hygiene, and overall demeanor; and speaking positively about the facility when out in the community.[9]

Trilogy's customer-service principles were reinforced monthly through posters and payroll stuffers, "something that will reintroduce and remind people of that principle," said Rhonda Sanders, a registered nurse and one of Trilogy's trainers. "Randy Bufford can have the vision, but it takes each person to make the difference," said Sanders, adding that at Trilogy, they talked constantly about the importance of each and every staff member.[10]

Employee Communications

In addition to training and education, Bufford invested in employee communications, which, he believed, was essential for gaining buy-in for company and facility goals. "The more investments we make in two things—training and communications—the better we get with our employees," he said. Employees received company and campus newsletters containing messages from Bufford. A bulletin board at each facility displayed messages about Trilogy goals and progress. Facility leaders routinely pulled aside five or six employees for "coffee breaks" at which they received coffee and donuts while learning about a new initiative or goal. Bufford believed that reaching employees in a small-group setting helped maintain a consistent message.

Recruiting

Bufford's efforts to create a culture focused on people—residents and employees—paid off: In 2008, Trilogy applied for the "Best Places to Work in Kentucky" program and was the number one company in the small/medium category; it repeated the feat the following year. Snatching the top spot two years in a row was a great morale boost; it also helped Trilogy compete for the best health care workers.

Bufford took recruiting seriously. "First and foremost, you have to get the right employees," he said and revealed that Trilogy had a simple question on its job application: "Do you love the elderly?" Bufford described the ideal candidate Trilogy was trying to attract:

We want to find somebody who's looking for a compassionate return, who is not there just to pick up a check, because that person is not going to find satisfaction in the difficulties we face. And we don't beat around the bush about the difficulties. We tell our potential employees, how many businesses are open 24/7, 365 days a year with customers who really don't want to be with us?

Lowering Employee Turnover
Trilogy's turnover was significantly lower than the industry norm, and a distinct advantage for Trilogy, which competed in an industry rife with transience. According to Bufford, employee turnover rates in the health care industry averaged between 90 and 150 percent a year. Trilogy's turnover rate in 2009 was only 36 percent, a figure Bufford planned to shrink to 25 percent by 2011.

Training and Retaining New Hires
The comparatively high employee retention rate at Trilogy was partly due to the time, care, and expense the company invested in the onboarding and training processes. In 2004, Trilogy launched a Caregiver Preceptor Program to help new hires acclimate. "We've got a buddy who's been specially trained in onboarding leadership, making sure new employees feel like they're part of the family," Bufford said. Trilogy preceptors also conducted culture and leadership training for new employees at off-site retreats.

Because approximately 80 percent of Trilogy's turnover took place in the first six months of employment, during that time the new hires wore blue name badges. "The idea behind it is that we all know you're new, we're giving you extra love, we're telling you that we want to celebrate that badge turning white with you," Bufford explained. Employees who satisfactorily completed six months on the job took part in a special celebration and became eligible for a base-wage increase and additional benefits.

More Effective Hiring Processes
Trilogy's management worked hard to address the issue of employee turnover by reviewing its hiring practices and trying to improve them. Bufford

admitted that the reason front-line employees left the company—or were asked to leave—was twofold:

We hire the wrong people, or the people we hire say the right things in the interview process, but they really don't mean it when it comes to how hard we work and not playing politics. So, some of that turnover is a result of us saying, after the 90-day trial period, "Hey, you're probably not the right person for us." And the other part is—we don't do a good job screening. We've never gotten great results out of the reference process, but we're trying to intensify that from a networking standpoint, trying to find people who have known this person in employment in our communities, versus what this person puts on their reference sheet.

To get a better shot at improving employee retention, Trilogy put in place an internal referral program and awarded its employees bonuses for referring candidates that the company brought on board, provided that they stayed for at least a year.

Trilogy's Growth Strategy
Trilogy grew its portfolio of senior-living communities by building brand-new health campuses in attractive markets and through acquisitions of well-run nursing homes, whose management and culture were in line with Trilogy's. After buying land adjacent to the newly acquired properties, Trilogy would then build state-of-the art facilities to replace the old ones.

Bufford's preference was to own Trilogy real estate rather than lease it. But when Trilogy was a start-up, it was so cash-starved that leasing was the only viable option. In 2008, however, the company was in a position to negotiate a purchase of 14 of its leased facilities. "It's a good time for us to buy since we have capital," Bufford said. "It's tough for them to raise capital so they're selling assets. We probably won't ever get to owning 100 percent but, I'd say, within two years we'll be pretty close to about 90 percent."

Bufford's expansion efforts centered on underserved, nonurban markets, where Trilogy was growing in clusters, "branching out from outposts, and filling in and backfilling," as Bufford explained it. In reviewing Trilogy's disciplined expansion strategy, Bufford attributed the company's success to "staying focused on how we grow the tight markets we are in, where they're located in proximity to other markets." He continued:

We've had a chance to go to a small town in Tennessee that on paper looks great, but it's a long way from Louisville, and we don't have any sister facilities there. We first determined the depth of the market around that location in Tennessee and whether we could get five facilities in that area. We studied Michigan that way, and we took our lone outpost to southern Michigan, near our Indiana properties, and we're now up to three properties with a fourth coming. That's our opportunities—to remain focused on our geographic area and do the filling in. We like clustering because it's easier to grow that way and transfer the culture.

Transferring the Culture

For Bufford, successful culture transfer started with getting the right people on a new facility's management team, which often meant pulling some of Trilogy's seasoned veterans from other locations. For example, when Trilogy opened a new health campus in Bellevue, Ohio, in 2008, four members of its 10-person team of department heads came from two other nearby Trilogy facilities.

But conquering new markets also required tapping the outside talent pool. "We look for what I call the 'providers of choice' to recruit from, primarily through cold calling, to see if we can find leaders who match up with our culture." The select candidates for top management positions were routinely invited to spend time on Trilogy's health campuses about 120 to 180 days before the hiring process started. Bufford explained:

They live in a hotel for a week or two at a time, visiting our four or five campuses. Just meet our people, understand what we do, and start capturing the culture and the leadership components by seeing it in action versus us sitting at a new location, telling them. We do peer reviews, which are twice a year inspections, so, for example, they would go and spend time on peer reviews.

Building the Management Team

When Bufford started hiring more senior people, the COO position was the toughest to fill. "We're an operations-oriented company, and the depth of talent in our sector is not that strong," Bufford said. The first COO, who came on board when Trilogy had only 10 health campuses, could not keep up with the growing company, and his job soon outgrew him. "I knew that he didn't have the capacity," Bufford said. "I pretty much had to set his agendas and follow up, and we need to be self-starters to grow."

In 2002, after an intensive search, Bufford hired Philip Caldwell, who proved to be the right man for the job. "He's been with us six years. I brought him in as co-COO while we worked the other gentleman into the idea that maybe he couldn't be the COO forever."

Bufford worked with Caldwell to ensure that Trilogy had a deep talent bench, "assembling that next layer of operational management," as he said and added, "We have four out of five, we're very solid. We have one gentleman who's willing to learn, so Phil and I are investing a lot of time with him, because we think it's probably easier to grow him into the position then to find somebody else."

Leadership of Continuous Improvement
Despite Trilogy's success, Bufford remained acutely aware that failure was always close at hand. He kept his finger on the company's pulse, making an effort to visit Trilogy campuses at least twice a year. "A big part of our business is that we don't run it out of a corporate office," Bufford said. He explained:

Even though we have a central office, our business really happens in the field. Our employees see a lot of me, and also the COO and the area managers. Occasionally, I'll sub in if we have an area manager's position open. I might grab two or three facilities and just take those under my wing, because it keeps me close to the business and sharp on management and things on the field level.

Bufford understood the dangers of success; he knew it could breed complacency and arrogance, which he worked hard to fight. For Trilogy to continue to thrive, he argued, its management had to lead by example, focusing on how to do things better. "We call it LOCI—Leadership of Continuous Improvement," Bufford said and then elaborated:

If I don't put my feet on the floor every day, thinking about how this organization's going to get better, and if our employees and our executives aren't doing the same exact thing, we got a good shot at going backwards. It's almost like you're on a treadmill and you better keep working it, because as soon as your employees think that it's not important to you, it becomes unimportant to them. As long as we continue to get better at each and every campus, we're going to continue to grow at eight or ten units a year. And I manage that way, I tell people we have lots of metrics and numbers, and the number really is not important to me; it's really the delta in the number. Everything we do is pretty much keyed around, "Are we getting better, and can we do that better?"

LESSONS FROM THE TRILOGY HEALTH SERVICES STORY

Randy Bufford understood that the silver bullet of business success was having highly engaged employees. He knew that to attain that result he needed to create the right culture and hire the right kind of people to manage and lead employees. He wanted humble servant leaders—people who would find satisfaction in serving others and not be focused solely on themselves and "what is in it for me."

Building and maintaining that environment took hard work. Aligning behaviors, communications, celebrations, hiring processes, onboarding processes, new employee mentoring, and employee hiring and referral programs all took focus and constant vigilance to ward off inconsistencies and bad behaviors. To build and maintain an environment that results in high employee engagement requires a culture of constant improvement.

Bufford's business was a service business, and I have learned that almost all businesses, no matter what they sell, are in reality service businesses because customers truly care about how they are treated. Highly engaged employees who care are more likely to treat customers with care. That can only happen if you care about your employees.

CHAPTER 9 TAKEAWAYS

1. Culture is the glue that binds employees together and to the business. Culture is the values, the mission, the "why" the business exists, and

the meaning of the business. The purpose of culture is to engage people in something that motivates them to excel, and money by itself does not accomplish that goal.

2. High employee engagement in the purposes of the business results in daily excellence and high performance. High employee engagement is the silver bullet of business success.

3. The research is compelling: highly engaged employees are happy employees, and happy employees create happy, loyal customers. Cultures either enable or inhibit high employee engagement.

4. Cultures are represented by words but are, in reality, behaviors. Employees model their behavior after their manager's behavior and the managers role model based on how the entrepreneur treats them. That is why the phrase "walk the talk" is so critical.

5. Culture sets the norms for personal and business conduct. Those proscribed behaviors must be measured and celebrated. Behaviors that violate those norms must be corrected and, in the case of major violations, lead to termination. Culture is not ad hoc or negotiable.

6. Cultures are inculcated through the hiring, training, and daily "huddle" processes.

7. Hire for "cultural fit."

8. Cultures are reinforced by aligning consistently one's culture with measurements and rewards.

9. High employee engagement is dependent on how employees are treated. Employees who feel that they are treated with dignity and respect, cared about as people, and who feel as though they have some control over their personal destiny are more likely to treat their work as more than a job. High employee engagement results from helping employees be all they can be.

10. Meaning, fun, showing appreciation, emotional rewards, and teaching all contribute to a culture that can result in high employee engagement.

11. Employees are not a means to an end, but, rather, they are the "end."

12. Money or more pay by itself will not buy a good culture or high employee engagement.

13. Culture is the environment that either enables or hinders high employee engagement. How employees feel about where they work will be transmitted directly or indirectly to customers.

I O   BUILDING AN EFFECTIVE
MANAGEMENT TEAM

CEO QUOTES

- "I have yet to be successful in putting somebody (manager) on a different seat on the bus and their ego being able to handle it."

- "Eighty percent of the people who started with me are no longer here because they could not grow with the business."

- "You have to dump stars who are not nice."

- "One negative person can impact five, ten, fifteen people in a small company."

- "My biggest mistakes were hiring too quickly and firing too slowly."

MULTIPLE HIRING MISTAKES

My DPGC research produced several surprising findings. One was the difficulty entrepreneurs had in hiring the right people for their management team. In fact, multiple hires—as many as four or five—were sometimes necessary to find the right person for the positions of chief financial officer, HR officer, chief sales officer, and chief technology officer. This extraordinary inefficiency wasted time, money, and opportunities and generated stress for the entrepreneurs and their employees.

    This pattern of multiple hiring mistakes can be traced to

1. poor hiring processes and inexperience in evaluating candidates' technical competencies;

2. inexperience in evaluating whether individuals would fit into the business culture;

3. underestimating the difficulty that managers with big company experience had transitioning to an entrepreneurial environment; and

4. failing to understand the importance of team play.

BUILDING A MANAGEMENT TEAM
THAT PLAYS WELL TOGETHER

A second surprise from my research was the difficulty entrepreneurs had getting good managers to work well together and have constructive conversations rather than engage in corporate politics and gamesmanship. To foster constructive team dynamics, for example, two firms that I studied had to hire executive coaches or psychologists to work with the management team. This need led one entrepreneur to state: "You have a choice: either build a star culture or a team culture."

Related to getting the management to play well together and drive results was the challenge of getting their compensation right. It took several iterations for many businesses to find the right balance between rewarding individual results versus team or company results.

OUTGROWING MANAGEMENT CAPABILITIES

Consistent with the reoccurring themes of change and evolution, the third surprising finding of my research was that companies frequently had to upgrade their management teams as they grew. Often managers who operated effectively at one revenue level of the business were unable to manage effectively at a much higher revenue level. The jobs simply outgrew their skills.

The need to upgrade managers to fit the expanding job demands was gut wrenching for many entrepreneurs because the now-ineffective manager had often had a successful history with the business but was now in over his or her head. Such cases presented personal and cultural tensions between the value of loyalty and need for effectiveness.

This tension was particularly difficult when the ineffective manager failed to transition back to a nonmanagerial role or to a lower-level management position. This difficulty caused tensions with employees, too, because many of them were comfortable and liked their manager—who was now going to be replaced by, in most cases, an outsider. Many entrepreneurs were surprised by the necessity of managing this dynamic.

WHOM TO HIRE FIRST?

When an entrepreneur can no longer manage the business alone, he or she must then decide what skills to hire first. The entrepreneur's expertise and the business needs will determine whether the answer to that is a finance, sales, HR, technology, sales, or operations person. In most cases, the entrepreneur will add a critical skill or competency that he or she does not have.

ASSESSMENT OF COMPETENCIES

In my study, many entrepreneurs chose to hire someone with functional experience and skills complementary to their own. For example, if an entrepreneur's strength was finance, then he or she hired a sales person or an HR person. If the entrepreneur's strength was sales, then he or she hired a finance person.

This decision heuristic, however, led to unanticipated shortcomings in the entrepreneur's ability to evaluate competencies outside of his or her specialty area. For example, how would one without a finance background evaluate the competencies of an experienced finance person in the first place, and, further, how does he or she subsequently evaluate that individual's proposals and work when they are on the team?

Another pattern in determining whom to hire was assessment of the critical business need. Was there a need for more revenue or more process? If the need was for more process, entrepreneurs hired either a finance or HR person. If it was more revenue, they hired a senior sales person.

HIRE FOR CURRENT NEEDS OR FUTURE NEEDS?

Many entrepreneurs also struggled with whether to hire someone who had helped another entrepreneurial company scale or to hire a person with experience in a much bigger company but who had no scaling experience.

The results here were mixed. Some entrepreneurs brought in people with too much experience too early. Others hired people from companies slightly bigger and found the person could scale a little but not three or four times. Several found that people making their first switch out of a big company had difficulty adjusting to an entrepreneurial environment.

Many found it particularly challenging to attract good, experienced managers during their expansion or, as one entrepreneur called it, the "adolescent" stage. As a result, many entrepreneurs had to rely on younger, less experienced managers with the drive and passion to learn on the job. Many had success by hiring people they already knew well from prior working experience. Others had success hiring those with big company experience and who had also at least one successful experience with a growing entrepreneurial company.

One entrepreneur stated: "We made mistakes hiring people whom we did not know well or who were not part of our network. Other mistakes were hiring people who gave us all the right answers but could not check their egos at the door."

One entrepreneur, who built a successful national franchise, stated his experience this way:

But as we started to go out and look for execution, we found out that no one really has any magic. I mean, magic is understanding your business, understanding your customer, understanding where you want to go, and being very passionate about it.

GOOD HIRING PROCESSES: A MUST!

Many entrepreneurs learned best-hiring practices from the book *Topgrading: How Leading Companies Win by Hiring, Coaching and Keeping the Best People* by Bradford Smart.[1] Commonly used good hiring practices aim to mitigate the natural inclination to hire people like oneself. Especially in a growth business, the tendency is to rush into a hiring decision because of the urgent need for more help. One lesson that came through clearly was to hire slowly (and fire quickly).

By bearing the financial and other business consequences of making sometimes frequent hiring mistakes, entrepreneurs learned the practical necessity of installing processes to put management applicants through a rigorous interview schedule, comprised of multiple-graded reviews by senior managers as well as other relevant line employees.

There was considerable variability in the approaches taken among the companies I studied, but all involved a systematic review of the likely fit of an employee with the business culture. For example, one consulting company's response to hiring mistakes was to require that all six senior executives interview every hire, regardless of the level of position. Further, to protect the culture, unanimous agreement on every hire was required as well.

Other companies chose to interview applicants in teams to get multiple views about the applicant's answers and behavior. Many used behavioral interviewing techniques, asking applicants to describe challenges faced and their responses or providing hypothetical situations for applicants to deal with. The goal of these techniques was to get past the "marketing ballet" of both the interviewee and the company.

Both of these examples of using multiple interviewers were designed, in part, to ensure a "cultural fit." Yet another entrepreneur made the need for "cultural fit" explicit by grading each management applicant based on his company's cultural scorecard. In some cases, entrepreneurs found that hiring mistakes lessened if the business only hired people known to trusted advisors or other managers. This route enhanced the likelihood of the candidate both having the substantive skills and fitting into the business culture.

Assessing the broader "cultural fit" and particular fit with the existing management team, when done well, was a time consuming process. To do this, many companies found that it was necessary to have different people conduct multiple interviews of the candidate over a period of time to get a good feel for a person and his or her values. These interviews included meetings outside of the workplace, over dinner or at social events. Lastly, frank discussions were held concerning what behaviors were expected of a member of the management team and what behaviors would not be acceptable, including how one should treat employees.

In addition to the challenge of getting a good "cultural fit," many entrepreneurs found it difficult to evaluate technical proficiency outside their functional area of expertise. This was especially true in the areas of finance and technology. Entrepreneurs were able to solve this problem by either using highly competent specialized executive recruiters or enlisting a third party functional expert to grade the technical expertise.

REALISTIC EXPECTATIONS

Context is so important in hiring. A growth company needs to have management expertise and experience. The need is generally urgent, and the risk of hiring the wrong people is particularly high because many entrepreneurs have little experience in hiring those with the appropriate skills to take the business to the next level.

In addition to these skills, the candidate should have at least an appreciation of entrepreneurial business as well as a broader understanding of what it takes to grow and develop a business. Many entrepreneurs fail to understand the weightiness of these early hiring decisions. One stated: "It takes one set of skills to start a business and a different set of skills to grow a business."

One's approach to the hiring processes should maximize a good "cultural fit" and minimize surprises for both the company and the interviewee after the hire. It takes time and several interactions with the candidate to achieve this goal. Almost every entrepreneur in my study that was scaling his or her first company and who hired managers they did not know well found this process surprisingly difficult and fraught with error.

MANAGEMENT TEAM DYNAMICS

Every new management-level hire creates multiple new interpersonal relationships among management team members, introducing change into an existing team. The need to attend to management team dynamics was a surprise and a major challenge for most entrepreneurs. And it was time consuming.

Unfortunately, many entrepreneurs lacked the interest or natural inclination to manage the interpersonal dynamics of the management team. Managing team dynamics and interpersonal dynamics takes emotional intelligence, the ability to understand each team member as an individual, and the ability to tailor the message to get the right result. In the beginning, many entrepreneurs were clueless about how to tailor the message or even its necessity. Many entrepreneurs viewed managing management teams as detracting from what they thought were the important tasks of running the business. But they soon learned that focusing on the people was the important stuff.

Having difficult conversations, holding team members accountable for results, and dealing with responsibility and compensation issues proved difficult. In the best of these cases, entrepreneurs accepted the need to do this as well as their own limitations and hired outside executive coaches or psychologists to teach the management team how to work well together. Most entrepreneurs also based a meaningful part of each manager's incentive compensation on team performance and company financial results rather than only individual performance.

Having learned from prior mistakes, one serial entrepreneur knew that he wanted to foster direct, open conversations among team members. As he said, "I want a stab-me-in-the-chest culture not a stab-me-in-the-back management culture." Another entrepreneur said that he taught his managers that *respectful* dissent and disagreement was expected. What was critical was that the management learn to deal directly and honestly with issues.

FIRE QUICKLY

No entrepreneur in my study reported that he or she made a mistake by firing someone too quickly. To the contrary, most said that their biggest mistakes were firing too slowly, in hopes that the person would improve or that they could teach the person to be what was needed. Unanimously, entrepreneurs reported erring on giving a poor fit too much time in a position and making their biggest managerial mistakes by not firing faster. Having the wrong person in the job was costly in time, personnel dynamics, lost opportunities, and finances.

Entrepreneurs were constantly conflicted on the issue of firing someone that was not working out. Were they being fair? What message would it send to the organization? Could the person fit somewhere else in the organization? Some of this hesitancy to fire can be traced to the unpleasantness of the act of firing and the resulting bad feelings, debates about performance, or even the potential of legal actions. But hesitance can also result from the entrepreneur not wanting to admit that he or she made a mistake. Likewise, sometimes the hesitancy is rationalized by thinking one is too busy now to do it, so it is better to postpone it to a slower business time, which in some cases never really happens. In the meantime, the person continues to be a poor fit for either his or her job or the organization as a whole, infecting the organization and causing a risk for more damage.

UPGRADING THE MANAGEMENT TEAM

Another challenge for most entrepreneurs was the need to upgrade the management team as the business grew. Many found that their managers could "not grow as fast as the business grew." For many businesses, the need to upgrade the management team was not a one-time event. As the business grew to different levels of revenue, often greater experience and sophistication was needed in the areas of finance, HR, technology, and sales than could be provided by those who had performed well in those roles in earlier phases.

The need to upgrade managers caught many entrepreneurs by surprise. It was not planned for, nor even contemplated. Consequently, in some cases, entrepreneurs made the wrong hiring decisions by hiring people who had little or no experience in scaling a business to three or four times its size. As a result, the skill and experience level of the hire was quickly exceeded.

The limitation in hiring individuals with experience for the longer term was often money—how much experience the business could afford to invest in with one hire at that time. Getting the balance right was not easy and frequently was thought about more in hindsight than foresight by many first-time entrepreneurs.

A common progression of finance in growing businesses was to move from having a part-time accountant to a full-time controller, to a vice-president of finance, to a chief financial officer (CFO). When entrepreneurs reached the need for a CFO, many had to find someone more sophisticated in the skills they needed and hired someone who had been through revenue growth levels beyond where the business now was.

For human resources, companies generally progressed from a single general administrative person, to a junior full-time HR person, to an HR person with experience in a much bigger company. In sales, it was often the case that a good salesperson does not necessarily make a good sales manager. Likewise, a good sales manager at a certain revenue level cannot necessarily transition to make a good vice-president of sales at a much higher level.

These transitions were difficult because often the incumbent had done a good job earlier in the company's growth. Now, however, that individual was eased out and another, more senior hire was his or her replacement. Understandably, this loss of position and status was hard for many incumbents to accept and, if not well managed, impacted other employees' morale—especially those who reported to the now-displaced incumbent. Entrepreneurs learned that morale was fragile and that, in some cases, the incumbent had to leave the company.

Many entrepreneurs were unprepared both for the interpersonal challenges raised in this chapter of getting the right people in place to successfully grow a company and the challenges addressed in Chapter 8, which addressed the need for entrepreneurs to change their role(s) in the business and manage the managers. Many had never thought deeply about how most businesses are really nothing more than groups of people learning how to work together to produce something of value to sell to other people. Many entrepreneurs found that building a management team was an ongoing process with new team dynamics emerging with the addition (or subtraction) of team members.

SECUREWORKS[2]

Mike Cote was a seasoned executive who was brought into SecureWorks by its institutional investors to grow the business. He was tasked with many things, including building a management team that could work together.

SecureWorks was a privately held company in Atlanta, Georgia, specializing in information-security services. It was launched in 1999, during the first Internet gold rush, by two former CompUSA employees: Joan Wilbanks and Michael Pearson.

The startup's technology established it as an expert in preventing external Internet attacks on commercial computer networks and attracted large investors. The two co-founders raised $30 million from Mellon Ventures, GE Equity, and other investors.

The technology focus, however, was a double-edged sword. Secure-Works' management was so busy with the company's technical development that it neglected sales and marketing efforts and revenue suffered. At the end of 2001, SecureWorks had fewer than 100 clients and was burning roughly $900,000 a month on less than a million in sales with only $9 million of the original cash raised left in the bank.

In February 2002, Wilbanks stepped down as CEO and made room for Michael Cote. A high-tech industry veteran with a strong financial background, Cote brought in a new management team, changed the sales strategy, and, most important, developed a strong, customer-focused culture. Under Cote's leadership, client retention became SecureWorks' number one goal. "[It's] pure gold—it's between 96 and 97 percent," Cote said.[3]

The payoff was tremendous. Sales for 2003 topped $8 million. Since then, the company saw triple-digit growth, year after year. Unlike many fast-growth companies, SecureWorks had grown through increased sales, rather than through mergers and acquisitions. Its client base included organizations of all sizes with more than 10 percent of them listed on the Fortune 500. In 2008, SecureWorks had more than 2,000 customers worldwide and pulled in $53.9 million in revenue.

In 2009, *SC Magazine* honored the 300-employee company with a Reader Trust Award for the Best Managed Security Service for the fourth year in a row. In addition, SecureWorks had earned the spot on the *Inc. 500*, *Inc.* 5,000, and Deloitte Technology Fast 500 lists of fastest-growing companies.

Company History

SecureWorks co-founders Joan Wilbanks and Michael Pearson met at CompUSA, Inc., a personal-computer retailer headquartered in Dallas, Texas. Wilbanks, a sales director for CompUSA's integration team, and Pearson, a technical-account executive, became aware of a market void in Internet-security systems for small and medium-sized companies.[4]

In the late 1990s, large companies were forking over millions of dollars to fortify their computer networks against unauthorized use by increasingly sophisticated intruders. Smaller companies that did not have the resources to install firewalls and other protective systems, which required trained personnel to monitor them, were virtually defenseless against computer-network attacks, and the big Internet-security players had little interest in addressing their needs.

Sensing a business opportunity, Wilbanks and Pearson decided to start a company that would offer affordable Internet-security systems to this largely neglected customer base. In March 1999, they launched Secure-Works in Atlanta, Georgia, with Wilbanks as president and CEO and Pearson as chief technology officer.

Rounding Up Capital

Consulting provided early funding. Wilbanks coached sales teams at large security-software providers, such as Internet Security Systems, on how to improve their pitches.[5] But the serious money started flowing in when SecureWorks attracted the attention of an Atlanta-based venture-capital firm at a local technology trade show.

The early round of funding from Noro-Moseley Partners, Alliance Technology Ventures, and ITC Holdings generated more than $10 million for the startup. In November 2000, SecureWorks snagged an additional $20 million in a second round of funding, which was led by Mellon Ventures of Mellon Financial Corporation and included investors such as General Electric's GE Equity and SBK Capital.[6]

Developing the Technology

Flush with capital, SecureWorks now could develop the technology to deliver cost-effective, round-the-clock Internet security monitoring and response service. The service was ideal for companies with 250 or fewer network users per location, such as medical and law practices, accounting firms, insurance agencies, and other businesses that handled sensitive information but did not have in-house IT security personnel to protect their computer networks against denial-of-service attacks, information and identity theft, Website vandalism, and viruses.

In addition to managing the intrusion-detection systems and providing firewalls, which protected its clients' networks from unauthorized access, the startup's security center could respond to security breaches in real time, thanks to its proprietary iSensor technology.

Engineers at SecureWorks made sure the technology met the needs of small companies. The security system they developed did not take too much bandwidth on the small companies' networks, and the user-friendly Web interface enabled small-business owners who had little technical expertise to easily review the data.[7]

The Revolving Door at the Top

The young company had technology that worked and a market hungry for its services. It also had cash and a solid investor base. But all was not well at SecureWorks. In August 2000, the board brought in a former MCI WorldCom executive as the new president and chief operating officer in charge of building distribution channels and directing sales, marketing, operations, and finance.[8] In February 2001, co-founder Wilbanks stepped down as CEO, retaining her role as chairman of the board.[9] Robert Minkhorst, former CEO of Atlanta-based Philips Consumer Electronics for North America, took over the reins of the fledgling company.[10]

At the end of 2001, SecureWorks was a weak regional player with fewer than 100 clients. It was losing $800,000 to $900,000 a month on less than $1 million in sales. There was little doubt among board members that, unless they challenged the status quo, the troubled startup was not going to survive in the long term.

Enter Michael Cote

When Michael Cote took the helm of SecureWorks on February 1, 2002, he was the company's third CEO in three years. Cote explained what attracted him to the startup:

I came for several reasons. I believed that Internet security had good potential, and the SecureWorks technology was up and running, not just a gleam in somebody's eye. I was impressed with the company's investor group, which has turned out to be one of the best I've run across. SecureWorks had cash, which meant there wasn't a working-capital issue, and I didn't have to go out and look for money. And finally, I felt the company needed to be redirected and focused from a sales and marketing perspective.[11]

Despite having no CEO experience, Cote had a track record of growing innovative technology companies in CFO and COO roles. A graduate of Boston College with a double major in computer science and accounting, Cote started his career as a certified public accountant. He spent two years in London, England, with KPMG Peat Marwick and five years as the chief financial officer of a public company that grew from $50 to $750 million in revenue. During his tenure as partner and COO of a privately held software company MSI Solutions, Inc., revenue growth topped 75 percent every year. Prior to joining SecureWorks, Cote was a CFO at Talus Solutions, a pricing and revenue-management software firm acquired by Manugistics Group, Inc., in 2000.

During a career that spanned nearly 20 years, Cote negotiated the sale of two companies in which he was a shareholder and senior officer: one for $450 million and another for $65 million. He completed 41 acquisitions worth $1.6 billion and led equity offerings that generated $261 million.[12]

First Things First

The newly minted CEO had his work cut out for him. "The most important thing I knew we had to drive was to get the right people on the bus, and in the right seats," Cote said, describing his priorities during the first 90 days of his tenure at SecureWorks.[13] "And then we had to focus on driving the revenue," he said. "Because that's what we needed in order to survive."

Getting the Right People on the Bus in the Right Seats

Among Cote's initial tasks was to interview each SecureWorks employee to find out what they did. "When I met with the guy who was running sales," Cote recalled, "he looked at me and said 'I've never run sales before. I don't want to be in this position. I hope you can move me somewhere else where I can produce.'" The unhappy sales director was transferred to the product-management area, where he ended up excelling. "That was an example of putting someone in the right seat," Cote said. Filling the top executive positions, however, was more challenging. In order to "get the right people on the bus," Cote had to tap the talent pool outside the company.

Finding the right CFO was a high priority for Cote. "I spent nine years in public accounting and then was a CFO of a public company, so I came up through the finance route," Cote said and noted the importance of financial discipline. In February 2002, he hired Michael Vandiver as SecureWorks' CFO. Vandiver, whom Cote had met a year before during his own job search, had "broad experience dealing with venture-backed, privately held, and public technology companies," Cote said.[14] In March 2002, Cote brought in Chris Coleman as CMO. Coleman was a former owner of the largest technology-marketing company in the southeast and had more than 25 years of marketing experience.

With the help of an executive recruiter, Cote found Tyler Winkler, a vice president of sales at SafeNet, a manufacturer of hardware and software for corporate-network security located in Belcamp, Maryland. "[He] had years of experience selling Internet security space," Cote said.[15] Winkler joined SecureWorks in April 2002 as senior vice president of sales and business development.

The new management team was fully assembled by June 2002. In a cost-cutting effort, Cote reduced the SecureWorks headcount from approximately 80 employees to 40 employees. "Then, I put a new budget in front of the board starting July 1st of 2002," Cote said.

Driving Revenue

Cote was painfully aware that that the startup would not survive without a focused effort on driving revenue and that his cost-cutting efforts could only go so far. He explained:

We are a heavy fixed-cost business. I have backup diesel generators. I'm in a fully redundant, biometric secured facility because we do 24 × 7 × 365 managed Internet security. I've got a lot invested in technology. I could not cut costs there. If we didn't drive revenue, we were done—we were out of business. And we had a nine-month life when I joined.

Cote could not drive revenue with what he had inherited, however; the sales and marketing departments were in need of big overhauls. The company was technology-focused and, as Cote said, "It had the most dysfunctional sales and marketing departments I had ever seen."[16] Rather than selling directly to businesses, the company sold through distributors and resellers, which did not make any sense to Cote. "If we can't sell our services directly, how can we expect someone else to sell them? And we are a service business; we have to touch our clients," he said.

But, at the time, no one at SecureWorks seemed to realize that. "When I joined," Cote recalled, "the company had no idea who they were. They didn't know if they were a software company or a licensing company or a service company or what they did." He continued:

The biggest thing that I struggled with then, and, quite frankly, has become a struggle with us, is focus and business model. We're not in the software business. We're not in the product business. We're a service company. Our goals have been pretty much the same for six years: daily living our team values of integrity, service excellence, reliability, open honest communication and innovation, client retention rate, and our growth and revenue because with growth comes excitement and profitability. And for six years now, those are posted in our offices.

Making Over the Sales Department

Cote had hired Tyler Winkler to attack the problem of low sales. To Winkler, the solution was clear: a top-to-bottom makeover of the sales department. Rather than continuing to sell exclusively to channel partners, SecureWorks adopted the direct-to-customer sales model. In addition, the startup narrowed its focus to four markets: banks, credit unions, hospitals, and utilities, which enabled it to be "narrow and deep, rather than wide and shallow," Cote said.[17]

Winkler was appalled by the lack of accountability and sales processes in place and set specific goals for the people in sales. He greeted the sales team with: "Make your numbers in three months or you're out." But he made sure they were ready for the fight by making sure all sales reps received intensive training from internal and external trainers. They were also given a new tool—a Webinar presentation for potential clients.[18]

Now, a sales representative who brought in $5,000 in sales in a month despite a quota of $50,000, "was gone that afternoon," Winkler said.[19] Out of a staff of six salespeople, he fired four. Yet, his militant approach produced results: Within nine months after he took over the sales department, revenues for 2002 totaled $1.9 million. Two years later, the department had grown to 30 employees, while the number of SecureWorks' clients had grown tenfold.

"Tyler has grown and developed," said Cote in 2008. "And today, he not only has all sales and business development, he recently picked up our consulting-services group and has somewhere in the neighborhood of 75 of our 300 people working for him."

And the salespeople? "They have commission checks in a month today that are bigger than what they used to make annually," said Cote.[20]

HR Issues

Revenue growth meant growing headcount. In 2007, the company hired 120 new employees, and 40 more in the first few months of 2008. To handle an influx of employees, the company had a full-time recruiter who "did nothing but recruit and focus on bringing the people onboard and making sure we pay them and all that," Cote said, adding that SecureWorks used Automatic Data Processing, Inc., (ADP) for payroll services. ADP also managed the company's benefits package and dealt with "reviews and interviews and that type of thing." Cote said.[21]

Compensation

SecureWorks took compensation management seriously, using it as a way to improve performance and manage talent. Cote understood that offering the right compensation for each person was critical to attracting and retaining high-quality employees. "I have a very personal vested interest in how we compensate people and what the benefits are," Cote said.

The total compensation at SecureWorks had three components: base pay, variable compensation, and equity. "My philosophy is, look to go on the lower end of base from a market perspective—the bottom 50 percent. And then have variable compensation that can bring you above or at the high end of the total market," Cote said.

Compensation was tied to individual and corporate performance. "It's 60 percent tied to the company performance, 40 percent individual," Cote said. "But there are hurdles the company has to hit for you to be eligible at all. The bonuses typically get paid out in the spring after the audit has

been completed." In the fall, the employees were paid the equity component of their entire compensation. "I've granted equity to the entire employee base in some shape or form every fall," Cote said.

Turnover

The turnover rate at SecureWorks ran "somewhere in the neighborhood
of 15 percent, both voluntary and involuntary," Cote said. He admitted
that because SecureWorks was a "high-energy, heavily driven" organization, it attracted a certain type of driven, high-producing individual. "And
what happens is that if somebody joins the team and is not producing at
the same caliber that others on the team are, they tend to push them out,"
Cote said. In some cases, those who did not fit in SecureWorks' fast-paced,
high-charging culture left on their own. "But I don't think we lose a lot
of people for other reasons, such as them being recruited away," Cote
said, adding that, although he had let the marketing executive he hired in
2002 go, the CFO and the SVP of sales and development had been with
the organization almost as long as he had.

Cote's Management Style

As SecureWorks grew, so did the man at the helm. The CEO's evolving
leadership role was "one of the things we struggle with a lot and talk
about a lot here," Cote admitted. A believer in open communication, Cote
created a PowerPoint-slide presentation titled "Who Am I?" intended for
members of SecureWorks' board and executive team. "If I'm the one running this ship, and I'm the chairman, CEO, and president of the company,
you'd better know who you're working with and what my management
style is," said Cote.

One of the tag lines in Cote's presentation was, "Stop talking before
I stop listening." "I don't have a lot of time to waste," Cote explained.
"And if you want to come in, let's talk, but get to the point." He continued:

The second thing is, don't strap me in the copilot seat. Don't look for me to solve
your problems. I'm paying you good money to run a department. And if you
want to talk about something, then that's fine. Come in and say, "I don't have the
answer and I want to run this by you." But it is your problem, and you come up

with a solution. I don't manage my folks. I look to hire high-quality people. Just like I manage the board; I look for them to manage me.

The SecureWorks executive team consisted of twelve members, including the CEO, but only six of them reported directly to Cote: the CFO, the CTO, the CMO, and the heads of operations, engineering, and sales and business development. As Cote told the members of his executive team, "As a CEO, I shouldn't be making routine decisions."

The same principle applied to the members of his executive team: Cote wanted SecureWorks executives focused on making strategic decisions and for their direct reports to handle the easy ones. He devoted a lot of the time in meetings with his executive team on questions such as, "What am I spending my time on? What *should* I be spending my time on? And if that's the case, what should *they* be spending *their* time on? And how do I get the reports or information from them? And how do we get our relationship to work?"

Cote worked well with people who valued open communication and transparency in the same way he did. In his opinion, the ability to communicate well, which required good rapport and a certain level of "mutual respect, trust, and understanding," was an essential element of a good work relationship. To describe his philosophy of working with the executive team, Cote said:

I'm the leader of the team, but we're all in this boat together. The enemy's not in the room. And we're all executive people looking to drive this thing. And we need to be able to have a rapport and work well together and understand where we're all driving. And there's a clear handoff from one department to another of what's being done and where we're going.

Managing Time

As the company grew, one of the challenges Cote faced was deciding how to allocate one of his scarcest resources: his time. He said, "Probably the most difficult part is figuring out what *not* to do." He continued:

It's not that I'm not delegating. But I may be doing things or looking over someone's shoulder where, quite frankly, it doesn't matter anymore; I can't afford to put my time in that area. The one thing I perhaps do not do frequently enough is try and sit back and ask, "Where am I spending my day, and is it effective?" I'm trying to make sure I divide my time between . . . how I am working with the board, how I am thinking through how we're going to grow five times the size we are today, interviewing new board members, and dealing with how I pull the most out of what the next stages are.

In 2006, Cote hired an executive assistant—he did not have one for the first four years—with whom he sat down regularly and reviewed his schedule. Now he said, "No, I can't meet with this person. With 15 companies that want us to buy them and 20 companies that want us to partner with them, these people can't be on my calendar anymore."

Cote also reorganized SecureWorks every 18 months, in part to give himself time to devote to the things that mattered most for the growing company. In 2008, Cote said, "I had nine direct reports six months ago. I've reorganized down to six." He tried to limit the time he was available to direct reports seeking his advice. "My calendar's booked. Schedule it later," he told them. "And my hope is that in many of those instances they end up making the decision, because I've blocked out my calendar so I can't meet with them for two or three days," Cote said.

Information Management

For years, Cote had used Excel spreadsheets and "long hours of smart people" to help make sound financial and managerial decisions. Then, in July 2008, he implemented the Microsoft's Great Plains accounting and business software to produce the data for SecureWorks' financial statements.

Cote, who had been CFO with enough companies with revenue ranging from $800,000 to $800 million to know, said that "there are different stages and different elements of where you can kind of manhandle your way through it." He added:

You sort of hit a wall with $5 million in revenue. And you sort of hit another wall in that $10- to $15-million threshold. And then my experience in buying companies is that companies are paid a higher multiple once they cross to $25 million in revenue because with $25 million in revenue it can't be manhandled anymore. You have to have systems, policies, and procedures in place. So that's sort of where we began to hit the next threshold.

One of the tools critical in the management-decision-making process at SecureWorks was the board book, which was distributed to the directors in advance of meetings. Cote said:

We have a board book that's pretty extensive. Our business is like an insurance company as far as predictability. One client is over 2 percent of our revenue. We've only missed one month a year from a sales perspective or a new contract perspective and have never missed an EBITDA monthly target. But it's a pretty diverse client base, pretty easy to predict. And we trend a lot—there are a lot of graphs and a lot of financial information in our board book.

Internal Controls
Cote set up adequate financial controls immediately after he took over as CEO. "From the control-of-cash perspective, the first thing I did was make sure the only two people who were allowed to sign on behalf of the company were the CFO and myself," he said. Cote added that "pretty tight controls" were put around anything that could put the company at risk. He continued:

We work heavily on the budget. Each department head has control over their expenditures. They're tied to their variable comp plan. They each have their own expenses and, if applicable, their revenue budget. And that rolls up to full corporate finances. But if it's things that relate to serving the client, running a department, there's a fair amount of latitude that has been given.

For example, the sales representatives had the authority to discount the service 10 percent off the list price. The two vice presidents of sales had the authority to discount another five points, and the CFO could take off 25 points. "And anything over that, he brings it to me," Cote said. "So there are some discounting functions in place like authority to sign the company, big critical things of that nature. My operations guy may give away two, five months of free service. And I've never questioned them on any of that."

Because client retention was the company's number-one goal, Cote gave SecureWorks employees the authority to make decisions that had an impact on the client relationship. "We're human. We make mistakes," he said and recalled an exchange he had had with a staff member in charge of operations: "I asked him, in front of his staff, 'What do you think your authority is in order to fix a problem that we created relating to a client relationship?' And he looked at me and said, 'I don't know.' And I said, 'When have I ever said no to you on anything you've ever wanted to do?' It's whatever you want to do and whatever you think needs to be done."

Managing Growth
Under Cote's leadership SecureWorks experienced stellar growth. In May 2008, he said, "Today, we have almost 300 employees and about $50 million in revenue. And we'll do about $70 to $80 million in bookings or contracts this year."

In addition to a stable client base, which was a source of recurring revenue, SecureWorks was winning new clients, including international ones, every day. "As all of that grows, I have a lot of open direct conversations with my executive team. Some of this may sound exciting and sexy. But I want to make sure they truly understand what international travel means if we get to that point," Cote said.

In 2008, one of the biggest challenges facing Cote was taking the company to the next level—from $50 million to $250 million in revenue. The issues related to managing growth were the focus of many board meetings. "We spend a lot of time on whether we have the right people. And if they are the right people, what things they need to work on to make sure they've got the skill set to take them to the next level," Cote said.

One of Cote's 2008 hires was the vice president of human resources, whose mandate was to work with members of the executive team to identify their constraints and deficiencies and ensure they received the right training to succeed in their evolving roles. Cote explained:

Of the twelve people on the executive team, there's only one who's been in [his current] role in a quarter of a billion dollar company before. I've been in an $800 million publicly traded company, but as the CFO, not the CEO. And some folks on the executive team, it's sort of 50/50 that they will be the ones running their departments four or five years from now. They may be here in different roles, or they may be able to continue to evolve as we grow as a company. I was with a company, in the CFO position, that we grew from $40 million to $800 million in revenue in three-and-a-half years, all through acquisitions. So I lived through situations where we grew beyond people's capabilities. And we ended up promoting them too far, and, eventually, we had to fire them. So, when it comes to making people decisions . . . pull the trigger quicker.

In July 2009, SecureWorks acquired VeriSign's managed security-services division to increase its market share and boost its international presence. According to Cote, the acquisition also resulted in an addition of "some technical capabilities and name brand enterprise accounts."

As of October 2009, the company had approximately 2,700 clients, $110 million in run-rate revenue, and about 525 employees in offices in Atlanta, Georgia; Chicago, Illinois; Providence, Rhode Island; Myrtle Beach, South Carolina; and London, as well as partnerships in Spain, Mexico, South America, Taiwan, and Saudi Arabia.

Staying Focused

With success came new challenges. Early on, Cote had helped the troubled startup find its focus; six years later he strove to maintain it. Cote said:

The biggest issue for the leadership—the thing I harped on six years ago, and I'm harping on again—is focus. Does this fit who we are? Does it fit what we're doing? We've gone from one service line to seven or eight service lines. But we're not trying to be everything to everyone. We are a value-added Internet security-service provider—we are not your low-cost provider. Our gross margin runs in the mid-70 percent range. We've got to know who we are, know what we're do-ing, and stay focused on our knitting.

Cote admitted that it was hard to stay focused on what was important when confronted with all the opportunities that accompanied exponential growth. The dozens of high-tech companies interested in partnering with SecureWorks or wanting to be acquired by it presented distractions. "If we don't stay focused, we end up getting ourselves all wrapped around where we are as an executive team and find the whole organization spend-ing time on stuff that's a waste of time," Cote stated.

To help the organization stay true to what it was and not lose sight of its core values, the executive team developed a culture book and distributed it to all SecureWorks employees. All new hires received a copy during orientation.

It's All About People

At the beginning of 2002, SecureWorks was one of a few dozen information-security startups. With its sales stagnant and totaling under $1 million, it was on the verge of extinction; under new leadership, however, the company found its focus and thrived.

By 2008, SecureWorks emerged as one of the three or four survivors in the industry it had helped kick-start, along with companies such as ISS and CipherTrust. "We are clearly the largest and fastest-growing company from an organic growth perspective. I often get asked, 'Why have you guys been able to do it?'" Reflecting on the driving force behind SecureWorks' success, Cote answered:

If you boil all of it down, its people, people, and people. It's the passion we have. And we've got a focused business model. We know who we are, what we do, and what we don't do. Everybody in the company knows that if clients call, they'd better be doing cartwheels to respond to them. We may not be able to fix the problem. We may not be able to put in a new feature they want. But we're going to be open, honest, and communicate with them. And if we make a mistake, we're going to admit it and apologize. We're going to figure out how to make it right. We've got probably the best technology in the industry. But the only reason we have that technology is because we have people. We're able to focus on what clients want, and we'll continue to improve it.

LESSONS FROM SECUREWORKS

SecureWorks is a great concluding story for this book because it illustrates several of the key themes of the book:

1. Growth is change and businesses evolve as they grow.

2. To grow, both a business's way of doing business—its processes—and its people have to evolve and the people have to either grow or be replaced.

3. Strategic focus and managing the pace of growth are mission critical.

4. Building a management team is hard and takes time.

5. Management team dynamics have to be worked on and the leader must focus on mentoring management.

6. Scaling is the key way to grow a business to a much larger size.

7. Figuring out what not to do is as important as figuring out what to do.

CHAPTER 10 TAKEAWAYS

1. Businesses are collections of people coming together to produce something of value to other people. Most businesses do business through employees and with customers.

2. Businesses, as they grow, need managers. Building the management team is hard.

3. Hiring the right managers requires finding people with both the right experience and skills and the right personal fit with your culture.

4. Many growth companies make bad hiring decisions because they have bad hiring processes.

5. Hire slowly and fire quickly.

6. Entrepreneurs need help in evaluating technical skills when hiring candidates for areas in which the entrepreneur has no experience.

7. Even if you hire the right person, that hiring requires the entrepreneur to focus on and manage the management team's personal dynamics. Getting managers to be good team players and engage in constructive dialogue with each other takes work.

8. The SecureWorks, Global Medical Imaging, and Trilogy Health Services stories all demonstrate the importance but difficulty of getting the right people in the right positions, working together for the common good.

9. As businesses grow, many times the management skills needed are beyond the capabilities of the current managers, and the difficult process of upgrading people must occur.

10. A business cannot grow unless its people grow.

REFERENCE MATTER

REMINDERS FOR THE ENTREPRENEUR

1. Too much growth too fast can destroy your business.

2. Focus everyday on quality, cash flow, and engaging your employees in being better.

3. Delegate and audit.

4. Do not have a single point of failure.

5. Put out the fire and always leave a process behind.

6. Hold teaching huddles every morning.

7. Institutionalize your "firehouse" time.

8. Make hiring a science.

9. Align desired behaviors, measurements and rewards.

10. Understand your personal and financial tolerance for risk.

11. Never, never stop learning and improving.

12. Engaged happy employees create happy customers.

13. It is not about you—it is about them: customers and employees.

14. Use the Growth Risks Audit at least every four months.

15. The DNA of growth is constant improvement.

16. The turbocharger of growth is scaling.

17. For a business to grow, you have to grow.

18. Money is not enough.

19. Hire for "cultural fit."

20. Improve or die.

21. Every day is game day.

22. Two most important words for building a business: Thank you.

23. Most businesses are people businesses—people helping other people meet their needs.

24. Lead by example and remember that actions speak louder than words.

25. Stuff happens—what counts is how you react to it.

CHAPTER 2

1. All quotes from the Darden Private Growth Company Research project are anonymous.

2. Robert M. Solow, "The Neoclassical Theory of Growth and Distribution," *BNL Quarterly Review* 215 (2000): 349.

3. Paul A. Geroski, "Understanding the Implications of Empirical Work on Corporate Growth Rates," *Managerial and Decision Economics* 26, no. 2 (2005): 129–38.

4. Edward D. Hess, Robert K. Kazanjian, eds., *The Search for Organic Growth* (Cambridge: Cambridge University Press, 2006), 147–48; Louis K. C. Chan, Jason Karceski, and Josef Lakonishok, "The Level and Persistence of Growth Rates," *Journal of Finance* 58, no. 2 (2003): 643–84; Mark Lipton, *Guiding Growth: How Vision Keeps Companies on Course* (Boston: Harvard Business School Press, 2003), 36–37; Matthew S. Olson, Derek van Bever, *Stall Points: Most Companies Stop Growing—Yours Doesn't Have To* (New Haven, CT: Yale University Press, 2008); Robert R. Wiggins and Timothy W. Ruefli, "Sustained Competitive Advantage: Temporal Dynamics and the Incidence and Persistence of Superior Economic Performance," *Organization Science* 13, no. 1 (2002): 81–105; Robert R. Wiggins and Timothy W. Ruefli, "Schumpeter's Ghost: Is Hypercompetition Making the Best of Times Shorter?" *Strategic Management Journal* 26, no. 10 (2005): 887–911; Sven Smit, Caroline M. Thompson, and

S. Patrick Viguerie, "The Do-or-Die Struggle for Growth," *McKinsey Quarterly* 3 (2005): 35–45.

5. Paul M. Romer, "The Origins of Endogenous Growth," *Journal of Economic Perspectives* 8, no. 1 (1994): 3–22.

6. Edith Penrose, "The Theory of the Growth of the Firm," *International Encyclopedia of Business and Management* (Oxford: Oxford University Press, 1996), 2440–48.

7. Kim S. Cameron, Jane E. Dutton, and Robert E. Quinn, eds., *Positive Organizational Scholarship* (San Francisco: Berrett-Koehler, 2003); Jane E. Dutton, *Energize Your Workplace: How to Create and Sustain High-Quality Connections at Work* (San Francisco: Jossey-Bass, 2003); James L. Heskett, W. Earl Sasser, Jr., and Leonard A. Schlesinger, *The Value Profit Chain: Treat Employees Like Customers and Customers Like Employees* (New York: Free Press, 2003); James L. Heskett, W. Earl Sasser, Jr., and Leonard A. Schlesinger, *The Service Profit Chain: How Leading Companies Link Profit and Growth to Loyalty, Satisfaction, and Value* (New York: Free Press, 1997); Edward D. Hess, "Organic Growth: Lessons from Market Leaders," (Working Paper, 2007); Edward D. Hess, *The Road to Organic Growth* (New York: McGraw-Hill, 2007); Edward D. Hess and Kim S. Cameron, eds., *Leading with Values: Positivity, Virtue and High Performance* (Cambridge: Cambridge University Press, 2006); Charles A. O'Reilly III and Jeffrey Pfeffer, *Hidden Value: How Great Companies Achieve Extraordinary Results with Ordinary People* (Boston: Harvard Business School Press, 2000).

8. Jeffrey D. Arendt, "Adaptive Intrinsic Growth Rates: An Integration Across Taxa," *Quarterly Review of Biology* 72, no. 2 (1997): 149–77; John Henry Clippinger III, ed., *The Biology of Business: Decoding the Natural Laws of Enterprise* (San Francisco: Jossey-Bass, 1999), 7; José M. Gómez, "Bigger Is Not Always Better: Conflicting Selective Pressures on Seed Size in *Quercus Ilex*," *Evolution* 58, no. 1 (2004): 71–80; Stephen A. Arnott, Susumu Chiba, and David O. Conover, "Evolution of Intrinsic Growth Rate: Metabolic Costs Drive Trade-Offs Between Growth and Swimming Performance in Menidia Menidia," *Evolution* 60, no. 6 (2006): 1269–78; Karl Gotthard, "Increased Risk of Predation as a Cost of High Growth Rate: An Experimental Test in a Butterfly," *Journal of Animal Ecology* 69, no. 5 (2000): 896–902; Stephan B. Munch and David O. Conover, "Nonlinear Growth Cost in Menidia Menidia: Theory and Empirical Evidence," *Evolution* 58, no. 3 (2004): 661–64.

9. Arseniy S. Karkach, "Trajectories and Models of Individual Growth," *Demographic Research* 15, no. 12 (2006): 347–400.

10. Arnott et al., "Evolution of Intrinsic Growth Rate," 1269–78; Munch, Conover, "Nonlinear Growth Cost," 661–64.

11. Shona L. Brown and Kathleen M. Eisenhardt, "The Art of Continuous Change: Linking Complexity Theory and Time-Paced Evolution in Relentlessly Shifting Organizations," *Administrative Science Quarterly* 42, no. 1 (1997): 1–34; Shona L. Brown and Kathleen M. Eisenhardt, *Competing on the Edge: Strategy as Structured Chaos* (Boston: Harvard Business School Press, 1998).

12. The Eyebobs story is adapted from Edward D. Hess and Gosia Glinska, "Eyebobs Eyewear, Inc.," Case Study UVA-ENT-0139. University of Virginia Darden School Foundation, Charlottesville, 2009.

13. Melissa Colgan, "People Who Do Cool Things: Julie Allinson," *Minneapolis St. Paul Magazine* (January 2008) http://www.mspmag.com/style/stylemakers/peoplewhodocoolthings/82877.asp.

14. Ibid.

15. Ibid.

16. Ibid.

17. TXAllie Shah, "Eye-Conoclast: Meet the Brains Behind Some of the Wackiest Glasses You'll Ever See," *Star Tribune* (August 24, 2006).

18. ENK was the leading fashion-industry tradeshow organization, conducting twenty-five events per year. Upscale fashion retailers representing specialty and department stores from around the world attended ENK events.

CHAPTER 3

1. Susan Feller's story was adapted from Edward D. Hess, "3 Fellers Bakery," Case Study UVA-ENT-0137. University of Virginia Darden School Foundation, Charlottesville, 2009.

CHAPTER 4

1. Michael E. Gerber, *The E-Myth Revisited: Why Most Small Businesses Don't Work and What to Do About It* (New York: HarperCollins, 1995).

2. Edward D. Hess, "Defender Direct, Inc.: A Business of Growing Leaders," Case Study UVA-ENT-0115. University of Virginia Darden School Foundation, Charlottesville, 2009.

3. The Global Medical Imaging story is adapted from Edward D. Hess and Gosia Glinska, "Global Medical Imaging," Case Study UVA-ENT-0143. University of Virginia Darden School Foundation, Charlottesville, 2009.

4. Kathy Brown, "Sonic Was the Tonic For This Fixer-Upper," *Business-North Carolina,* November 1, 2005.

5. Lindsay LeCorchick, "Imaging the Possibilities," *Greater Charlotte Biz*, December 2004, http://www.greatercharlottebiz.com/article.asp?id=477.

6. Brown, "Sonic Was the Tonic."

7. LeCorchick, "Imaging the Possibilities."

8. Brown, "Sonic Was the Tonic."

9. Ibid.

10. Michelle Said, "Global Medical Imaging," *24x7*, May 1, 2006.

11. Global Medical Imaging Web site, http://www.gmi3.com/.

12. Kaihan Krippendorff, "Save Your Clients Money—What Could Be More Economic?" *Fast Company*, May 28, 2009.

13. Bradford D. Smart, *Topgrading: How Leading Companies Win by Hiring, Coaching, and Keeping the Best People* (New York: HarperCollins, 2005).

14. Lindner, Andrew, "Entrepreneurs Talk About What They Do and Why They Do It," *Charlotte Business Journal,* October 6, 2006.

15. Jim Collins, "Good to Great," *Fast Company*, October 2001.

16. Lindner, "Entrepreneurs Talk."

CHAPTER 5

1. The Enchanting Travels story is adapted from Edward D. Hess, Monidipa Mukherjee, and Sanju Jacob, "Enchanting Travels," Case Study UVA-ENT-0144. University of Virginia Darden School Foundation, Charlottesville, 2009.

2. Michael Porter, "What is a Strategy?" *Harvard Business Review* (November–December, 2009): 64.

3. The Sammy Snacks story is adapted from: David Eakes (revised by Timothy M. Lasater and Gregory B. Fairchild), "Sammy Snacks (A)," Case Study UVA-OM-1177. University of Virginia Darden School Foundation, Charlottesville, 2005; Edward D. Hess, "Sammy Snacks (B)," Case Study UVA-OM-1350. University of Virginia Darden School Foundation, Charlottesville, 2008; Edward D. Hess, "Sammy Snacks (C)," Case Study UVA-OM-1398. University of Virginia Darden School Foundation, Charlottesville, 2009; and Edward D. Hess, "Sammy Snacks (D)," Case Study UVA-OM-1399. University of Virginia Darden School Foundation, Charlottesville, 2009.

CHAPTER 6

1. The C. R. Barger & Sons, Inc. story is adapted from: Edward D. Hess, "C. R. Barger & Sons, Inc. (A)," Case Study UVA-ENT-0106. University of Virginia Darden School Foundation, Charlottesville, 2008; and Edward D. Hess,

"C. R. Barger & Sons, Inc. (B)," Case Study UVA-ENT-0107. University of Virginia Darden School Foundation, Charlottesville, 2008.

2. Greg Snapper, "Lessons from the 'Little Guy': Smaller Precasting Outfits Like Barger & Sons Inc. Are Marketing Just Like the Big Guns," *MC Magazine* (July/August 2006): 42.

3. Snapper, "Lessons from the 'Little Guy,'" 44.

4. ACI stood for American Concrete Institute. Founded in 1904, ACI managed 14 certification programs to develop, share, and disseminate the knowledge and information needed to utilize concrete to its fullest potential.

5. ASTM stands for the American Society for Testing and Materials. This association sets international standards for a wide range of materials, products, systems, and services.

6. C. R. Barger and Sons. "Company Information." http://www.bargerand sons.com.

7. Snapper, "Lessons from the 'Little Guy,'" 42.

8. Bridget McCrea, "Parrot's Best Friend," *Precast Solutions Magazine,* Spring 2006.

9. The Hass Shoes story is adapted from Edward D. Hess, "Hass Shoes," Case Study UVA-ENT-0142. University of Virginia Darden School Foundation, Charlottesville, 2009.

CHAPTER 7

1. Portions of this chapter are adapted from: Edward D. Hess, "Organic Growth—Lessons From Market Leaders" (Working Paper, 2007).

2. Edward D. Hess, "Organic Growth Index 'OGI' 1996–2006," 2008. Funded in part by the Batten Institute, Darden Graduate School of Business Administration; Edward D. Hess and Robert K. Kazanjian, eds., *The Search for Organic Growth* (Cambridge: Cambridge University Press, 2006): 147–48.

3. Hess and Kazanjian, *The Search for Organic Growth,* 147–48.

4. Edward D. Hess, "Why Everything You Think You Know About Growth Is Probably Wrong," Technical Note UVA-S-0172. University of Virginia Darden School Foundation, Charlottesville, 2010.

5. The Room & Board Story is adapted from Edward D. Hess, "Room & Board" Case Study UVA-S-0150. University of Virginia Darden School Foundation, Charlottesville, 2008.

6. Jena McGregor, "Room & Board Plays Impossible to Get," *BusinessWeek,* October 1, 2007.

7. Ibid., 80.

8. The Leaders Bank story is adapted from Edward D. Hess and Gosia Glinska, "Leaders Bank: Creating a Great Place to Work," Case Study UVA-ENT-0128. University of Virginia Darden School of Business, Charlottesville, 2009.

9. "Leaders Bank Demonstrates How Deeper Relationships Help Private Businesses" [Press release], 2009.

10. "Entrepreneur Magazine Ranks Leaders Bank as One of the Hot 100 Fast-Growth Businesses in the U.S." [Press release], 2008.

11. "*Entrepreneur* Magazine Ranks Leaders Bank as One of the Hot 100 Fast-Growth Businesses in the U.S." [Press release].

12. Jim Lynch, "Appreciation Ranks High with Employees," *Bank News*, July 1, 2001.

13. Milton Zall, "Empowering Employees," *Independent Banker*, January 1, 2002.

14. Lynch, "Appreciation Ranks High with Employees."

15. Ibid.

16. Ibid.

17. Marcus Buckingham and Curt Coffman, *First, Break All the Rules: What the World's Greatest Manages Do Differently* (New York: Simon & Schuster, 1999).

18. Lynch, "Appreciation Ranks High with Employees."

CHAPTER 8

1. The Defender Direct, Inc. story is adapted from Edward D. Hess, "Defender Direct, Inc.: A Business of Growing Leaders," Case Study UVA-ENT-0115. University of Virginia Darden School Foundation, Charlottesville, 2009.

2. Indianapolis Business Journal, "Indianapolis' Fastest Growing Companies: Defender Security Co.," *Indianapolis Business Journal*, September 15, 2003.

3. Michael Gerber, *The E-Myth: Why Most Businesses Don't Work and What to Do About It* (Cambridge: Ballinger Publishing, 1986).

4. Excerpted from Defender Direct Web site (http://www.defenderdirect. com/corporate.aspx).

5. Ibid.

6. Terri Greenwell, "*IBJ*'s Fastest Growing Companies," *Indianapolis Business Journal*, September 17, 2007.

7. Defender Direct Web site.

8. Jim Collins, *Good to Great: Why Some Companies Make the Leap . . . and Others Don't* (New York: HarperBusiness, 2001).

9. Bobby Knight, the coach with the most career wins in men's collegiate basketball history, led the Indiana University men's basketball team to three NCAA championships between 1971 and 2000.

10. "500/5000 Fastest-Growing Private Companies in America," *Inc.*, 2008.

CHAPTER 9

1. Kim S. Cameron, Jane E. Dutton, and Robert E. Quinn, eds., *Positive Organizational Scholarship* (San Francisco: Berrett-Koehler, 2003); Jane E. Dutton, *Energize Your Workplace: How to Create and Sustain High-Quality Connections at Work* (San Francisco, CA: Jossey-Bass, 2003); James L. Heskett, W. Earl Sasser, Jr., and Leonard A. Schlesinger, *The Value Profit Chain: Treat Employees Like Customers and Customers Like Employees* (New York: Free Press, 2003); James L. Heskett, W. Earl Sasser, Jr., and Leonard A. Schlesinger, *The Service Profit Chain* (New York: Free Press, 1997); Edward D. Hess, *The Road to Organic Growth* (New York: McGraw-Hill, 2007); Edward D. Hess and Kim S. Cameron, eds., *Leading with Values: Positivity, Virtue and High Performance* (Cambridge: Cambridge University Press, 2006); Edward D. Hess, "Organic Growth—Lessons from Market Leaders" (Working Paper, 2007); Charles A. O'Reilly III and Jeffrey Pfeffer, *Hidden Value: How Great Companies Achieve Extraordinary Results with Ordinary People* (Boston: Harvard Business School Press, 2000).

2. Marcus Buckingham and Curt Coffman, *First, Break All the Rules: What the World's Greatest Managers Do Differently* (New York: Simon & Schuster, 1999).

3. James C. Collins and Jerry I. Porras, *Built to Last: Successful Habits of Visionary Companies* (New York: HarperBusiness Essentials, 2002).

4. Ibid. 7–11.

5. The Trilogy Health Services story is adapted from Edward D. Hess and Gosia Glinska, "Trilogy Health Services, LLC: Building a Great Service Company," Case Study UVA-ENT-0122. University of Virginia Darden School Foundation, Charlottesville, 2009.

6. The U.S. Census Bureau has projected that the population of senior citizens will double between 2010 and 2030, from 35 million to 72 million; if these projections hold, one in five Americans will be sixty-five or older in 2030.

7. Jane Adler, "Trilogy Boosts Nursing and Assisted Care Holdings with $34.5 Million Purchase," *Penton Insight*, April 27, 2009.

8. Ken Blanchard, Paul J. Meyer, and Dick Ruhe, *Know Can Do! Put Your Know-How into Action* (San Francisco: Berrett-Koehler Publishers, 2007).

9. Marla Fern Gold, "New-Venture Profits Help Balance SNF Shortfalls," *Provider*, February 2003.

10. Ibid.

CHAPTER 10

1. Bradford D. Smart, *Topgrading: How Leading Companies Win by Hiring, Coaching, and Keeping the Best People* (New York: HarperCollins, 2005).

2. The SecureWorks story is adapted from Edward D. Hess and Gosia Glinska, "SecureWorks," Case Study UVA-ENT-0140. University of Virginia Darden School Foundation, Charlottesville, 2009.

3. "Michael Cote—SecureWorks Inc.: CEO Interview," *Wall Street Transcript*, April 26, 2004, http://www.twst.com/pdf/YAA600.pdf.

4. Nicole Harris, "Startup Offers Web Security to Smaller Firms," *Wall Street Journal*, February 2001.

5. Ibid.

6. "SecureWorks Receives $20 Million in Second-Round Funding," *PR Newswire*, November 16, 2000.

7. Harris, "Startup Offers Web Security."

8. "Former MCI WorldCom Executive Joins SecureWorks as President/COO," *PR Newswire*, August 17, 2000.

9. In February 2003, Wilbanks resigned from the SecureWorks board to head a startup in security patch management services.

10. "SecureWorks Names CEO," *PR Newswire*, February 22, 2001.

11. Michael Cote—SecureWorks Inc.: CEO Interview" (2004).

12. Ibid.

13. Jim Collins, *Good to Great* (New York: Harper Collins, 2001), 13.

14. Michael Cote—SecureWorks Inc.: CEO Interview" (2004).

15. Ibid.

16. "Seeing Double: How Four Companies Overhauled Their Sales Strategies to Spur Growth," *Sales & Marketing Management*, September 1, 2004.

17. Ibid.

18. Ibid.

19. Betsy Cummings, "The Whip Cracker," *FORTUNE Small Business*, October 1, 2004.

20. Ibid.

21. Automatic Data Processing, Inc., was a provider of HR, payroll, tax, and benefits administration solutions.

BIBLIOGRAPHY

Arendt, Jeffrey D. "Adaptive Intrinsic Growth Rates: An Integration Across Taxa." *Quarterly Review of Biology* 72, no. 2 (1997): 149–77.

Arnott, Stephen A., Susumu Chiba, and David O. Conover. "Evolution of Intrinsic Growth Rate: Metabolic Costs Drive Trade-Offs Between Growth and Swimming Performance in *Menidia Menidia*." Evolution 60, no. 6 (2006): 1269–78.

Blanchard, Ken, Paul J. Meyer, and Dick Ruhe. *Know Can Do! Put Your Know-How into Action.* San Francisco: Berrett-Koehler, 2007.

Brown, Shona L., and Kathleen M. Eisenhardt. "The Art of Continuous Change: Linking Complexity Theory and Time-Paced Evolution in Relentlessly Shifting Organizations." *Administrative Science Quarterly* 42, no. 1 (1997): 1–34.

———. *Competing on the Edge: Strategy as Structured Chaos.* Boston: Harvard Business School Press, 1998.

Buckingham, Marcus, and Curt Coffman. *First, Break All the Rules: What the World's Greatest Managers Do Differently.* New York: Simon & Schuster, 1999.

Cameron, Kim S., Jane E. Dutton, and Robert E. Quinn, eds. *Positive Organizational Scholarship.* San Francisco: Berrett-Koehler, 2003.

Chan, Louis K. C., Jason Karceski, and Josef Lakonishok. "The Level and Persistence of Growth Rates." *Journal of Finance* 58, no. 2 (2003): 643–84.

Clippinger, John Henry III, ed. *The Biology of Business: Decoding the Natural Laws of Enterprise.* San Francisco, CA: Jossey-Bass, 1999.

Collins, James C., and Jerry I. Porras. *Built to Last: Successful Habits of Visionary Companies.* New York: HarperBusiness Essentials, 2002.

Collins, Jim. *Good to Great: Why Some Companies Make the Leap . . . and Others Don't.* New York: HarperBusiness, 2001.

———. "Good to Great." *Fast Company,* October 2001.

Dutton, Jane E. *Energize Your Workplace: How to Create and Sustain High-Quality Connections at Work.* San Francisco, CA: Jossey-Bass, 2003.

Eakes, David. "Sammy Snacks." Revised by Timothy M. Lasater and Gregory B. Fairchild. Case Study UVA-OM-1177. University of Virginia Darden School Foundation, Charlottesville, 2005.

Gerber, Michael E. *The E-Myth Revisited: Why Most Small Businesses Don't Work and What to Do About It.* New York: HarperCollins, 1995.

Geroski, Paul A. "Understanding the Implications of Empirical Work on Corporate Growth Rates." *Managerial and Decision Economics* 26, no. 2 (2005): 129–38.

Global Medical Imaging Web site. http://www.gmi3.com/, accessed December 2, 2010.

Gómez, José M. "Bigger Is Not Always Better: Conflicting Selective Pressures on Seed Size in Quercus Ilex." *Evolution* 58, no. 1 (2004): 71–80.

Heskett, James L., W. Earl Sasser, Jr., and Leonard A. Schlesinger. *The Value Profit Chain: Treat Employees Like Customers and Customers Like Employees.* New York: Free Press, 2003.

———. *The Service Profit Chain: How Leading Companies Link Profit and Growth to Loyalty, Satisfaction, and Value.* New York: Free Press, 1997.

Hess, Edward D. *Smart Growth: Building an Enduring Business by Managing the Risks of Growth.* New York: Columbia Business School Publishing, 2010.

———. "Why Everything You Know About Growth Is Probably Wrong." Technical Note UVA-S-0172. University of Virginia Darden School Foundation, Charlottesville, 2010.

———. "3 Fellers Bakery." Case Study UVA-ENT-0137. University of Virginia Darden School Foundation, Charlottesville, 2009.

———. "Defender Direct, Inc.: A Business of Growing Leaders." Case Study UVA-ENT-0115. University of Virginia Darden School Foundation, Charlottesville, 2009.

———. "Organic Growth: Lessons from Market Leaders." Working Paper, 2007.

———. *The Road to Organic Growth*. New York: McGraw-Hill, 2007.

———. "C.R. Barger & Sons, Inc. (A)." Case Study UVA-ENT-0106. University of Virginia Darden School Foundation, Charlottesville, 2008.

———. "C.R. Barger & Sons, Inc. (B)." Case Study UVA-ENT-0107. University of Virginia Darden School Foundation, Charlottesville, 2008.

———. "Organic Growth Index 'OGI' 1996–2006." 2008. University of Virginia, Funded in part by the Batten Institute, Darden Graduate School of Business Administration, Charlottesville.

———. "Room & Board." Case Study UVA-S-0150. University of Virginia Darden School Foundation, Charlottesville, 2008.

———. "Sammy Snacks (B)." Case Study UVA-OM-1350. University of Virginia Darden School Foundation, Charlottesville, 2008.

———. "Sammy Snacks (C)." Case Study UVA-OM-1398. University of Virginia Darden School Foundation, Charlottesville, 2009.

———. "Sammy Snacks (D)." Case Study UVA-OM-1399. University of Virginia Darden School Foundation, Charlottesville, 2009.

———. "Hass Shoes." Case Study UVA-ENT-0142. University of Virginia Darden School Foundation, Charlottesville, 2009.

Hess, Edward D., and Kim S. Cameron, eds. *Leading with Values: Positivity, Virtue and High Performance*. Cambridge: Cambridge University Press, 2006.

Hess, Edward D., and Gosia Glinska. "Eyebobs Eyewear, Inc." Case Study UVA-ENT-0139. University of Virginia Darden School Foundation, Charlottesville, 2009.

———. "Global Medical Imaging." Case Study UVA-ENT-0143. University of Virginia Darden School Foundation, Charlottesville, 2009.

———. "Leaders Bank: Creating a Great Place to Work." Case Study UVA-ENT-0128. University of Virginia Darden School of Business, Charlottesville, 2009.

———. "SecureWorks." Case Study UVA-ENT-0140. University of Virginia Darden School Foundation, Charlottesville, 2009.

———. "Trilogy Health Services, LLC: Building a Great Service Company." Case Study UVA-ENT-0122. University of Virginia Darden School Foundation, Charlottesville, 2009.

Hess, Edward D., and Robert K. Kazanjian, eds. *The Search for Organic Growth*. Cambridge: Cambridge University Press, 2006.

Hess, Edward D., Monidipa Mukherjee, and Sanju Jacob. "Enchanting Travels." Case Study UVA-ENT-0144. University of Virginia Darden School Foundation, Charlottesville, 2009.

Karkach, Arseniy S. "Trajectories and Models of Individual Growth." *Demographic Research* 15, no. 12 (2006): 347–400.

Lipton, Mark. *Guiding Growth: How Vision Keeps Companies on Course.* Boston: Harvard Business School Press, 2003.

Munch, Stephan B., and David O. Conover. "Nonlinear Growth Cost in *Menidia Menidia*: Theory and Empirical Evidence." *Evolution* 58, no. 3 (2004): 661–64.

Olson, Matthew S., and Derek van Bever. *Stall Points: Most Companies Stop Growing—Yours Doesn't Have To.* New Haven, CT: Yale University Press, 2008.

O'Reilly, Charles A. III, and Jeffrey Pfeffer. *Hidden Value: How Great Companies Achieve Extraordinary Results with Ordinary People.* Boston: Harvard Business School Press, 2000.

Penrose, Edith. "The Theory of the Growth of the Firm." In *The International Encyclopedia of Business and Management*, edited by Malcolm Warner. Oxford: Oxford University Press, 1996.

Porter, Michael. "What Is a Strategy?" *Harvard Business Review* (November–December, 2009): 64.

Romer, Paul M. "The Origins of Endogenous Growth." *Journal of Economic Perspectives* 8, no. 1 (1994): 3–22.

Smart, Bradford D. *Topgrading: How Leading Companies Win by Hiring, Coaching, and Keeping the Best People.* New York: HarperCollins, 2005.

Smit, Sven, Caroline M. Thompson, and S. Patrick Viguerie. "The Do-or-Die Struggle for Growth." *McKinsey Quarterly* 3, August (2005): 35–45.

Solow, Robert M. "The Neoclassical Theory of Growth and Distribution." *BNL Quarterly Review* 52, no. 215 (2000): 349.

Wiggins, Robert R., and Timothy W. Ruefli. "Sustained Competitive Advantage: Temporal Dynamics and the Incidence and Persistence of Superior Economic Performance." *Organization Science* 13, no. 1 (2002): 81–105.

———. "Schumpeter's Ghost: Is Hypercompetition Making the Best of Times Shorter?" *Strategic Management Journal* 26, no. 10 (2005): 887–911.

RECOMMENDED READING

BOOKS

Building a Company

Bethune, Gordon. *from Worst to First*. New York: Wiley, 1998.

Chouinard, Yvon. *Let My People Go Surfing*. New York: Penguin Group, 2005.

Collins, James C. *Good to Great: Why Some Companies Make the Leap and Others Don't*. New York: HarperBusiness, 2001.

Collins, James C., and William C. Lazier. *Beyond Entrepreneurship: Turning Your Business into an Enduring Great Company*. Paramus, NJ: Prentice Hall, 1992.

Collins, James C., and Jerry I. Porras. *Built to Last: Successful Habits of Visionary Companies*. New York: HarperCollins, 1994.

Dell, Michael, and Catherine Fredman. *Direct from Dell*. New York: HarperBusiness, 1999.

Hess, Edward D. *Growing an Entrepreneurial Business: Concepts and Cases*. Stanford, CA: Stanford Business Books, 2010.

———. *Smart Growth: Building an Enduring Business by Managing the Risks of Growth*. New York: Columbia Business School Publishing, 2010.

———. *The Road to Organic Growth*. New York: McGraw-Hill, 2007.

Hess, Edward D., and Charles F. Goetz. *So! You Want to Start a Business*. Upper Saddle River, NJ: FT Press, 2009.

Marcus, Bernie, and Arthur Blank, with Bob Andelman. *Built From Scratch: How a Couple of Regular Guys Grew the Home Depot from Nothing to $30 Billion.* New York: Times Books, 1999.

Meyer, Danny. *Setting the Table.* New York: HarperCollins, 2006.

O'Reilly, Charles A. III, and Jeffrey Pfeffer, *Hidden Value: How Great Companies Achieve Extraordinary Results with Ordinary People.* Boston: Harvard Business School Press, 2000.

Roddick, Anita. *Body and Soul.* New York: Crown Publishing Group, 1991.

Schultz, Howard, and Dori Jones Yang. *Pour Your Heart into It.* New York: Hyperion, 1997.

Truett, Cathy S. *Eat Mor Chiken: Inspire More People.* Decatur, GA: Looking Glass Books, 2002.

Walton, Sam, with John Huey. *Sam Walton, Made in America: My Story.* New York: Doubleday, 1992.

Business Strategy

D'Aveni, Richard A. *Hypercompetition.* New York: Free Press, 1994.

Joyce, William F., Nitin Nohria, and Bruce Roberson. *What Really Works: The 4 + 2 Formula for Sustained Business Success.* New York: HarperBusiness, 2003.

Employee Engagement

Buckingham, Marcus, and Curt Coffman. *First, Break All the Rules: What the World's Greatest Managers Do Differently.* New York: Simon & Schuster, 1999.

Cameron, Kim S., Jane E. Dutton, and Robert E. Quinn, eds. *Positive Organizational Scholarship.* San Francisco: Berrett-Koehler, 2003.

Dutton, Jane E. *Energize Your Workplace: How to Create and Sustain High-Quality Connections at Work.* San Francisco, CA: Jossey-Bass, 2003.

Heskett, James L., W. Earl Sasser Jr., and Leonard A. Schlesinger. *The Service Profit Chain: How Leading Companies Link Profit and Growth to Loyalty, Satisfaction, and Value.* New York: Free Press, 1997.

Entrepreneurship

Drucker, Peter F. *Innovation and Entrepreneurship.* New York: HarperBusiness, 1993.

Gerber, Michael E. *The E-Myth Revisited: Why Most Small Businesses Don't Work and What to Do About It.* New York: HarperCollins, 2001.

Family Business

Hess, Edward D. *The Successful Family Business—A Proactive Plan for Managing the Family and the Business*. Westport, CT: Praeger, 2006.

Ward, John L. *Perpetuating the Family Business*. New York: Palgrave MacMillan, 2004.

Leadership

Badaracco, Joseph L. *Leading Quietly: An Unorthodox Guide to Doing the Right Thing*. Boston: Harvard Business School Press 2002.

Behar, Howard, and Janet Goldstein. *It's Not About the Coffee: Leadership Principles from a Life at Starbucks*. New York: Penguin, 2007.

Cameron, Kim S. *Positive Leadership: Strategies for Extraordinary Performance*. San Francisco, CA: Berrett-Koehler, 2008.

Collins, James C. *How the Mighty Fall: And Why Some Companies Never Give In*. New York: Jim Collins, 2009.

George, Bill. *Authentic Leadership: Rediscovering the Secrets to Creating Lasting Value*. San Francisco, CA: Jossey-Bass, 2003.

Gergen, David. *Eyewitness to Power: The Essence of Leadership: Nixon to Clinton*. New York: Simon & Schuster, 2000.

Goldsmith, Marshall, with Mark Reiter. *What Got You Here Won't Get You There: How Successful People Become Even More Successful*. New York: Hyperion, 2007.

Goleman, Daniel, Richard E. Boyatzis, and Annie McKee. *Primal Leadership: Realizing the Power of Emotional Intelligence*. Boston: Harvard Business School Press, 2002.

Greenleaf, Robert K. *Servant Leadership: A Journey into the Nature of Legitimate Power and Greatness*, edited by Larry C. Spears. New York: Paulist Press, 2002.

Hess, Edward D., and Kim S. Cameron, eds. *Leading with Values: Positivity, Virtue, and High Performance*. Cambridge: Cambridge University Press, 2006.

Sutton, Robert I. *Good Boss, Bad Boss: How to Be the Best—and Learn from the Worst*. New York: Business Plus, 2010.

Management

Bossidy, Larry, and Ram Charan, with Charles Burck. *Execution: The Discipline of Getting Things Done*. New York: Crown Business, 2002.

Finkelstein, Sydney. *Why Smart Executives Fail and What You Can Learn from Their Mistakes*. New York: Portfolio, 2003.

Kaplan, Robert S., and David P. Norton. *The Balanced Scorecard: Translating Strategy into Action*. Boston: Harvard Business School Press, 1996.

Magretta, Joan, with Nan Stone. *What Management Is: How It Works and Why It's Everyone's Business*. New York: Free Press, 2002.

Sullivan, Gordon R., and Michael V. Harper. *Hope Is Not a Method: What Business Leaders Can Learn from America's Army*. New York: Broadway Books, 1997.

Marketing and Sales

Kotler, Philip. *Kotler on Marketing: How to Create, Win, and Dominate Markets*. New York: Free Press, 1999.

Lencioni, Patrick. *Getting Naked: A Business Fable About Shedding the Three Fears That Sabotage Client Loyalty*. San Francisco, CA: Jossey-Bass, 2010.

Sheth, Jagdish, and Rajendra Sisodia. *The Rule of Three: Surviving and Thriving in Competitive Markets*. New York: Free Press, 2002.

ARTICLES

Collins, James C. "Level 5 Leadership: The Triumph of Humility and Fierce Resolve." *Harvard Business Review* 79, no. 1 (2001): 66–76.

Churchill, Neil C., and John W. Mullins, "How Fast Can Your Company Afford to Grow?" *Harvard Business Review* 79, no. 5 (2001): 135–42.

Drucker, Peter F. "Managing Oneself." *Harvard Business Review* 77, no. 2 (1999): 64–74.

Magretta, Joan. "Governing the Family-Owned Enterprise: An Interview with Finland's Krister Ahlstrom." *Harvard Business Review* 76, no. 1 (1998): 112–23.

McKenna, Jack, and Paul Oritt, "Growth Planning for Small Business." *American Journal of Small Business*, 5, no. 4 (1981): 19–29.

Porter, Michael E., Jay W. Lorsch, and Nitin Nohria. "Seven Surprises for New CEOs." *Harvard Business Review* 82, no. 10 (2004): 62–72.

Rogers, Paul, Tom Holland, and Dan Haas, "Value Acceleration: Lessons from Private Equity Masters." *Harvard Business Review* 80, no. 6 (2002): 94–101.

Slywotsky, Adrian J., and Richard Wise. "The Growth Crisis and How to Escape It." *Harvard Business Review* 80, no. 7 (2002): 72–83.